CONTEMPORARY JEWISH RELIGIOUS RESPONSES TO THE SHOAH

CONTEMPORARY JEWISH RELIGIOUS RESPONSES TO THE SHOAH

Edited by
Dr. Steven L. Jacobs, Rabbi

Studies in the Shoah

Volume V

University Press of America
Lanham • New York • London

Copyright © 1993 by
University Press of America®, Inc.
4720 Boston Way
Lanham, Maryland 20706

3 Henrietta Street
London WC2E 8LU England

Library of Congress Cataloging-in-Publication Data

Contemporary Jewish religious responses to the Shoah / edited by
Steven L. Jacobs.
    p.   cm. — (Studies in the Shoah ; v. 5)
    Includes bibliographical references.
  1. Holocaust (Jewish theology)   2. Judaism—20th century.
        I. Jacobs, Steven L.   II. Series.
  BM645.H6C66   1993   296.3—dc20   92–44748 CIP

ISBN 0–8191–8985–5 (cloth : alk. paper)

The paper used in this publication meets the minimum requirements of
American National Standard for Information Sciences—Permanence
of Paper for Printed Library Materials, ANSI Z39.48–1984.

For

Leo and Ella Jacob,

Grandparents,

Married July 29, 1920,

Murdered by the Nazis,

Late 1941 or Early 1942.

With Love.

And for My

Father,

Ralph Albert Jacobs

[May 1, 1921 - September 27, 1981],

The Saving Remnant

TABLE OF CONTENTS

Introduction: Why This Book?

Judaism and Christianity After Auschwitz   1
                            Steven L. Jacobs

In a World Without a Redeemer, Redeem!   23
                            Michael Berenbaum

Academia and the Holocaust   33
                            Alan L. Berger

After Auschwitz and the Palestinian Uprising   45
                            Marc H. Ellis

The Holocaust: A Summing Up after Two Decades of
                            Reflection   65
                      Emil L. Fackenheim

Voluntary Covenant   77
                            Irving Greenberg

Auschwitz: Re-Envisioning the Role of God   107
                            Peter J. Haas

Why?   135
                            Bernard Maza

Apocalyptic Rationality and the Shoah   157
                            Richard L. Rubenstein

Between the Fires   173
                            Arthur Waskow

Notes   181

Glossary   211

Bibliography   233

Questions   241

About the Contributors   245

About the Editor   249

INTRODUCTION

WHY THIS BOOK?

In 1988, there appeared a collection of philosophical essays dealing with the Shoah[1] entitled Echoes from the Holocaust: Philosophical Reflections of a Dark Time[2] . In examining its Table of Contents, only one of those essays, that of Hans Jonas--"The Concept of God After Auschwitz: A Jewish Voice" [pages 295-305]--reflected upon those years theologically. For, in truth, while many of those who had thought theologically and Jewisly about the implications of the Shoah, including many of those included here, had done so either in individual articles scattered about in a wide variety of publications, or in specific books, there did not exist a comparable collection of thoughtful essays from the perspective of Jewish religious or theological thought. Contemporary Jewish Religious Responses to the Shoah is an attempt to fill that void by bringing together many of the leading Jewish religious thinkers about the Shoah, allowing them the freedom to respond to two questions uppermost in the mind of this Editor: [1] "What are the questions which we as religious thinkers should be asking about the Shoah today?" and [2] "What are the answers which you yourself would give?" That all of those included were so readily willing to contribute their thinking to this project is an indication of the need for such a work.

Contemporary scholars in all disciplines have long recognized that the Shoah is a critical challenge to Christianity and Western Civilization, as well as a watershed event in Jewish history. The authors of the individual essays, as it were, speak of their own particular concerns to a wider audience than the Jewish community. In so doing, these essays serve to broaden the base of the reader's own thinking about the religious implications of the Shoah, and, thus, enter into dialogue with the reader. That the concerns expressed here are as varied as they are is a potent indication that now, five decades after the closure of the Second World War, there still exists no consensus as to the primary or central issues--theologically, philosophically or historically--when confronting the enormity of the Shoah in all of its many and varied aspects and dimensions.

When all is said and done, however, what comes through in these essays is the primacy of a renewed exploration of the ethical--in a very real and practical sense--over that of the intellectual task of "theologizing." The Shoah presented humanity not with its successful evolution of both intellect and technology, but with its failure to use both for the improvement and betterment of all humankind. What is now needed, given this reality of an historical experience testifying to the willingness of a given segment of the human community to go to any lengths whatsoever to eradicate another segment, is a renewed commitment to the teaching of ethics, at all levels of society, within a religious context, addressing the very concerns that should be the central focus of any faith: concern for the individual and group, regardless of their size and status; concern for the life's journey all human-ity shares; and concern for that which is common among all peoples--recognition of the partnership of humanity and planet earth in a universe beyond itself. The all-too-frequent repetition of genocidal acts subsequent to the Second World War [e.g. Tibetans, Ibos, Kampucheans, Bosnians, etc.] is eloquent testimony and witness that the world--both Western and Eastern--has learned precious little from the Shoah. The inherent danger, however, in not learning from the Shoah is not merely repeating the "sins of the past," but, with ever-increasing and ever more sophisticated technology, encom-passing wider and wider segments of humanity in the wake of its murderous design. Having committed itself continually to destroying specific portions of its own population, having increased the ability to do so exponentially, humanity appears to inch ever closer to turning in upon itself and destroying itself as well as its home. While no humanly crafted or created process is, ultimately, irreversible, one prays that Samuel Pisar, international lawyer and "graduate" of Auschwitz, author of the book Of Blood and Hope³, is proven wrong by the work and resolve of collective humanity. Should he be proven correct, however, that "the Holocaust is the pilot program for the end of humanity," neither books such as this one, nor all the prayers of all the world's peoples, will prove capable of preventing the long, dark night of destruction which will engulf it.

*

Difficult as this project has proven to be, pain-filled as the subject itself has proven to be, profound thanks and grateful acknowledgement are here-with extended to all those without whom it would not have seen the light of day.

To those who contributed their thinking to this book and who met every deadline and expectation asked and from whom I have learned so much; to Professor Zev Garber of Los Angeles Valley College and General Editor "Studies in the Shoah Series" who saw merit both in this project and in its publication; to my wife Louanne, daughters Hannah and Naomi, and son Shea, for their understanding, encouragement, and love; to all those who continue to wrestle and to struggle with the Shoah and the world of faith; and to those who own reading of these essays will further all the dialogues which must now take place. May the thinking contained within this book serve to inspire others to address the issue of our collective human survival on spaceship earth before it is too late.[4]

Steven L. Jacobs

Huntsville, Alabama

14 December 1992

In my own initial contribution, I attempt to briefly survey and respond to the major Jewish and Christian thinkers who have grappled with the enormity of the Shoah, after first having addressed an issue of crucial importance: the question of the theological and/or historical uniqueness of the Shoah. I conclude by enumerating those categories of Jewish religious concern which must be addressed in any attempt to reformulate a relevant and contemporary post-Auschwitz Jewish theology, suggesting, therefore, a preliminary direction for future Jewish thought: [1] God, [2] Covenant, [3] Prayer, [4] Mitzvah [Commandment], [5] Celebration of Festival-Calendar and Life-Cycle Events, and [6] Jews and Christians in dialogue.

JUDAISM AND CHRISTIANITY AFTER AUSCHWITZ[1]

Steven L. Jacobs

I. Introduction

That the events of the Shoah, specifically the years 1933-1945, which saw the deaths of approximately six million Jews, five million non-Jews, and twenty-million Russians--not to mention untold Allied and German military combatants and civilians--have profound theological implications is patently obvious. That those who, in their anguish and their pain, both Jews and non-Jews, have "chosen" [if that is, indeed, the correct word!] to wrestle with these implications are pitifully few in number should be equally as obvious. Names like Arthur Cohen, Irving Greenberg, Eliezer Berkovitz, Emil Fackenheim, Richard Rubenstein, and, of course, Elie Wiesel in the Jewish community; and Harry James Cargas, Alan Davies, Alice and Roy Eckardt, Franklin Littell, Michael McGarry, John Pawlikowski, David Rausch, Rosemary Radford Reuther, and John Roth in the Christian community, are known only to the initiated should, also, be obvious. For both Judaism and Christianity, whose very theological houses are built upon the premise of the God-who-acts-in-history, whatever else we may say of both God and faith, the Shoah is a frontal assault upon both. Might this, then, not be the first theological implication: That the events of the this very limited moment in history would cause such a fundamental and radical restructuring and rethinking of the entire historical understanding of both Judaism and Christianity that we best leave well enough along, save for the few, and get on with our lives, preferring not to deal with those implications rather than consider them?

Such would certainly seem to be the case for both Jews and Christians in the world today. For Jews, the miracle of the modern rebirth of the State of Israel on May 14, 1948, the phoenix literally arising out of the ashes of the Shoah, and its ongoing struggle for survival, have all but preoccupied Jews and Jewish energies, and is, in and of itself, by and large, a redirection of Jewish thinking away from the Shoah. For Christians, the ever-increasing encroachment of both secularism and third-world theologies, fundamentalism and the "electronic gospel," have directed Christian thinkers away from the events of the Shoah, if, indeed, they were truly of primary theological concern in the years following the Second World War. For both communities, the tragic history of relationship, culminating in the events of the Shoah, has distanced both communities from confronting directly the theological meaning of those events, allowing other lures and crises to supplant the two essential to which both communities have failed to respond adequately: [1] "Where was God in the Shoah?" and [2] "Where was humanity in the Shoah?" [Additionally, for Jews, "What covenantal relationship now exists between the Jewish People and God in light of the death camps?" And for Christians, "How does Jesus the Redeemer now present himself to an unredeemed world which could, seemingly, countenance a Shoah?"]

Before attempting my own conclusions, it will best serve our purposes to survey, however briefly, those aforementioned thinkers and respond to them individually and collectively. While those so surveyed are by no means all-inclusive, they are, in reality, the major thinkers who have attempted to grapple with the magnitude of the Shoah.

We begin, however, with the following caveat: In light of the Shoah, the post-Auschwitz theological enterprise must address these two questions: [1] The historical uniqueness of the Shoah--yes or no? and [2] Irving Greenberg's oft-quoted criterion, "No statement, theological or otherwise, should be made that would not be creditable in the presence of burning children"[2]. Rephrased by Cohen, "No God is worth a single child's life. How much the more so untold children?"[3]. Commenting on this very idea, Robert Sherwin writes:

> All the wisdom of all the philosophers, said Dostoyevsky, cannot explain the death of one innocent child. How, therefore, to explain the deaths of one million one hundred thousand children? Any statement would be an understatement. Yet the holocaust embraces a basic paradox. It imposes silence but demands speech. It defies solutions but requires responses.[4]

If such is, indeed, true, as I fully believe it is, then we must, likewise, agree with Cohen that:

> Any constructive theology after the 'tremendum' must be marked ny the following characteristics: first, the God who is affirmed must abide in a universe whose human history is scarred by genuine evil without making the evil empty or illusory not disallowing the real presence of God before, even if not within, history; second, the relation of God to creation and its creatures, including both, now include demonic structures and unredeemable events, must be seen, nonetheless, as meaningful and valuable despite the fact that the justification of life and struggle is now intensified and anguished by the contrast and opposition that evil supplies; third, the reality of God in his selfhood and person can no longer be isolated, other than as a strategy of clarification, from God's real involvement with the life of creation.[5]

Let us return, then, to the two caveats prior to surveying those Jewish and Christian thinkers who have had the courage to deal with the Shoah and their attempted reconciliation with their own understandings and their own tradition's understanding of the relationship between God, humanity, and the world.

II. The Theological-Historical Uniqueness of the Shoah

In my own teaching, I use the following definition of the Shoah: "The historically-validated, legalized, bureaucratic marriage of technology and death." This definition is predicated upon my understanding that the event is unique, both theologically and historically, in both Jewish and world history, though, to be sure, the result of an historically pre-prepared environment which evolved from generations of Western and Christian anti-Jewish and anti-Judaic sentiment, best summed up in Hilberg's schemata, "You [i.e. the Jews] have no right to live among us as Jews!" to "You have no right to live among us!" to "You have no right to live!"[6]

The very uniqueness of the Shoah marked, perhaps forever and all times, a radical shift in the understanding of who and what the Jew was: Prior to the rise of the Nazis, those who sought to do harm to the Jews-- either individually or communally--admitted that the Jew could change by surrendering his or her identity and adopting that of the larger society. In pre-Christian Egypt, Greece, and Rome, one born a Jew could renounce his or her Judaism and take on the coloration of that larger society, and, while he or she may have suffered social discrimination, one or two generations later, all was forgotten and forgiven. In Christian society up until the advent of the Nazis, renunciation of Judaism in favor of Christianity opened doors to integration into a new, non-Jewish world. Again, aside from the Marranos, whose questionable conversions were the source of their affliction, former Jews saw the integration of their offspring one to two generations later. Thus, almost all pre-Nazi Western European societies admitted the possibility of change from formerly Jewish identity to non-Jewish identity, and, with it, a subsequent loss of discrimination and oppression.

For the Nazis, however, this historical understanding of anti-Judaism was, essentially in error. Whatever else we may say of the so-called "racial theories" of the Nazis, they saw no way for the Jew to change. Previous manifestations of antisemitism, then, may be labelled "cultural antisemitism," "social antisemitism," "political antisemitism," and "theological" or "religious antisemitism." Now, for the first time in history, the Jews were confronted with "biological antisemitism." Not what they did, how they behaved, how they practiced their faith and its rituals and ceremonials was at issue, but what they were was the root of all that afflicted the Western world. "Jewishness" was a physical component of the individual, part of the very lifeblood of the Jew, and, thus, could no more be changed that could amputation of limb render the individual a whole human being.

"Race-mixing" between Jew and Aryan, according to the Nazis, had to result in an inferiorization and mongrelization of the Aryan race; there was simply no other way to perceive that negative relationship. This shift, then, from non-biological forms of antisemitism and anti-Jewish persecution and prejudice to biological antisemitism marks the Shoah unique on the world scene.[7]

There are, however, those within the Jewish community who do not so regard the events of the Shoah as unique, as there are those within the Christian community who, equally, perceive the events of the Shoah as part of some, as yet unknowable, Divine plan. Daniel Polish writes:

> As we reflect on how to understand God after the 'shoah,' then, I reject the proposition that we treat it as being of a different order of reality from anything that preceded it, thus needing theological responses of a wholly new order. I regard it as being different in magnitude but not in kind, from cataclysms that the people had known before in its history.[8]

I would, however, contend that the concerns of those who reject the Shoah as unique is not with history, but with maintaining the structures of historical Jewish faith as previously presented by generations of Jews. David Weiss, writing in Sh'ma: A Journal of Jewish Responsibility, sees the Shoah as a continuation of the sad and tragic story of Jewish persecutions, but not unique.[9] And he is not alone in his thinking! Martin Cohen enumerates those whose response to the Shoah is, even today, to think in historically-traditional terms:

> Thus, Ignatz Maybaum, emphasizing the role of the Jews as the Suffering Servant, view the Holocaust as a divine visitation to being an end to a decaying era and to usher in a new, utopian world. Menahem Hartom explain the Holocaust as punishment for Jewish assimilation and sets the state of Israel as its intended outcome, although the Jewish people 'was not worthy of it by its conduct.' Bemoaning the tendencies to irreligiosity in Israel's secular nationalism, Hartom warns against another retributive visitation.
>
> Joel Teitelbaum, leader of the anti-Israel Satmar Hasidim, goes so far as to blame secularist Zionism for the divine visitation of the Holocaust. David Chomsky shares Hartom's faith, but rejects his fear of assimilative trends in Israel. On the contrary, he sees the possibility of the Jews in secular Israel becoming a 'kingdom of priests and a holy people.' Issachar Jacobson hears in the Holocaust a call for Jews to renounce all attempts at rational explanation of its events and to reaffirm their Jewish belief 'to

remain people of faith, fearing God and always doing good, for in these ways alone can we grasp something of God's wisdom.'

Similarly, Jacob Rothschild calls on the Jew to rise above the natural human desire for explanation of daily events to a strong and unquestioning faith in human history under the guidance of God.[10]

For the traditionally-minded believer, everything that occurs, occurs as the result of the God-who-acts-in-history. Certainly no event of the cataclysmic proportions of the Shoah escaped Divine attention. All continues to be theologically and historically as it has always been theologically and historically. Jewish and Christian religious responsibility becomes the integration of attempts to fathom the meaning of these events within a God-controlled world. To reject these events as, somehow, outside the purview of the Divine is to reject, consciously or otherwise, the whole theological enterprise as it has historically evolved.

Yet questions abound which admit of no easy answers: [1] Why did this controlling Deity permit these events to take place? [2] Did God, in actuality, so construct these events as a means of punishing an errant Jewish community according to the classical lines of the Covenant? [3] What sin have the Jews committed that warranted such punishment?[11] [4] And, if not the Jews alone, what sin had others--Gypsies; political enemies of the Third Reich; sincere Christians, including clergy--likewise committed that warranted their own horrendous deaths? [5] Did the Deity, in fact, choose Adolf Hitler and his minions to do Divine bidding?

For those who affirm the historically-traditional notions of faith, the only creditable conclusion is that the Shoah is punishment. Whether we like it or not, whether we wish to accept it or not, this notion of God's relationship with humanity answers all relevant questions and remains intact. The Shoah was punishment for sin, though we know not the nature of the sin which merited such punishment. That there are others, Richard Rubenstein most particularly, and even Elie Wiesel, who reject such a notion should be obvious. I would classify myself among them.

In commenting himself on his interview with Dean Heinrich Gruber of the Evangelical Church of West Berlin, himself an avowedly anti-Nazi who suffered physically because of his opposition, Richard Rubenstein experienced the very "crisis of faith" which rendered the historically-traditional understanding of God and God's relationship with humanity passe, which is at the heart of the quest for a relevant, rethought theological response:

Having commenced with his biblical interpretation of recent history, he could not stop until he had asserted that it had been God's will to send Adolf Hitler to exterminate Europe's Jews. At the moment that I heard Gruber make this assertion, I had what was perhaps the most important single crisis of faith I have ever had. I recognized that Gruber was not an Antisemite and that his assertion that the God of the Covenant was and is the ultimate Author of the great events of Israel's history was not different from the faith of any traditional Jew. Gruber was applying the logic of Covenant Theology to the events of the twentieth century. I appreciated his fundamental honesty. He recognized that, if one takes the biblical theology of history seriously, Adolf Hitler is n o more nor less an instrument of God's wrath than Nebuchadnez-zar....

     If one accepts the doctrine that God is distinctively involved in the history of Israel, the fundamentalist Christian may indeed be right in asserting that the sorrows of the Jews have been inflicted upon them for rejecting Jesus. Whether one is a fundamental Christian or a traditional Jew, it is impossible to regard the sorrows of Jewish history as mere historical accidents. They must in some sense express the will of God as a just and righteous Creator. Either such a God is a sadist who inflicts pain because he enjoys it or he has a reason for the misfortune he inflicts. The only morally defensible motive for a superior to inflict pain on an inferior would be punitive chastisement which has as its purpose altering the victim's mode of behavior. If one takes Covenant Theology seriously, as did Dean Gruber, Auschwitz must be God's way of punishing the Jewish people in order that they might better see the light, the light of Christ if one is a Christian, the light of Torah if one is a traditional Jew.[12]

     The Shoah may, also, be perceived as unique because of its very modernity on two accounts: [1] The operative concept of "surplus populations" so well orchestrated in the writings of Richard Rubenstein[13], and [2] The very use of technology which made of the concentration camp process of death the ultimate epitome of the assembly line, to wit:

     Efficiency was at its peak in the concentration camp process: In the morning, you stepped off the train. In the evening the corpse was buried or cremated. Clothing was packed away, after having been sorted and repaired, if necessary, for shipment back to Germany. People were killed on an assembly line basis.[14]

     The theological implications of both--declaring any population outside the context of human community and the use of technology for totally negative purposes--have not been explored to any great degree by Jewish and Christian thinkers, though Catholic theologian Michael Novak has begun to explore the theological implications of the corporation[15], and Richard Rubenstein himself seems to heading in this direction in his The Age of Triage.

Having now, concretely, established the uniqueness of the Shoah as a theological concern, we move, of necessity, to the second pre-concern: That the construction of any valid post-Auschwitz theology must confront the historical reality of evil death, most poignantly, the useless deaths of so many children, Jewish or Christian.   Such a theology must wrestle, even unsuccessfully, with the enormity of these deaths--in ovens, in gas chambers, by bayonet or bullet, often in the presence of parents or grandpar-ents, often accompanied by the very adults who represented for these children the only safety and security permitted them in their nightmare world.   The death of any child poses enormous theological difficulties, though both Jewish and Christian traditions continue to affirm the reality of the God-who-acts-in-history when confronted with such.   The deaths of one million children below the age of twelve, and an additional one-half million if we raise the age to eighteen, is a double frontal attack to which neither has responded, even inadequately.

III. Jewish Thinking About the Shoah

We begin, most appropriately, with Elie Wiesel's Night, most particularly that passage most often viewed as the fullest literary expression of the theological dilemma:

> One day when we came back from work, we saw three gallows rearing up in the assembly place, three black crows. Roll Call. SS all around us, machine guns trained: the traditional ceremony. Three victims in chains--and one of them, the little servant, the sad-eyed angel.
>
> The SS seemed more preoccuppied, more disturbed than usual. To hang a young boy in front of thousands of spectators was no light matter. The head of the camp read the verdict. All eyes were on the child. He was lividly pale, almost calm, biting his lips. The gallows threw its shadow over him.
>
> This time the Lagerkapo refused to act as executioner. Three SS replaced him.
>
> The three victims mounted together onto the chairs.
>
> The three necks were placed at the same moment within the nooses.
>
> "Long live liberty!" cried the two adults.
>
> But the child was silent.
>
> "Where is God? Where is He?" someone behind me asked.
>
> At a sign from the head of the camp, the three chairs tipped over.
>
> Total silence throughout the camp. On the horizon, the sun was setting.

"Bare your heads!" yelled the head of the camp. His voice was raucous.

We were weeping.

"Cover your heads!"

Then the march past began. The two adults were no longer alive. Their tongues hung swollen, blue-tinged. But the third rope was still moving; being so light, the child was still alive....

For more than half an hour he stayed there, struggling between life and death, dying in slow agony under our eyes. And we had to look him full in the face. He was still alive when I passed in front of him. His tongue was still red, his yees were not yet glazed.

Behind me, I heard the same man asking:

"Where is God now?"

And I heard a voice within me answer him:

"Where is He? Here He is--He is hanging here on this gallows...."[16]

Rubenstein in rejecting Gruber's conclusions, and along with them the historically-traditional Jewish response, and Wiesel in presenting in starkly dramatic form the very same picture, seem to me to be saying that the previous ways in which we have thought about God, about God's rela-ti-onship with humanity, in particular the Jewish people, have now become passe, that the very categories of relationship no longer suffice to explain or incorporate into their schema new, contemporary historical evidence that what happened during those dark years is, quite literally, beyond the scope of those understandings. What is now called for are new ways of thinking and understanding the universe and the place of both God and the Jewish people--and Germans and Christians and everyone else--in it.

Rubenstein's honest, pain-filled willingness to confront the Shoah direct-ly in theological terms, independent of his conclusions, has called forth his share of critics and defenders: Seymour Cain applauds him for cogently raising the questions he raises, but, equally, argues that his proposals were contradictory and confusing, bordering on the irrelevant.[17] Michael Wys-chogrod takes him to task for the very divisiveness within the Jewish community that his writings sew:

The sin [sic] of Rubenstein is, therefore, that he permits Auschwitz further to divide the Jewish people at a time when survival is paramount if Hitler is not to be handed a posthumous victory, and survival deamnds unity.[18]

Because Rubenstein can no longer believe after Auschwitz as his ances-tors believed, he labels himself a 'pagan', though, to be sure, his paganism is an existential paganism whereby he also affirms his place as a member of the Jewish people who must now rely on their own resources to survive:

> I am a pagan. To be a pagan means to find once again one's roots as a child of earth and to see one's own existence as wholly and totally an earthly existence. It means once again to understand that for mankind the true divinites are the gods of earth, not the high gods of the sky; the gods of space and place, not the gods of home and hearth, not the gods of wandering, though wanderers we must be.[19]

Pagan or not, Rubenstein's break with historically-traditional notions and ideas continues to subject his theology to a veritable "conspiracy of silence" today in institutional Jewish life.

Wiesel, on the other hand, is relatively untouchable. After all, he is, by his own admission, a storyteller, and does not venture into the realms of academic-intellectual discourse confined to philosophy and/or theology. He offers no systematic response to his experiences, but pre-fers to simply tell the story and energize the moral commitments necessary to prevent repetition, leaving to others their own avenues of responsibility.[20]

A somewhat different tack is that taken by Orthodox Jewish thinker Eliezer Berkovitz, author of Faith After Auschwitz.[21] For him, the traditional notions of God, Covenant, and Jewish people remain intact. For him, for whatever the reason, always unknown to us, God chose "to turn HIs face away from us, to hid His face"--perhaps as the ultimate expression of commitment to human freedom--and the resultant perversion of that freedom was the events of the Shoah. Thus, to ask the question "Where was God?" according to Berkovitz becomes the wrong question. God is where He has always been: Waiting for faltering humanity to mature in its responsibilities. The question we must ask and continue to ask is "Where was humanity?" and how can that humanity overcome its potential for future repetitions?

What is surprising about Berkovitz is the very radical understanding he has of human freedom as, somehow, beyond the arena of Divine accountability, and his acceptance of hester panim [God's "hidden face"] as speaking meaningfully to the human condition. The God who cares is, seemingly, willing to maintain His distance even when humanity so desperately needs that involvement and caring for its own salvation. Could it be, then, that having removed Himself from humanity--out of that commitment to human freedom--the Deity is no longer capable, not to mention unwilling, or re-entering into relationship? Berkovitz provides us no answer. Also, other than for the initial act of creation which merits thanksgiving, how do we enter into a meaningful relationship with a God who [arbitrarily?] removes

Himself? And why bother to do so--since He has seemingly rejected any involvement with the affairs of humanity?[22]

This same question might very well be asked of Irving ["Yitz"] Greenberg who, in his own writings, speaks of a "voluntary covenant" with God in light of Auschwitz. This Orthodox thinker, too, like Eliezer Berkovitz, essentially negates all previous Jewish understandings of Covenant, which is perfectly acceptable--except that he wishes to maintain his place within that same Orthodox community which continues to speak in historically-traditional ways. Commitment to the Jewish people, to be involved with the Jewish people and its ongoing struggle for survival, to continue to affirm time-honored religious forms, as well as innovative forms, is not Covenant, no matter how well-intentioned the covenanter. That Covenant of Jewish tradition is predicated upon a God who will provide and protect its adherents so long as they own up to their responsibilities as members of a covenanted community. Now, since we voluntarily have the option of choosing to accept this covenant, we, also, have the option of rejecting that very same covenant, and God may not necessarily be a part of either decision. Stripped to its barest bones, Greenberg's position may only be a more contemporary rejection of the notion of the Shoah as expression of Divine punishment for a people who failed to honor its historic covenant.

Emil Fackenheim, on the other hand, sees no voluntarism at all, though he does not speak in covenantal terms, but, rather, in emotionally-historical ones. For Jews to reject their Jewish identity and merge with the larger culture and society is to grant Hitler and his minions that very victory which was his ultimate goal all along: To make the world 'Judenrein'!

> I believe that whereas no redeeming voice is heard at Auschwitz, a commanding voice is heard, and that it is being heard with increasing clarity. Jews are not permitted [By whom?--SLJ] to hand Hitler posthumous victories. Jews are commanded [By whom?--SLJ] to survive as Jews, lest their people perish....-They are forbidden [By whom?--SLJ] to despair of God, lest Judaism perish....Jewish survival, were it even for more than survival's sake, is a holy duty.[23]

Emotionally powerful words, indeed--but spoke only to those who have already made the commitment to positively affirm their Jewish selves. The essential problem with Emil Fackenheim is two-fold: [1] For the Jew for whom the Shoah is an "uncomfortable bit of history," at the very least, appeal to it will not build a house of positive Jewish commitments and/or practices; and [2] As the events of 1933 to 1945 recede further and further into history, transmission of those horrific events to succeeding generations becomes even more difficult to teach, and becomes a theological absurdity upon which to affirm Jewish faith. Essentially, the Jewish voice which speaks at Auschwitz speaks to those who have always heard such voices and who continue to incorporate into their own Jewish 'weltanschauung' Jewish historical experiences. The newer adherents to Jewish commitment because of such events remain pitifully few.

In brief, then, these are some of the significant Jewish thinkers who today continue to grapple with the theological meaning of the years 1933 to 1945. They have been subject to serious critique, some more than others, some less than others. Before, however, examining my own thinking, let us address those Christian thinkers who have, likewise, attempted to, somehow, deal with the Shoah in light of their own religious traditions.

IV. Christian Thinking About the Shoah

Catholic Gerard Sloyan writes of Christian history:

> More than eighteen hundred years of Christian antipathy for Jews for alleged theological reasons were followed by an attempt unique in history to exterminate them. Whether or not a direct causality can be proved becomes an indifferent matter. The sequence alone requires that Christians purge from their faith and theology and not merely from their behavior anything that could have led to this demonic outcome. On any reading of Christianity, one would think that the motivation so to act cannot be found in divine revelation.[24]

While agreeing with Sloyan as to the re-examination required of Christianity when confronting the Shoah, I do not agree that "causality" is "an indifferent matter." It is the very essence of the challenge to Christian faith: Whether, in point of fact, inherent in Christianity's presentation of itself to the world is an antisemitism potentially so virulent that the right set of historic and environmental factors could bring about a repetition of the Shoah. If such is true, and antisemitism is not yet expunged, then it is only a matter of time before we realize that repetition. If, on the other hand, there is no causality, not foundation on which to build the house, then the examination is one of relationship between the ideas and practices of Christianity and the various aberrations which have been inflicted upon the Jewish people for the past two thousand years. Either way, the task at hand is not easy, nor is it free of pain. But the failure to examine the past is prelude to the future. Irving Greenberg writes:

> Nothing less than a fundamental critique and purification of the Gospels themselves can begin to eliminate Christianity as a source of hatred. What the Holocaust reveals is that Christianity has the stark choice of contrition, repentance, and self-purification or the continual temptation to participate in or pave the way for genocide.[25]

John Pawlikowski, also a Catholic, calls for a re-examination of the Catholic understanding of God and humanity in light of the Shoah, but equally stresses that the Church itself must rethink its relationship with non-Catholics, especially Jews, because of the Shoah. To maintain the kind of successionism and triumphalism that has been part and parcel of Christianity's history is, today, morally wrong and theologically objectionable.[26]

Harry James Cargas, on the other hand, not a priest, is, along with Rosemary Radford Reuther, the most radical critic of the Roman Catholic Church in the aftermath of the Shoah. Calling himself a "post-Auschwitz Catholic," he writes of his "obsession" with the Shoah, and presents sixteen proposals for forging new links between Jews and Catholic Christians, among which are the following:

> [1] The Catholic Church should excommunicate Adolf Hitler.
> [2] The Christian liturgical calendar[s] should include an annual memorial service for the Jewish victims of the Holocaust.
> [8] The Vatican's historical archives for the twentieth-century need to be opened to historians.[27]

Rosemary Reuther, even more a radical theologian than Cargas, calls for a restructuring of Christian thought because her own examination of the texts of Christianity have led her to conclude that, indeed, the Gospels are antisemitic and do contain within them the seeds of historical anti-Judaism. In Faith and Fratricide: The Theological Roots of Anti-Semitism, she calls for nothing less than a total re-evaluation and rethinking of the theological relationship between Judaism and Christianity, revolving around a new understanding of Christology as the "key issue" in that relationship.[28] She shares that concern with Michael B. McGarry, whose Christology After Auschwitz surveys Roman Catholic opinion subsequent to the Second World War in light of the momentous import of Vatican II, and, hesitatingly, makes some predications as to future directions.[29] He does not, however, go far enough in his own thinking, though he, too, realizes that a rethinking of the place of Christ in Christian theology, most particularly a down-playing of triumphalist successionism, presents enormous problems within all facets of Christianity.

Anglican priest Alan Ecclestone, in his own book Night Sky of the Lord, likewise tries to deal, albeit unsuccessfully, with the theological dilemmas for Christianity posed by the Shoah.[30] He calls for the following new agenda for the Christian community, like the others noted previously: [1] an acknowledgement and understanding of anti-Semitism; [2] the abandonment of anti-Jewish theology; [3] "the recovery of the Hebraic understanding of the creation and the nature of human life"; [4] "the religious significance of

Jesus"; and [5] "the problems [sic] posed by the State of Israel". While his book is an attempt to expand upon his agenda, his desire for Jews to rethink Jesus and discover worth in him nullifies his desire to further dialogue. His difficulty, like so many, appears to be the difficulty in accommodating within a Christian world-view an equally-valid expression of the God-human encounter of which Christ has no part, as well as a general unwillingness to deal with the raw notion that Christianity may have had a direct relationship and responsibility for those pre-1933 events which led to the Shoah.

Protestant thinkers Franklin H. Littell and David A. Rausch have written companion volumes attempting to explore the meaning of the Shoah for non-Catholic Christians: Littell's The Crucifixion of the Jews: The Failure of Christians to Understand the Jewish Experience[31] and Rausch's A Legacy of Hatred: Why Christians Must Not Forget the Holocaust[32] start from the standpoint of history, acknowledging in the process Christian complicity and responsibility for the events which led to the ovens and the gas chambers of World War II. Though both texts are well-organized and provide exacting documentation for their conclusions, neither Littell nor Rausch have worked through the theological implications of their studies, nor provided a thorough reconstruction of non-Catholic Christianity for their readers. Such continues to remain the primary task for both Catholic and non-Catholic theologians in light of the Shoah.

Seminal to any discussion of antisemitism in a Protestant religious framework has been A. Roy Eckardt's Elder and Younger Brothers: The Encounter of Jews and Christians.[33] Small wonder, then, that both Eckardt and his wife Alice Lyons Eckardt have turned their attention to the Shoah with Long Night's Journey into Day: Life and Faith After the Holocaust.[34] Calling for a radical rethinking of the Christian faith, the primary focus is the Crucifixion-Resurrection phenomenon as centrally and uniquely decisive. A concise summary of their work to date is contained in an article entitled "Post-Holocaust Theology: A Journey Out of the Kingdom of Night".[35] It likewise represents an excellent summary of the theses, questions, and future directions for serious Christian theolog-ians attempting to integrate the historical event of the Shoah into any Christian post-Auschwitz theology.

Eckardt posits five basic theses essential to any Christian understanding of the Shoah:

> [1]   The Holocaust--the Nazis' decision and systematic measures to annihilate all Jews anywhere within their reach, and to remove all evidences of the Jewish presence and testimony-- was unique in both world and Jewish history.
> [2] At the same time, the Holocaust could not have occurred [I am convinced] without the centuries of Christian teaching ["the teaching of contempt"], ecclesiastical decrees, laws rooted in and

justified by the church's theology and urged by church officials, and the ever-growing demonization of the Jew within Christian society.

[3] The Shoah was--and is--an absolute event, because it was meant to be final: an end, an absolute end.

[4] The Holocaust is and must be recognized as a decisive event in and for Christianity.

[5] The Shoah challenges the faithful of both Christianity and Judaism at fundamental levels.[36]

Acceptance of these five theses for the Christian theologian mandates a rethinking of Christianity at its most basic level: At the very point where Christ redeems the world. And yet, except for the thinkers noted above, decidedly in the minority, such calls for rethinking go unheeded and unheard. Even so significant a book as John Roth's A Consuming Fire: Encounters with Elie Wiesel and the Holocaust[37] fails to address this troubling question, as I noted in my review of the book:

> Yet even here [in Roth's commentary to Wiesel's One Generation After], Roth falls far short in the power of his own witnessing and testimony in response to the question he himself poses, "Jesus--God in Christ--has overcome the world?" If Roth would have us understand the life and death of Jesus as the reaching out of God in order "to give hopeless men a momentary future and even hope for a future," then confronted with Wiesel's child-God on the gallows, he has not achieved his objective. The Christian theological dilemma of the redemptive Christ versus an unredeemed world which would countenance a Holocaust remains unresolved.[38]

Having left this central question unresolved, what then are Christians to make of the questions Eckardt herself asks further on in her article:

> --How are we to understand a German cardinal's letter sent to his clergy following the November 1938 Kristallnacht telling them that this nation-wide attack on Jewish places of worship, businesses, homes, and persons was not a matter for the church or clerical persons?
>
> --How are we to grasp the fact that in the years between 1939 and 1945 the only two references the Jesuit periodical Civita Cattolica [published by the Vatican] made to the Jews were in denunciatory ways in connection with the trial and crucixion of Jesus?
>
> --How are we to countenance The Christian Century's editorial comment after Kristallnacht that not only was it "highly

inadvisable to let down our [American] immigration barriers" but "Christian....citizens [of the United States] have no need to feel apolegetic for the limitations [on immigration]?"

--How are we to accept that the best Pastor Martin Niemoller was able to say regarding the "alien and uncongenial" Jews was a grudging acknowledgment that "God has seen fit to reveal Himself to the Jew, Jesus of Nazareth," and therefore this "painful and grievous stumbling block has to be accepted for the sake of the Gospels?"

--How are we to appropriate the truth that while the Warsaw Ghetto inhabitants were making their desperate stand against machine guns, poison gas, flame-throwers, artillery, and planes, the Christian part of the city observed Holy Week, and churchgoers paused on their way to or from Easter services to watch as Polish Jews hurled themselves from burning buildings?

--How are we to dealt with the reality that on each 28 December during World War II Christians were able to continue blithely commemorating the death of the Holy Innocents at Bethlehem, while showing such little concern, even after the news had reached them, that millions of other innocents were being done to death by a modern Herod at Belsen and Auschwitz?

--And when a rabbi went to a local priest to plead for his intercession with the authorities to stop the deportation of Jews to Auschwitz, or at least to do something to save the innocent children, the cleric's response was: "There are no innocent Jewish children. You are all guilty of the Lrod's death, and unless you confess this and enter the church, you will suffer these punishments deservedly." How can we live with this knowledge?[39]

Such poignant questions only jaggedly scratch the surface of the tragic history of Jewish-Christian relationships. Examples abound of Christian indifference and insensitivity to Jewish suffering. Yet, when these very questions are asked by Christians, when sincere and committed Christians learn of such tragic examples, they cry out for response, at the very least a theological response. And, like every other Christian theologian--Catholic as well as non-Catholic--who has wrestled with the profound theological implications of the Shoah, Eckardt considers the following "essentials of such a restructured and revitalized theology":

First, the church needs to put an end to all teachings of superiority and claims of exclusive possession of the menas of salvation.

Second, the church and its theologians must cease finding comfortable ways of meeting the negation of Judaism built into both its traditions and its own addition to Scripture, the New Testament.

Closely allied to the foregoing argument that the church must abandon its displacement claims is a third essential corrective: the church must cease once and for all its presentatin of the Jewish people as the enemies of God and the children of Satan, as well as the Christ-killers or murderers of God, for the issue is far more than a religious one.

Fourth, we must stop asserting that the cross constitutes the ultimate in human suffering.

A fifth point is that the Holocaust not only exposed the extent of the church's anti-Jewish theology, but it also revealed the shallowness of its own devotion to its own ethic.

There is a sixth point. Is it enough to rediscover the historical Jesus, a hasid, or to affirm that it is through this Jesus that we Gentiles have--by a strange process--been brought into the original Covenant with God and Israel?....Can one affirm the Resurrection without at the same time continuing the displacement theology of the church?[48]

Having now presented her theses, asked her questions, and enumerated her "essentials," Eckardt has, in fact, presented the Christian community with its theological agenda for the twenty-first century. That precious few will heed her call, in light of the Shoah and its theological implications, is a continuing tragedy of the first magnitude, one best left to Christians, rather than Jews, to respond.

V. Personal Conclusions

For me personally, as I have indicated at the beginning of this essay, the Shoah is a unique event in both Jewish and world history. Having come to this conclusion growing up in the home of a survivor of the Shoah, meeting other survivors, having studied this phenomenon beginning in my teenage years, having had the opportunity to teach this material on the college and university level, having now written both articles and book reviews dealing with the Shoah, and continuing to research various aspects of the Shoah, I have, also, concluded that it is unique theologically as I have struggled with my own Jewish identity. Certainly for Jews; most particularly for Christians. Having so concluded, I have now committed myself to try and understand both that singular uniqueness as well as the historical and theological implications of the Shoah. What follows, then, are my own theological conclusions which, at the very least, chart for me my own future theological agenda. As one committed to and ordained to serve the Jewish people, I continue to try and reconcile the experiences of Jewish history--in particular one cataclysmic, rupturous event--with the evolving nature of Jewish belief which I now understand to move in a direction significantly different than the historically-traditional notions of the past being emulated, largely without thought, in the present.

[1] I can no longer believe or accept the notion of the God-who-acts-in-history, the very foundation upon which both Judaism and Christianity have built and maintain their faiths. Indeed, I can no longer pray to such a notion of God, for I no longer regard this notion as the true and correct understanding of Divine reality or the Divine-human encounter. Not only did Six Million of my brothers and sisters die during the Shoah, as well as five million non-Jews, but the historically-traditional notion of God also died in the concentration camps which puncture the landscape of Europe. What is now demanded in the realm of theological integrity is a notion of Deity compatible with the reality of radical evil at work and at play in our world, a notion which also admits of human freedom for good or evil without false appeal to a Deity who "chose" [?] not to act because He or She could not act. To continue to affirm the historically-traditional notion of faith in God as presented by the Biblical text and subsequent religious history is to ignore the Shoah with all of its uniqueness and to ignore those who, like myself, continue to feel the pain of family loss, who remain committed to Jewish survival--not because a Deity wills it, but because without this community, we are cut off from even this most fragile of moorings.

[A] A possible source of affirmation of Deity, therefore, in light of my own--and others'--rejection of past notions, lies in the concept of a "limited Deity" who could neither choose nor reject action during the years 1933 to 1945, but, rather, who could not have responded to those humanly-created and crafted processes--even if He or She had wanted to do so. Such a notion, however, must for me be allied with the notion of a Creator-God who, having initiated such a process, prepared an earthly environment wherein so much that has happened historically continues to be possible. Whether this same Creator-God chose to begin this process through the act of self-limitation, or even out of a genuine desire and commitment to human freedom, and cannot now, as evidenced by history, reverse the process is, ultimately, secondary. We human beings are here for however long we now choose to have this planet endure, and no appeal to that Deity--rational or emotional--will now overcome our technological fury should be choose to unleash it. Samuel Pisar, a "graduate of Auschwitz" and author of the book Of Blood and Hope, is, indeed, correct, when he writes that the Shoah is a pilot project for the end of humanity.[41]

Here, too, is a theological lesson gleaned directly from the Shoah: The technology which resulted in the deaths of millions in concentration camps and elsewhere has forever shattered the easy appeal to a Deity who will, somehow, curb the limits of human intellect for good or evil and prevent repetition of the Shoah. If anything, the reverse is now possible: Having let the genie of destructive technology out of the bottle of human ignorance, our best hope for survival lies not in the heavens but in we ourselves, in our ability to educate the next generation to evince the same intellectual expertise to creative measures as we have thus far evidenced to destructive measures.

[B] The notion of Covenant, too, now becomes redefined. Green-berg's "voluntary covenant" becomes an option for those who wish to so enter it--as does its opposite, a rejection of the entire enterprise. Covenant with Deity whereby both Divine and human partners agree to certain stipula-tions in order to maintain harmony and equilibrium is no longer applicable. We can no longer trust God to keep the enemy from crouching at our door--to use the prophetic metaphor--not can Deity trust us not to act in ways that would prove a violation of sacred trusts regarding the living things of our planet. If we are to enter into a covenant in a religious framework, it must now be with each other--as individuals, as communities, as nation-states. Possessing the potential to destroy each other, we must guard against making use of that potential by our willingness to engage in continual dialogue despite our differences as well as our rejection of the value-systems held by others. Just as we would have the Russians and Americans engage in continual dialogue on issues of nuclear arms, so, too, must Jews and Christians, Jews and Arabs, Jews and Germans, Jews and Jews, Christians and Christians engage in continual dialogue with each other. Appeals to Deity will not make such conversation possible. Appeals to each other will.

[C] Prayer, too, must be rethought. Appeals to Deity to correct present situations or to dramatically alter future possibilities will have now become of no avail. Having not responded to words spoken in earnestness and fervor during the long, dark night of Nazism's all-too-successful reign, to expect that same God to respond on a less frightful level to less critical pleas is theological absurdity. Prayer will now have to become an internal plea for recognition that the universe does manifest certain harmonies if we are but receptive to them; that creation allows us more possibilities for human growth than destruction; that aesthetic appreciation of our world enhances our pleasure at being a part of it; that the poetic words of our predecessors, now reinterpreted, likewise increase our understanding of the shared yearnings of all of humankind for peace; that the disciplined gather-ing of like-minded groups in celebration can help energize us to confront the challenges of our own day; that we need not suspend our intellect nor deny historical realities when we engage ourselves in prayer.

[D] The Jewish notion of mitzvah as "commandment" or "Jewish religious obligation" will now have to be reinterpreted. No longer can this concept of Divine commander have merit for those for whom such respon-sive behaviors merited such sadistic contempt from their Nazi oppressors. Again, Fackenheim's "commanding voice," heard only by those who are already listening, will not be heard by those not already sensitized to their Jewish responsibilities because of the events of the Shoah. Besides, even Fackenheim himself would not have the temerity to maintain that this voice is even remotely akin to the Bat Kol of Jewish talmudic tradition, the Divine voice which spoke to the rabbis of the ancient academies in an effort to resolve their disputes. As I have written previously, the only mitzvah now incumbent upon the Jewish in light of the Shoah is the mitzvah of study, the responsibility to know in order to make informed decisions in this post-Auschwitz age.[42] But the notion of mitzvah as the religiously-commanded act of Deity to creation, imposed upon the Jewish people by an historically-bound and committed authority structure, is yet another casualty of the Shoah. To include only those who are now willing to maintain those structures is equally as pernicious as excluding those who no longer wish to do so. What is of relevance is those Jews who, freely, are willing to make commitments, who are now willing to practice those forms of historically-traditional behaviors which they themselves find meaningful, both individually and collectively. But to presume guilt to-wards those who no longer think and act in accord with the ways of the past is to deny the present. The focus must be inclusive rather than exclusive if this people, so devastated by the enormity of its losses, is to again regain its equilibrium given the contemporary pressures with which it is currently confronted.

[E] Celebration, then, of festival-calendar events, as well as life-cycle events, will now have to be rethought, not so much for the specific manner in which they are celebrated, but for the rationale behind their celebration. No more can this or that holiday be celebrated or sanctified for the historically-traditional reasons previously supplied. No more can given life-cycle events be celebrated for similar reasons. Though the actual practices themselves may not vary one iota from previous patterns of behavior, the whys and wherefores in light of the Shoah now demand a degree of intellectual consistency coupled with theological integrity heretofore unknown in the past. No more can the Passover, for example, be seen as God's liberation of the Jewish people from the slavery and bondage of Egypt when the slavery and bondage of Nazi Germany resulted in the deaths and degradations of so many. No longer can the ritual of circumcision of an eight-day old Jewish male be understood as entering into covenant directly with God when those already committed to that covenant realized its impotence throughout Nazi-occupied Europe. New words are needed to address new realities; if not new words, then new interpretations of old words--not for all, but certainly for those of us for whom the old ways can no longer be maintained or resurrected.

[2] Lastly, a similar agenda must be presented to the Christian communities by the Christian communities and for the Christian communities. For Jews, what must be rethought is the whole notion of God and the Covenant and the Jewish people. For Christians, what must be rethought is the whole notion of God the Father, His Son Jesus the Christ, and the relationship of that Christ to this unredeemed world; and the Christian community to the Jewish people given the history of non-relationship which led to the Shoah, and the relationship which now must exist subsequent to it. Now

more than ever, serious, studious, open and honest dialogue is needed between Jews and Christians, not to erase the past but to understand it, and to chart new directions away from its repetition and continuation.

For Michael Berenbaum, the lesson of the <u>Shoah</u> is clear: The world is an unredeemed place and will [forever?] continue to remain so. While critical of the fervent messianic pretensions and predilections associated with militant Orthodox Judaism, particularly in Israel, the ongoing task of humanity is not to wait for--or believe in--the coming of the Messiah [<u>beviat ha-Maschiach</u>], but to take upon itself the responsibilities to act as re-deemers ["It is too late for the Messiah. The God who was silent then should be ashamed to act now."] Indeed, if the world possesses any pos-sibilities at all of redemption, they will come about by dint of human effort and not by appeals to religious faith.

IN A WORLD WITHOUT A REDEEMER, REDEEM!

Michael Berenbaum

I. Introduction: Israeli Zionism and Orthodox Messianism

The easiest affirmation I make as a Jew is that this world has not yet been redeemed. The evidence is so overwhelming--especially after the Shoah--that the point is just not worth arguing. This world has not been redeemed.

Jewish have been making the very same point since the beginning of the common era. We have been denying the Christ in its various forms, including Jesus of Nazareth, the nation-state, and, most recently, the Soviet state.[1] Yet the attraction to the Christ is equally strong, and, at moments, the yearning becomes most intense.

Even though it is much more difficult to believe in the Messiah and in redemption than to deny their presence in this world, Jews have striven for the redemption in diverse forms of religious life ranging from mili-tary revolution to quietistic piety. In the past, we have embraced for brief periods of time false Messiahs, often with disastrous results. From Bar Kokhba[2] to Sabbatai Sevi[3], the lure of a Messianic figure has been danger-ous. Yet to resist this religious infatuation has been equally difficult.

Were one attempting a history of contemporary Judaism three decades ago, as did Arthur Hertzberg in his anthology on Zionism The Zionist Idea[4], one could have written with confidence that, for the modern Jew, Messianism has become secularized, and only in its secular form has it achieved a modicum of success.

Certainly Zionism was built--directly and subliminally--on the Messianic impulse of the Jewish people. Theodor Herzl was received in Eastern Europe with the enthusiasm of a Messianic leader--secularized but Messianic nonetheless. The rabbinic leadership that resisted Herzl under-stood the true implications of his mission. They taught that Zionism was a human usurpation of divine prerogatives, an anti-religious revolution in Jewish life. Herzl, too, misjudged the character of his movement. He soon found himself forced to be mindful, if not respectful, of the Messianic impulse of the masses of Jews who would settle for nothing less than the historic land of Israel. They rejected the Uganda proposal approved by the Zionist leadership.

Zionism, Marxism, Freudianism, and even some aspects of Reform Judaism imply a secularization of the Messianic impulse, and, hence, its limited realization. However, over the past thirty years, the greatest Messianic movements have been seen as the non-secular and anti-secular religious movements that have arisen in Israel and shaped a Messianic politics of settlements in Judea and Samaria and conflict with Arabs and between Jews.

These Messianic movements have been joined in recent years by an intensified Messianic urgency among Lubavitch Hasidim, who may be concealing or slowing revealing the Messianic role of their current Rebbe, Menachem Mendel Schneerson, now reaching his mid-eighties. Childless, he is without an apparent heir. Quite often, his followers in Israel will be awakened in the middle of the night and sent scurrying to the [Western] Wall to pray, and thus, according to believers, many disasters have been averted. Lubavitch Hasidim live with a considerable sense of agitation and those of us with contacts in the movement know that over the past few years, some followers have even spoken openly about the Rebbe's Messianic role.

There is considerable division within Orthodoxy as to the meaning of the modern State of Israel. In some quarters, Zionism is still condemned as anti-Jewish, a human abrogation of God's role to bring about the redemption. Nothing galls these leaders more than to see the Jewish people led by a brazenly unobservant and secular leadership. Neturei Karta and the followers of the Satmar Rebbe are the most notable adherents to this doctrine, but there are others and their presence within the religious community, and especially within the world of the Yeshivot, is prominent. Recently, they have sought to embarrass the State by attracting as converts--penitents--the elite fighters of the Israel Defense Forces [IDF], its pilots.

Rabbi Joseph Dov Baer Soloveitchik, the acknowledged dean of Yeshiva University Orthodoxy [which was once known as "modern Orthodoxy" and more recently as "centrist"], has written of the modern State of Israel as kol dode dofek, "the knock of my beloved'[6]. The State is, perhaps, a manifestation of the Divine Presence within Jewish history. The evidence of God's presence is slight--only a knock--yet quite suggestive, but Soloveitchik is reluctant to stretch the evidence or to speak of the immediate implications of that Presence.

In the early years of the Yishuv, the first Chief Rabbi of Palestine, Abraham Isaac Kook, compared the Zionist enterprise to the building of the ancient Temple--even the least pious of workers was able to move about freely on the entire Temple mount, including the Holy of Holies, the most sacred site in the consecrated Temple. The Holy of Holies could be entered only once a year and only by one man: On Yom Kippur, the High Priest would enter this most sacred site only after a period of penitence and cleaning as prescribed in the a demanding ritual. So, too, Kook ruled, to build the new Holy of Holies, it is permissible to work with secular Jews until the moment of its consecration.[6] Kook thus bridged the gap between the Yishuv and non-Zionist Orthodoxy, granting only transient legitimacy to the early pioneers. He did conceive of the Zionist endeavor as reishit tzemichat geulatainu, the "first flowering of our redemption," language that was later incorporated into the official prayer for the State authored and sanctioned by Israel's Chief Rabbis. Kook's vision of re-demption was gradual, proceeding by this worldly and rather unorthodox means and linked directly with the Land of Israel. Kook made peace with the necessity of Zionism even while he denied its longevity.

Some students of Kook, such as the late Zvi Yaron[7], argue that Kook's chosen metaphor was more designed to appease the Orthodox than to make a directly theological statement, but it seems clear that he never accepted the legitimacy of the Zionist enterprise in an ultimate sense, as a permanent and acceptable way of sustaining the Jewish future.

The tension in Kook's initial position has come back to haunt his followers, most especially his late son Rabbi Zvi Yehudah Kook[8], who became the spiritual force behind the settler movement, many of whose members were trained in his Yeshiva, Merkaz Harav.

Two events intervened, the twin revolutions of modern Jewish history, the Shoah and the rise of the modern State of Israel. Elsewhere, I have written of the revolutionary impact of both events, and these writings need to be repeated here.[9] Suffice it to say, that no generation of Jews has lived history quite as intensely as ours, save, perhaps, the ancient Israelites who went from Egyptian servitude to the Event at Sinai, and spent the next forty years attempting to understand precisely what had happened. No future Jewish theology will be credible without grappling with both the Shoah and Israel. And certainly both loom large in the imagination and identity of every Jew.

The Shoah remains in the background for Rabbi Zvi Yehudah Kook and his disciples. Yet even for them--no less than for the post-Shoah theologians--Auschwitz poses serious theological dilemmas. Unwilling to forsake their belief in God and Torah, Zvi Yehudah Kook and his followers are forced to reunderstand the timetable of history. The Shoah is thus approached as the apocalyptic event, the great battle between the forces of good and evil, between Gog and Magog. An event of such magnitude forces thinking to a different level of interpretation. Apocalyptic catastrophe sets the stage for the redemptive events of Israel.

While for many secular Jews, 1948 marks a turning point in Jewish history, the event of modern Jewish history for the younger Rabbi Kook and his Gush Emunim disciples is not the foundation of the modern

State with its secular Declaration of Independence, but the miraculous victory of 1967, the reunification of Jerusalem, the restoration of the Temple Mount to Jewish rule, the return of that same Jewish rule to the ancestral lands of Judea and Samaria, and the religious resurgence that followed this mammoth victory. Thus, the Hallel Psalms will be recited on the 28th of Iyar, Yom Yerushalaim, on the day of the reunification of Jerusalem, but not on the 5th of Iyar, Yom Haatzmaut, Israel's Independence Day.

I vividly recall the sixth day of the Six Day War, the Shabbat on which the war ended. On Friday evening, we gathered in the old Hillel House building on Balfour Street in Jerusalem. The synagogue was filled with student soldiers, many enjoying a few moments of free time, ready to being the Kabbalat Shabbat Service, when the then-President of Israel, Schneur Zalman Shazar, walked in accompanied by the then-Chief Rabbi of the Israel Defense Forces, General Shlomo Goren. Naturally they were invited to speak. Goren, who was to introduce the President, spoke of Shazar as the first President of a unified Jerusalem and of an Israel restored to its land. He also declared that, on Monday, Shazar would be the first to greet the Messiah of Israel as he rode down Jaffa Street in Jerusalem. Goren had had a busy week. He had blown the shofar at the [Western] Wall on Tuesday; he had flown to the Sinai on Wednesday and again blew shofar from atop one of the hills which we had declared the site of the theophany. And while anything was believable in the euphoria of Jerusalem on June 10, 1967, Goren seriously believed that the Messiah would arrive imminently. He was not alone. And in twenty years, the ardor of some has only intensified.

In contrast, Shazar spoke in measured, poetic tones. Known for his long-winded, sermonic addresses, Shazar was uncharacteristically brief and crisp. "All my life," the Israeli President--a fellow traveller though not a disciple of Lubavitch--whispered, "I prayed, 'clothe yourself with the garments of majesty, O Jerusalem', and today I lived it. "Rav lach shevat beamek habachah, 'you have sat enough in the valley of tears'" he said with tears in his eyes, paraphrasing the words of Lecha Dode. His expectations, unlike those of Rabbi Goren, were modest and simple. His joy intense yet sober. Shazar reflected that day, the other dimension of the victory: the sober, cautious realism of those given to fervor but not to Messianic abandon.

The tensions between his views and Goren's persist to this day within religious circles.

Yonina Talmon has argued that Messianic movements are never the product of catastrophe alone. They are born of the imbalance between expectation and reality, of the disappointments that follow a period of sustained hope.[10] During the past half century, Jews have endured quite a buffeting.   Victims of the epitome of inhumanity in a governmentally-sponsored and systematically-structured mass genocide, we have also witnessed the flourishing of hope with the rebirth of the Jewish people in its ancestral land only three years after the destruction. Yet even the history of the State has also been characterized by cycles of despair and hope--war and armistice, then war and triumph crowned by the return to Jerusalem, followed by an enormous explosion of energy and enthusiasm and then followed by two devastating wars less than a decade apart. Attacked on the most solemn day of the Jewish year, Israel lost 2,500 soldiers in the Yom Kippur War along with a sense of its invulnerability. Nine years later, it lost one fifth as many men, but something almost as important as well--confidence in the righteousness of its cause, the wisdom and integrity of its deeds.

Religious Messianism in Israel is nourished by social realities. In Israel there are four parallel--separate but equal--school systems, a secular Jewish school system, a religious school system sponsored by the State, an ultra-Orthodox system sanctioned by the State but with minimal governmental involvement, and an Arab school system. Almost without exception, religiously-observant Jews attend a religious school system. They also belong to religious youth movements and can serve in the Army in a program that permits them to both study at Yeshiva and engage in army study at one and the same time. Thus, Israeli Orthodox youth are raised in self-segregated societies designed to preserve their religious world-view. Often they reach their early twenties without encountering secular peers with a cognitively dissonant world-view. Increasingly as well, they live in neighborhoods segregated according to religious observances: ultra-Orthodox enclaves, religious neighborhoods, and secular areas.

For the better part of a half century, the ideology that dominated Israeli society and provided it with its core of values was secular Zionism. During the past twenty years, the motivating power of this world-view has waned as the four basic promises of secular Zionism remain unrealized despite the incredible triumph of the State of Israel. Secular Zionism has promised normalcy, independence, an end to Jewish vulnerability, and the ingathering of the exiles. Yet Jewish life continues to be abnormal and the State of Israel remains abnormal as a state among the nations of the world. "A nation set apart," rather than "a people like any people" defines the reality of contemporary Israel.   So, too, Israel received independence precisely as the world has become interdependent and the sovereign state finds itself interdependent with the Diaspora--whose demise Zionism had predicted--for financial and political support, and interdependent, if not dependent, on the United States for an economic, political, and military lifeline.[11]

Furthermore, power and sovereignty have not ended Jewish vulnerability; they have altered the means by which we combat our vulnerability. An unanticipated sense of vulnerability persists. Finally, while Israel has absorbed more than two million immigrants, over the past twenty years, the number of yordim has exceeded the number of olim. There are more Israelis in New York than in Jerusalem. And Israelis increasingly come westward for an encounter with cosmopolitan culture just as American Jews come as pilgrims to Israel in search of their Jewish roots. Mutual exchange rather than absorption has characterized Israel's relations with the North American Diaspora. So total has been the collapse of the secularist Zionist vision that Zionism is often treated as a term of derision rather than a lofty ideal.[12]

Militant nationalism and religion have stepped into the vacuum created by the decline of Israel's civil religion of secular Zionism. Both never expected normalcy nor did they fully believe that Jewish vulnerability could be ended. They never sought to be integrated into the world, but rather to stand apart from the world--either by necessity or because of a national religious vocation. In the movement of Gush Emunim, they have fused into a Messianic, nationalist movement.

II. The Theology of Yehuda Amital

Perhaps the most interesting--though not necessarily the most influential--theological exposition of the Messianic religious Zionist perspective was presented by Rabbi Yehuda Amital, the head of Yeshivat Har Etzion, a Talmudic academy set in the rebuilt Etzion block destroyed by the Jordanians in 1948. Amital's Hamaalot Memaakim, Ascent from the Depths, is a slim, powerful collection of addresses on the religious meaning of war and his speeches to the Yeshiva students on the meaning of the hour.

From the Six Day War, Amital argues, we learned that war can serve a redemptive purpose, since, without any desire on Israel's part, and following a specific request to King Hussein that Jordan stay out of the war--the Jewish people were restored to the city of Jerusalem and all the sacred sites. Although the Yom Kippur War at first appears to be an anti-redemptive manifestation of history, the opposite may be the case in so far as Israel's military victory was greater than in 1967.[13]

The choice of the Yom Kippur as the day to begin the war, Amital reasoned, was an implied attack on Jews and Judaism--an assault by Islam against the Gold of Israel--yet the Western nations were the real losers of the war. The false Western God--the god of technology--was clearly addicted to oil and cheap supplies of energy. Israel's massive victory against powerful armies and overwhelming odds was a great act of divine salvation, Amital told his students. The purpose of the war was to mold and purify the Jewish people into a spiritually pure unit able to withstand the pressures of the Messiah's footsteps.   He called for a reintensification of efforts, a deepening commitment that is equal to Messianic stakes.

Amital was politically astute in his assessment of the West, yet stubborn in his refusal to see the war as stemming from real grievances and fought for military/diplomatic purposes.   He returns to the language of a pre-secularized warfare, a language sanctioned by tradition yet one which classical Zionism sought to overturn.   He has further immunized his disciples and their fellow travellers from responding to political pressures, viewing all such compromises as a retreat from a divinely-mandated task.

Amital's position is even more interesting because he moderated his views after the war in Lebanon.   Given the militant patriotism of the hesder Yeshiva students [those to divide their army service between the Yeshiva study and military duties], they volunteered for the elite units of the IDF often replacing or serving alongside Labor Zionism's elite, the kibbutzniks.   In Lebanon, for the first time, Yeshiva students were on the front lines and suffered disproportionately high casualty rates.   Amital's response was bold.   He told his students that Jewish responsibilities to the Land of Israel must be balanced by a commitment to the Torah of Israel and the people Israel.   If the former is emphasized to the exclusion of the other commitments, then the future of Israel is misconstrued.   While the war in Lebanon may have hardened many positions, it moderated at least one. Amital was immediately ostracized by his former political allies.

III. Catastropic Implications and the Shoah

It is understandable that a non-secularized Messianic striving in contemporary Israel has led to idealism and self-sacrifice.   It has also led to terrorism and to fundamental assaults on Israeli democracy and the rule of law.   It sustains a climate in which apocalyptic politics can become the norm for a significant segment of society and apocalyptic politics in a nuclear age is a sure prescription for catastrophe.   Given the scope of such serious and disciplined Messianic movements, we must again understand the full implications of the Messianic impulse.

After the Spanish Expulsion, the religious response to catastrophe took the form of Lurianic Kabbalah, which deepened our understanding of exile and made more difficult, though also more concrete, the task of redemption. According to Lurianic Kabbalah, exile was ontological--part of the primordial experience of creation.[14]   The divine sparks were scattered by a cosmic catastrophe.   And redemption was gradual, almost painfully slow, acts of tikkun, of restoration, reuniting one by one the divine sparks with their source.

If such was the response to Expulsion, what then should be our response to the Shoah? It is too late for the Messiah. The God who was silent then should be ashamed to act now. Jews can no longer afform what Gershom Scholem called the anti-existentialist posture of Messianism.[15] Both Gush Emunim and Lubavitch have joined secular Zionism and American Judaism in their commitment to a religious and political life of activism. They have become active in forcing the "hand of God"[16]. Jews can no longer wait for God but must become the initiator. On this we concur.

Yet, while it may also be too late for redemption in a global sense, but it is certainly not too late to redeem.

Emil Fackenheim returned to the Lurianic tradition when he sought to describe the post-Shoah reality of life. Where Rabbi Isaac spoke of shevirate hakelim [the breaking apart of the vessels--Ed.], Fackenheim writes of the rupture and returns to the image of tikkun, translated as "mending" rather than restoration, to describe the aftermath of the rupture.[17] The garment may be sown whole, but the original rent remains even after tikkun. It will never become whole again in an unbroken seamless fabric. On Purim, 1967, three months before the war, Wiesel described Auschwitz as the breaking of the covenant established at Sinai.[18] Richard Rubenstein's image was even starker: Auschwitz was nothing less than the death of the God of history--at least within the experience of the believer.[19] In my own work, I have preferred the image of the void, absence where presence has been.[20] Other radical images of the Jewish condition have also been offered. As with the generation after the Expulsion, we live at a time of shattering, of broken vessels, where the reality of exile--of non-redemption--is decisive.

Our response must be equally clear. After the rupture, mend, Fackenheim tells us. The possiblity of mending--even the model of mending--was offered amidst the darkness, so we know what has to be done. Mend the rupture, he exhorts us.

Unlike Maurice Friedman[21], I believe that Wiesel offers no more compelling image of the redemptive task that when he writes in The Town Beyond the Wall:

> To say 'I suffer, therefore I am' is to become the enemy of man. What you must say is 'I suffer therefore you are.' Camus wrote somewhere that to protest against a universe of unhappiness you had to create happiness. That's the arrow pointing the way: it leads to another human being and not via absurdity.[22]

So, too, he wrote in 1967:

> In a world of absurdity, we must invent reason, we must create out of nothingness. And because there is murder in the

world--and we are the first to know it--and we know how hopeless our battle may appear, we have to fight murder and absurdity and give meaning to the battle, if not our hope.[23]

While in his later work, Wiesel may flirt with the Messiah and return to traditional langauge with intensified urgency, the task of redemption has been reduced to a human scale. God has been replaced by the human image, "the image of a people who have routed defeat and survived in community, in celebration, in solidarity, in hope, in despair, in pain and in violence."[24]

In my own religious life, the Sabbath plays a much more significant role than the Messiah because the Sabbath is part of the week, in dialogue with the week, a foretaste of what can be, a moment of redemption that points back to the world rather than away from it. And the Sabbath does not make promises that it cannot keep.

In Evil and the Morality of God, Harold Schulweis has suggested a predicate theology. Instead of speaking of God, we speak of godliness and instead of speaking of redemption, Schulweis suggests, we go about the business of redeeming, deed by deed, person by person, spark by spark. The Messiah is therefore neither a person nor an event, but a series of actions that heal, save and console, that create hope after despair and empower the powerless and redeem the oppressed rather than consecrate those who have arrived.

I do not believe with a complete faith in the coming of the Messiah, but while he/she tarries, I will strive to redeem every day until....

Perhaps God will surprise us. Perhaps not. But the human task is clear and the Jewish task is our covenant with history and with memory made more urgent by what we have experienced and more poignant by the longings of generations.

A decade ago I wrote: "perhaps for Wiesel, to be a Jew after Auschwitz is to hope for a Messiah and to work for a Messiah while knowing full well that the hope is for naught."[25] Over the past decade, it has become less true of Wiesel and more and more true of my own life especially as I grow increasingly fearful of the politics of those who would work for a Messiah in the traditional sense. I remain convinced that the task is both necessary and vital--but only if it grounded in the sober realism of the work that is not redeemed nor likely to be. From the Shoah we can learn the urgency of the task. From Messianism in contemporary Israel, we must learn the dangers of religious infatuations. From our Lurianic forebears, we can learn much about modesty and humility--and also about the duration of the struggle.

All those who have contributed to this volume, as well as to <u>Contemporary Christian Religious Responses to the Shoah</u>, have a university or college connection, either full-time or part-time. Those who will read and ponder these two volumes, primarily, will be teachers and students in our institutions of higher learning. Alan Berger's essay reminds us that individual and collective ethical responsibility cannot be divorced from such teaching, and, by extension, from learning--not only in those courses which deal centrally with the <u>Shoah</u>, but, equally, with those in the humanities and sciences as well. He further reminds us that academic objectivity, long a hallmark of scholarly work, is, like rationalism itself, a casualty of the Second World War. "Practically speaking, the question is: What is the relationship between teaching and being human?" In so asking the question and framing his critique, he returns us, once again, to a contemporary religious response to the <u>Shoah</u>, invites a re-thinking of the process of learning as presently structured, and suggests a new direction for the future.[1]

ACADEMIA AND THE HOLOCAUST

Alan L. Berger

I. Introduction

This essay is a reflection on the relationship of Hitler's years of slaughter--what is infelicitiously termed Holocaust[2]--to the assumptions of university life and its methods of teaching. I am convinced that universities are at best marginal and, in certain cases, poor places to discover and to teach values and I wish, therefore, to argue that academics need to reexamine the foundations of their scholarship. Moreover, the Holocaust, having become grist for the academic mill, is now threatened with death by a thousand qualifications. For example, Elie Wiesel has observed that "yesterday people said, 'Auschwitz, never heard of it." "Now they say, 'Oh yes, we know all about it.'" The second statement underscores the perils involved in attempting to teach about the annihilation of the Jews.

Technological sophistication coupled with linguistic impoverishment has left academics ethical unmusical. Like the inhabitants of Plato's cave, university professors are transfixed by illusions. Academia's shadow idols are abstraction and generalization, professionalism and objectivity. The academy strives to understand while simultaneously shunning the particularity which alone can grant access to broader areas of knowledge. Scholarship which loses sight of the human ends as intellectual fascism.

The two poles around which Holocaust studies revolve have been articulated by Elie Wiesel and Richard Rubenstein. Wiesel, the survivor, views the Holocaust as a sacred subject. "One should take off one's shoes," he observes, "when entering its domain, one should tremble each time one pronounces the word."[5] However, there is another and frequently unexplored dimension to Holocaust implications. Rubenstein writes:

> Until ethical theorists and theologians are prepared to face without sentimentality the kind of action it is possible freely to perpetuate under conditions of utter respectibility in an advanced, contemporary society, none of their assertions about the existence of moral norms will have much credibility. To repeat, no laws were broken and no crimes were committed at Auschwitz....no

Reprinted from JUDAISM: A Quarterly Journal of Jewish Life and Thought Volume 31, Number 2, Spring Issue 1982, pages 166-176. Permission granted.

credible punishment was meted out--Truly, the twentieth century has been the century par excellence that is beyond good and evil.[4]

Both Wiesel and Rubenstein, despite their vastly different conclusions view the Holocaust as a novum. Wiesel compares the enormity of Auschwitz to the revelation at Sinai. Rubenstein, on his part, demystifies the Holocaust, claiming that the Nazis successfully breached a hitherto unbreachable moral and political barrier [exterminating the Jews] owing to their highly developed bureaucracy and their superior technology. Both positions form part of the total event. Rather than struggle with this tension, academics, apparently embarrassed by notions of holiness, stress social science categories, finding them more amenable to objectivity.

II. Academia and Objectivity

Academic rightly distinguishes itself from society at large by refraining from the easy temptations of sloganeering and provincialism when dealing with crucial civilizational issues. Dispassionate research broadens the horizon, enabling new constellations of possibilities to emerge. Removed from the intense passions of the moment, academics are able to supply analogies, furnish historical antecedents and, most important, lend perspective. But, too often, this dispassionate condition results in a kind of moral abstentionism. University professors frequently end as bystanders forever tentative, fearing a moral stance as an assault upon their professional status.

Objectivity, learned from Greek culture, heralded by seventeenth-century science and carefully nurtured in succeeding centuries, has attained a semi-sacred status not only among academics, but is, as well, a societal norm, having become the guideline for attorneys, bureaucrats, corporate executives, and physicians, among others. However, objectivity is based upon a presumption of rationality which is, itself, another victim of the gas chambers and ovens. Ethically unanchored objectivity frequently metamorphosizes into moral betrayal. In short, universities uphold objectivity--which is dignified as professionalism--but which is, in reality, only pseudo-professionalism, without a similar stress on compassion.

Elitism, another unspoken assumption of university existence, may be equally culpable. Universities have a right to demand excellence and, if this is what is meant by elitism, there can be little definitional quarrel. However, elitism among intellectuals frequently breeds indifference. Commitment and concern for community are the first casualties of intellectual fascism.

Man has increasingly become the measure of all things. His pro-methean arrogance, coupled with great technological skill, has produced power but not compassion, order without meaning, and progress instead of salvation. Somewhere along the way universities began producing parts for the societal machine, at the expense of living the "examined life." Congratulating themselves on attaining objectivity, the universities have admitted a Trojan Horse. It needs to be recognized that what apostasy is to theology, elitist objectivity [pseudo-professionalism] is to teaching.

Writing in The Origins of Totalitarianism, Hannah Arendt reports the emergence of a nineteenth-century tendency which is distressingly contemporary among academics:

> The cynical or bored indifference in the face of death or other personal catastrophes, the passionate inclination toward the most abstract notions as guides for life, [and a] general contempt for even the most obvious rules of common sense.[5]

Specifically concerning the Holocaust, Bruno Bettelheim reflects on the guilt of physicians in the so-called medical experiments in various death camps, lamenting their pride in professional skill and knowledge irrespective of moral implication. He views this as dangerous. "Auschwitz is gone," observes Bettelheim, "but as long as this attitude remains with us we shall not be safe from the indifference to life at its core."[6] His utterance is, I fear, prophetic. Universities accentuate and multiply skills courses while regularly deemphasizing and eliminating courses in ethics. Although frequently performed as ethically neutral acts [a course's fate typically depends upon enrollment], the results are disastrous. Skills are refined without any moral limit on their use.

III. A Literary Perspective

The need for academics to engage in a prolonged period of soul-searching is urgent, but is expression appears muted. For example, only two fictional Jewish professors react to the Holocaust--Moses E. Herzog and the less well-known Sol Nazerman. Saul Bellow's Herzog is an academic unimpressed by the "commonplaces of the Wasteland outlook, the cheap mental stimulants of Alienation, the can and rant of pipsqueaks about Inauthenticity and Forlornness." Herzog does not enjoy the respect of his academic colleagues. They are upset by his emotionalism which is perceived as an irrelevant concern from everyday truths, and by his refusal to engage in chic apocalypticism. Herzog, for his part, is bitterly critical of spurious elitism. Writing to Professor Shapiro, he denounces such elit-ism, holding it at least partly responsible for European totalitarianism and

> ....reaching at last the point of denying the humanity of the industrialized "banalized" masses. It was easy for the Wastelanders to be assimilated, to be assimilated to totalitarianism. Here the responsibility of artists remains to be assessed. To have assumed....that the deterioration of langauge and its

debasement was tantamount to dehumanization led straight to cultural fascism. [page 76]

Few academics recognize the validity of Herzog's warning: "How quickly the visions of genius become the canned goods of the intellectuals." Sol Nazerman, the Pawnbroker, is, like Herzog, a victim. Unlike him, Nazerman is a death camp survivor. Edward Lewis Wallant employs the figure of a displaced academic, professor of history of ideas prior to the cataclysm, who metamorphosizes after the war as front man for a major crime figure. Nazerman has abandoned, and been abandoned by, the morally corrupt and ideologically bankrupt university value system. He bitterly warns his assistant against the seductions of so-called culture: "I do not trust God or politics or newspapers or movies or art." He is most suspicious of "people and their talk, for they have created hell with their talk...." Although failing to pursue the implications for academics, is Wallant [perhaps subconsciously] portraying the role played by academics in Nazi Germany? What are the ethical moorings of scholars and teachers who, when faced with the choice of losing their university positions or supporting the Nazis, chose, in the vast majority, the latter course.[7] Would contemporary academics act differently?

IV. Pseudo-Professionalism and Objectivity in Nazi Germany

Pseudo-professionalism and objectivity were commonplace in Nazi Germany. How they came about and what they resulted in are questions of more than passing interest. If the past is but prologue, we owe to our present, and stake to our future existence, the obligation not only of learning history's lessons, but determining their contemporary implications. Only one generation separates us from the Holocaust. Surely that is too soon to forget the lessons of perverted professionalism. The preponderance of academics, corporate executives and physicians among the murderers raises the most fundamental questions about modernity. Civilizational assumptions in modernity, owing, no doubt, to the fact that man inhabits a desacralized world--Herzog laments the "decay of the religious foundations of civilization"--have less to do with illumination and are more concerned with attaining technological competence. Value-free performance is a hallmark of modernity. It is instructive to recall Raul Hilberg's description of the murderous Einsatzgruppen [SS] leadership:

These men were in no sense hoodlums, delinquents, common criminals, or sex maniacs. Most were intellectuals. All we know is they brought to their new task all the skills and training which, as men of thought, they were capable of contributing. These men, in short, became efficient killers.[8]

V. Three Examples

Dr. Joseph Mengele, the infamous "angel of death" at Auschwitz, attended a pregnant woman prisoner. According to an eye-witness account, Mengele:

> took all correct medical precautions during childbirth, rigorously observing all aseptic principles, cutting the umbilical cord with greatest care, etc. But only half an hour later he sent mother and infant to be burned in the crematorium.[9]

The corporate elite also had no difficulty divorcing skills from values. Five of I. G. Farben's top executives inspected I. G. Auschwitz, the firm's slave labor factory.[10] Passing two Jewish scientist inmates, one of the directors said to an SS man, "This Jewish swine could work a little faster." Another director, not to be outdone by his companion, added, "If they can't work, let them perish in the gas chamber." Dr. Lohner-Beda, one of the Jewish scientists, was pulled from his group, then beaten and kicked to death.[11]

The record of German academics, nowhere systematically report-ed, is equally appalling. Max Weinrich writes that "German scholarship provided the ideas and techniques which led to and justified this unparalleled slaughter."[12] It is a pity that there was no Nuremberg Trial against professors as such.[13] Few academics and intellectuals have learned to accept responsibility for the consequences [political and otherwise] of their ideological preachments. This divorce of academia from reality is nowhere clearer than in the statement of Martin Heidegger, one of the ranking philosophers in the world. His scholarship is read, studied, and pondered with great care in contemporary universities. Yet how many professors assigning Heidegger's works know, or care, about his actions as Rector of Freiburg University? In that capacity, Heidegger wrote to his students admonishing them:

> Not doctrines and "ideas" be the rules of your being. The Fuhrer himself and alone is the present and future German reality and its law. Learn ever deeper to know: that from now on each and everything demands decision and every action responsibility. Heil Hitler![14]

Ironically, Heidegger's call for decision and responsibility was made to those who had been barred from all possibility of self-responsibility and freedom of choice.[15]

The above record appears to suggest rather strongly that education has abandoned its humanizing task. The new product is described by Franklin H. Littell as a technically competent barbarian, whose education has "trained him to think in ways that eliminate questions of ultimate responsibility."[16] The aphorist, Elias Canetti, states the problem in its fundamental terms: "We have no standard any more for anything, ever since human life is no longer the standard." Is this situation reversible? Dare we think of values in a radically disenchanted world, a world in which there appears to be no restraint upon man's actions?

Values imply standards. Ideally, education is training in human potential and responsibility. What possible meaning could this goal have in the post-Holocaust world? Wiesel reports seeing himself in a mirror after the war, for the first time since he had been taken from the ghetto. "From the depths of the mirror," he writes, "a corpse gazed back at me." Is this the contemporary image of man?

Practically speaking, the question is: What is the relationship between teaching and being human? Professors and students must constantly ask what values are illuminated by the application of skills. The dissonance between what is taught and the world we live in seems overwhelming.

VI. Holocaust Specificity

Wiesel correctly notes that the Holocaust has become a "desanctified theme." Perhaps this was inevitable. Though I do not completely share his view that the Holocaust is "Holy History," I do emphatically agree that the murdered demand respect. What is done with the data reveals much about the nature of society. For example, at Babi Yar, where the earth opened to receive the bodies of 30,000 Jews whom the Nazis had machine gunned to death, the Soviets have put a plaque commemorating not the Jews, but the "victims of fascism."

Distortion of the Holocaust occurs with the very use of that term to describe what happened to Europe's Jews. Derived from the Greek holo-kautoma, "burnt offering," Holocaust came into use sometime in the late 1950s. This antiseptic word implies a Christian understanding of Jewish history. Six million sacrifices to God Almighty; no grosser falsification of Isaiah was ever proposed. Judaism, for its part, speaks of the trauma differently and in its own idiom. Hurban [day of awe] is a Yiddish word which carries with it memories of the destruction[s] of the Jerusalem Temple. Shoah is Hebrew. It means desolation of cosmic proportion. Theologically, the Holocaust remains a mystery. Wiesel has written that "perhaps some day someone will explain how, on the level of man, Auschwitz was possible; but on the level of God, it will forever remain the most disturbing of mysteries."[17]

Two pedagogical goals are elimination of ignorance and a striving for clarity of understanding. The Holocaust, an irrational act implemented in a highly rational bureaucratic manner, challenges at least the second goal. This is not to invalidate further research nor does it denigrate the enormous quantity of post-World War II documents which are coming to light. In fact, scholars continually penetrate ever deeper into the how of mass murder, including the reactions of victim and victimizer, but the why remains elusive.

It is for this reason, I suggest, that Wiesel contends that "....the Holocaust teaching nothing." But there is much to learn from it. The Holocaust is a looking glass which reflects civilization and ourselves, simultaneously revealing and unraveling the fabric of our civilization. Post-Holocaust requires us, at the very least, seriously to question any a priori comparison of Holocaust to other tragedies. On the other hand, while scrupulously particular in nature [ridding the world of Jews], the Holocaust does have universal implications, especially for the survival of civilization itself. Rabbi Irving Greenberg analogizes the Holocaust to an early warning system, the treatment of Jews serving as a harbinger.

> The Holocaust was an advance warning of the demonic potential in the very power and magnetism of modern culture. If one could conceive of Hitler's coming to power not in 1933 but in 1963, after the invention of hydrogen bombs, then the Holocaust would have been truly universal. It is a kind of last warning that if humanity will perceive and overcome the demonism unleashed in modern culture, the world may survive. Otherwise, the next Holocaust will embrace the whole world.[18]

VII. Uniqueness: Particularity and Universalism

Academics have a penchant for classifying which tends to obscure rather than illumine issues, seeking always that which is most general while stumbling over the unique. How, then, will they teach the Holocaust? Does one quantify an abyss? Language itself is a victim of the disaster. In teaching and learning about the Holocaust one needs to steer a course between the Scylla of mystification and the Charybdis of business as usual. Yehuda Bauer argues persuasively against mystification, noting a two-fold danger:

> If what happened to the Jews was unique, then it took place outside history, and it becomes a mysterious event, an upside-down miracle, so to speak, an event of religious significance in the sense that it is not man-made as the term is normally understood.[19]

This is mystification. On the other hand, Bauer warns of the historical and moral failure, or refusal, to confront the Holocaust. For example, Holocaust must be distinguished from genocide. Although there is no difference for the victims, more than semantics is at stake here. Genocide means ruthless, "even murderous, denationalization." Holocaust is systemic and total destruction: complete eradication from the face of the earth. Jews were the only group so designated for this fate.[20] Failure to realize the uniqueness of the Jewish situation is obscuring history.

The attempt to subsume the Holocaust as one example of man's inhumanity to man, thereby making it comparable to Hiroshima, Wounded
Knee, Mai Lai, Cambodia, among others, is at best a misreading of history
which generalizes human suffering and easily lends itself to distortion.
Academics would render more service to genuine objectivity if they re-call-
ed Wiesel's admonition: "Every tragedy deserves its own name." However,
neither false universalism nor bad faith can sidestep what the Nazis themselves called the Endlosung. Elimination of Jews was viewed by Hitler and
his devotees in eschatological terms. The question for professors is how to
avoid the pitfalls of singularity and mystification, both of which place the
Holocaust beyond the realm of human responsibility.

VIII. Contemporary Pseudo-Objectivity and the Holocaust

Two examples of pseudo-objectivity--one personal and the other or-
ganizational--have surfaced recently in association with so-called revisionist
history and the Holocaust.[21] Noam Chomsky, pioneer in meta-linguistics,
influential academic, and selective defender of human rights, recently signed
an appeal defending the civil rights of Robert Faurrison, a former professor
of French Literature in Lyon. Faurrison has made a career out of "debun-
king" the Holocaust. Lecturing and publishing on two continents, he denies
the reality of the gas chambers, charging that the Holocaust is a lie of
Zionist doing. Anne Frank, argues Faurrison, was a fake. Yet Chomsky, in
a letter to Professor Dawidowicz, expressed complete agnosticism on the
validity of Faurrison's views, claiming that he [Chomsky] was insufficiently
involved in the issue to evaluate or pursue it.[22]

The Organization of American Historians [OAH] received protests from
some members over the sale of the OAH mailing list to the neo-Nazi Journal
of Historical Review; other members defended the sale, citing academic
objectivity. To resolve the issue, well-qualified historians were to analyze
the JHR concerning its use of evidence and its contributors' credentials.
Then the OAH's Executive Board would report to the membership. Dawidowicz asks the key question.

> Report what is not quite clear. Perhaps that the Neo-Nazis
> did not have proper academic credentials, or that they failed to use
> primary sources? Again one wonders: Would the OAH have
> reacted the same way to a pseudoscholarly journal publishing KKK
> propaganda?[23]

It is tempting to dismiss these reports as merely exempla of endemic
anti-Semitism. There have always been, and there always will be, anti-
Semites. Self-hating Jews are, likewise and unfortunately, all too frequent
a part of the post-Enlightenment landscape. Moreover, the existence of evil
is hardly news. But there is, I think, more to the matter. Does academia
itself not only encourage but institutionalize attitudes of indifference?

Students are urged to eliminate or suspend ["bracket"] their own feelings and opinions while researching and writing papers. Those who most completely remove their attitudes, feelings, and values from their work receive A's. Universities reward indifference and neutrality in areas where an expression of concern would make students more fully human. Consequently, university training frequently leads to moral numbness and the dulling of personal responsibility. Accurate reporting [true objectivity] has, in our time, become confused with ethical objectivity.

IX. The Task Before Us--Types of Instruction

Western education is at a pedagogical as well as financial cross-road. The ancient Greek struggle between spiritual learning and technological skills is today, post-Holocaust, more intense even if less articulated. Our technological society is devoted to models and prototypes in areas outside of academia; why not within? Ananda Coomaraswamy remarks, somewhere, on the difference between Eastern and Western models of teaching. Eastern education requires a harmony between the thinker and his mode of living. Westerners deem sufficient the production of an internally coherent world-view, disregarding or downgrading the manner in which one's life is lead. My own view is that this is a contributing factor to the emergence in the East of the master-disciple rela-tionship with its emphasis upon instructor as personal ideal and disciples as "representatives of humanity." For example, Gandhi's way was unexceptional--in terms of method--whereas Martin Luther King, Jr., seemed so exotic to us. Master-disciple also is a specifically religious mode of instruction, requiring a cosmic orientation and self-understanding. Know-ledge and being are inextricably linked.

On the other hand, we in the West have adopted the teacher-student model. The teacher's skill or knowledge exercises prestige. He is irreplaceable only if, in Joachim Wach's words, "It is merely that none can actually be found to take his place." The teacher's life is irrelevant to, and may actually compete with, the skills that he wishes to communicate. Contemporary universities are built upon the teacher-student model. The danger is that frequently we confuse the two models, mistaking an accumulation of knowledge for a foretaste of salvation. Knowledge need not be wisdom. Educational schizophrenia can result in civilizational disaster.

Values are learned. While German professors were upholding the Fuhrer--and maintaining their jobs--Dr. Janusz Korczak, educator and physician, chose to accompany the orphans in his care to the gas chambers. Social scientists and psychologists may speculate on differences in behavior. But one thing is certain: when personal obligations and human compassion are sacrificed for utilitarian goals and job enhancement, society is in peril. Ideally, the Holocaust is a course in civic responsibility and personal virtue. Therefore, teaching such a course involves not only history, but equally important, its stress upon current events.

X. Conclusion

One seeks in vain a clear societal signal. Reduced financial support of arts, education, and the humanities are pervasive, ranging from drastic curtailment of federal funding to the elimination of courses in art and music at the secondary level. In universities, skills and vocational courses attract students but minimize ethical concerns. A journalism major reports that her news writing course spend one day--the last session of the semester--on the ethical aspects of reporting. Class responses to the query, "What would you do if the subject of your story threatened suicide upon the story's publication?" were mixed. There was greater clarity in response to the question, "What is the publication of your story would lead to its subject's dismissal?" All class members said they would refrain from publishing. On the other hand, there are more Holocaust courses, seminars, and institutes than at any other time since 1945. Jewish-Christian interchange is also a topic of great interest and scholarly concern. The answer to the question: "Where is our society headed?" is unclear. Numbers alone reveal little. The Holocaust shows the ease with which people may be desensitized to critical moral and ethical concerns.[24] Awareness of the blunting of aesthetic sensibilities is not high on the national agenda.

If teaching and learning are once again to become humanizing experiences, then professors must reconceive their goals and how to achieve them without doing irreparable violence to personal virtue and human responsibility. Students, for their part, must not be content merely to train for a vocation but should prepare themselves to ennoble their chosen field. What constitutes the ethical life? Old definitions pale before the enormity of Auschwitz. Recall the Nazi practice of giving three yellow work permits [which entitled the bearer to live an extra day] to a married father of four children, telling him to distribute those permits.

Honesty compels the admission that after Auschwitz the world is not the same. The task of renewal is urgent and the state of the world is unredeemed. Professional competence is necessary, but so is the realization that being human requires its own full measure of competence. Professors and students could benefit in their soul-searching from the advice given in Pirkei Avot: "Be deliberate in judgment [thoroughly study an issue from all angles], raise up disciples [teach and be what you know], and made a hedge for the Torah" [protect the divine from assault, making higher values accessible for contemplation].

Marc Ellis' challenging and provocative essay criticizes Shoah theology for not going far enough in its legitimate concern for Jewish survival, dealing as it does only with the Jew as victim and for becoming a political "tool" in the hands of both the Israeli and American Jewish communities. Like Rosemary Radford Reuther in Volume II, "Theological and Ethical Reflections on the Shoah: Getting Beyond the Victim-Victimizer Relationship," he focuses on the newly-empowered State of Israel and its supporters in the American Jewish community, both of which he chastises for only learning Jewish lessons of victimization from the Shoah and ignoring the legitimate and rightful claims of the Palestinian people--without, however, detailing their own abuses towards the Israeli people. In so doing, however, he reasserts the role of theology as questioner of the meaning of historical events, painful though the events may be, and the implications to be derived therefrom.

AFTER AUSCHWITZ AND THE PALESTINIAN UPRISING

Marc H. Ellis

I. Introduction

The decisive victory of Israel in the June 1967 Six Day War crystallized certain trends in Jewish theological understanding. In a sense, the war itself heightened the dialectic of Shoah and empowerment present in Jewish life since the discovery of the death camps and the emergence of the State of Israel. Many Jews felt that a revolution in theological thought was needed to match the revolutionary change in the Jewish condition characterized by the loss of European Jewry, the shift in diaspora Jewish power to North America, and the reality of a Jewish state. After the Six Day War, that revolution was accompanied by Shoah theologians who, in despair and courage, chartered a theology that is now normative for the Jewish community throughout the world.[1]

In the years after the 1967 war, Shoah theology, as pioneered by Elie Wiesel, Emil Fackenheim, Richard Rubenstein, and Irving Greenberg, was radical and incisive. It named the collective trauma the Jewish people had experienced as a, or often as the, formative event of Jewish history. Though diverse and often at odds with one another, Shoah theologians generally juxtaposed the Shoah with the Biblical origins of the Jewish community to pose the question of God's fidelity to a covenanted people. Among other ideas, they challenged the Rabbinic tradition both in its theo-logical analysis of the diaspora condition and the type of leadership, or lack thereof, it provided in the Shoah. At the same time Shoah theologians critically analyzed the other side of modernity with its landscape of mass dislocation and mass death.[2]

If the formative event of the Shoah made necessary retrospective probing of traditional Jewish understandings in the theological and political realms, it also called for the development of a framework for sustaining Jewish survival in the present. Shoah theologians understood quite correctly that the Shoah was the most disorienting event in Jewish history. Thus in the midst of broken lives and shattered faiths, Shoah theologians began to articulate a future for the Jewish people.[3]

Herein lies the genius of the Shoah theologians: they understood that the prospective search need be as radical as their retrospective probings. Within the radical questioning of past and future, the Jewish people would continue to need a sustaining faith, but Shoah theologians recognized that this would no longer be overtly theological in the present. Hence, in order to survive in the face of a disorienting event, Shoah theologians had to redefine what it meant to be Jewish. The ancient definition of a practicing Jew as one who engaged in study, ritual, and observance of the Law was no longer adequate, and Shoah theologians knew it. At the same time, they also understood that religious affiliation or non-affiliation after the Shoah was an insufficient test of fidelity to the Jewish people. What Shoah theologians offered instead was a framework to integrate diverse experiences and outlooks into a strong solidarity with the future of the Jewish people. No longer would the primary commitment to synagogue, to liberal/radical politics, or to an assimilationist indifference suffice. Instead, Shoah theologians broached a broad and energetic commitment to the commands of the Shoah experience: memory, survival, and empowerment, especially as embodied in the State of Israel. It was these commands that allowed for the continuation of the people so that at some point in history, there would be a context for the resolution of the questions posted by the Shoah. In a sense, Shoah theologians gathered the people together for the only kind of Sinai experience possible after the Shoah.[4]

The new Sinai, in gathering Jews of different persuasions into a transformed covenant, demanded a radical probing of the diverse worlds Jews lived within, including the worlds of Christianity and modernity. Indictment of historical Christianity was simple enough, at least in its overt institutional capacity; apathy toward, complicity in, and solidarity with the murderers was the order of the day. The "righteous gentiles" were clearly a minority to be mentioned, though often in passing and surely as exceptions. The collapse of European culture and values, the need to emphasize the dark side of the ideology of progress, the failure of the democracies to respond to massive Jewish refugee populations--these were more difficult issue to face. Modernity, as a promise to the world of human betterment and freedom, and especially emancipation for the Jewish people, needed a radical analysis as well. Thus, Shoah theologians confronted a dual crisis of massive proportions involving the shattering of the Jewish people and modernity.

Just as they responded to the crisis of Jewish life by creating a framework for solidarity among the Jewish people, Shoah theologians responded to the crisis of modernity by envisioning a solidarity for those consigned to the other side a century of progress. Richard Rubenstein and Irving Greenberg have crystallized this struggle to articulate a theological thesis for our time: "The passing of time has made it increasingly evident that a hitherto unbreachable moral and political barrier in the history of Western Civilization was successfully overcome by the Nazis in World War II and that henceforth the systematic, bureaucratically administered extermination of millions of citizens or subject peoples will forever be one of the capacities and temptations of governments." They explained further that the "victims ask us, above all, not to allow the creation of another matrix of values that might sustain another attempt at genocide." The terrible tragedy of the Shoah thus lay in the future as much as in the past.[5]

By the mid-1970s Shoah theologians had addressed the crisis of the Jewish people and modernity, proposed a framework for solidarity among the Jewish people and others suffering around the world, and thus had outlined the essential dimensions of Shoah theology as we inherit it today. Shoah theologians had succeeded in the task that faces all theology: to nurture the questions that allow us to understand the history in which we are participating and creating. Yet it was at this moment, the time when Shoah theology became normative for the Jewish people, that its critical edge became elusive. Shoah theology was succumbing to that to which all theologies inevitably succumb: it no longer could address the questions critical to the history the Jewish people were creating. The reasons for this failure are complex and beyond the scope of this essay. Suffice it to say here that Shoah theology emerged out of a situation of powerlessness that demanded a mobilization of psychic energy and material activity toward empowerment; the dialectic of Shoah and empowerment acted as a counterbalance and a critique of weakness and empire. However it did not have within it a way of analyzing power once it had been achieved. Because of the experience of Shoah, the theology lacked objectivity regarding power in Jewish hands. It could not and does not address the case of Jewish empowerment.[6]

In fact, as the situation in Israel changed over time, with expanded borders, two decades of occupation, the invasion of Lebanon, and an increasing role in global arms sales and foreign policy intrigue, Shoah theology's dialectic remained as it had crystallized at the moment of the 1967 triumph. What did change was its emphasis on empowerment. The critical role of the Shoah diminished. We might say that in this process the Shoah became the servant of power, called upon to legitimate activity that hitherto was seen as unethical, even immoral. Jewish in the United States were in the most difficult situation of all diaspora communities: maintaining highly visible support of Israel and creating the climate for an expanded American role in support of that state as necessary for its survival while being relatively powerless to affect Israeli domestic and foreign policy, even when in profound disagreement.[7]

As Shoah theology lost its ability to enter critically into the contemporary situation of the Jewish people, its reliance on empowerment became more and more obvious. A strange paradox ensued that continues today: a theology that poses the most radical religious and ethical questions functions politically in a neo-conservative manner. Not only are the most articulate Shoah theologians neo-conservative in their political stances; they help to legitimate the shift of Jewish intellectuals from the left to the center and right of center on the political spectrum. Even Shoah theolog-ians with previous liberal credentials bear analysis: by the 1980s Irving Greenberg, who wrote so eloquently about the prophetic call of the victims of the Shoah in the 1970s, was essentially supporting the re-emergence of American power under Ronald Reagan. At the same time, he warned against the misuse of the prophetic to undermine the security of the State of Israel: "There is a danger that those who have not grasped the full significance of the shift in the Jewish condition will judge Israel by the ideal standards of the state of powerlessness, thereby not only misjudging but unintentionally collaborating with attempted genocide." The subliminal if not overt message is clear: those who dissent carry a heavy burden, even to the point of creating the context for another Shoah.[8]

II. Memory as Burden and Possibility

For many Jews, especially since the Palestinian uprising and its brutal suppression by the Israeli government, the burden of proof has shifted. Instead of criticizing dissenters as Shoah theologians are wont to do, more Jews are beginning to analyze the politicized use of the Shoah as a way of crushing dissent and mobilizing the community to repress Palestinian aspirations to human dignity and justice. If Shoah theologians recognized and articulated the Jewish desire to cease to be victims, others are recognizing a similar Jewish desire not to oppress another people. Though this has not as yet reached a theological articulation, criticism of the politicized used of the Shoah in relation to the State of Israel may lead to such a theology. In short, recent discussion of the Shoah beyond Shoah theology opens up the essential choice before the Jewish people: if the memory of suffering is to be a burden to us and to others or a possibility for healing and justice.

In a recent essay Phillip Lopate, a Jewish essayist, reopens what for Jews is an extremely emotional subject. He begins with a most provocative title: "Resistance to the Holocaust." Lopate's intention is less to speak of the atrocities of the Nazi era, which are to his mind "enormous and unforgivable," than to address the cultural, political, and religious uses to which the disaster has since been put. Born after World War II, but before the term "Holocaust" had become commonplace, Lopate as a child heard "concentration camp; gas chambers; six million Jews; what the Nazis did ." Some might see it as an improvement to use a single designation for the event. Yet for Lopate, placing a label on such suffering serves to tame the experience. As use of the term Holocaust became more common in the mid-sixties, Lopate found it to have a self-important, almost vulgar, tone: "Then, too, one instantly saw that the term was part of a polemic and that it sounded more comfortable in certain speakers' mouths than in others; the Holocaustians [sic--Ed.] used it like a club to smash back their opponents....In my own mind I continue to distinguish, ever so slightly, between the disaster visited on the Jews and the 'Holocaust.' Sometimes it almost seems that 'the Holocaust' is a corporation headed by Elie Wiesel, who defends his patents with articles in the Arts and Leisure section of the Sunday Times."[9]

Taken in a certain context, Lopate's words seem almost too easy. Yet it is clear throughout that he is participating in the most ancient of Jewish practices: refusing idolatry insofar as the Shoah, or the use of it, become crystallized, untouchable, almost a God. What suffers, of course, when everything is reduced to the Shoah or analogous to the Shoah is the ability to think through the issues that confront the Jewish people. As Lopate notes: "The Hitler/Holocaust analogy deadens all intelligent discourse by intruding a stridently shrill note that forces the mind to withdraw. To challenge the demagogic minefield of pure self-righteousness from an ironic distance almost ensures being misunderstood. The image of the Holocaust is too overbearing, too hot to tolerate distinctions. In its life as a rhetorical figure, the Holocaust is a bully."[10]

The Shoah as a bully can also become Shoah as kitsch. The Israeli author Avishai Margalit explores this theme in an essay titled "The Kitsch of Israel." According to Margalit, kitsch is based on an easy identification of the represented object; the emotion evoked in the spectator comes simply from a reference to the object. Although genuine art always maintains a distance from the represented object, thus involving the spectator in interpretation and allowing a variety of perspectives to emerge, the idea of kitsch is to arouse a strong emotion from the spectator's relation to the original object. Thus, in the Jewish context, a glimpse of Masada, or the Wall, or the Temple Mount is enough to move the "Jewish heart," and the marketing of Israel takes full advantage of these images. Kitsch can also be politicized and become, in Margalit's terms, part of a state ideology whose "emblem is total innocence." The image of the Israeli soldier and the Wailing [i.e. Western--Ed.] War are two such items of kitsch, evoking easy emotional identification with the important secondary understanding of a beleaguered nation. Of course, as Margalit points out, the opposite of total innocence is total evil: "The innocent and pure with whom we sympathize have to be relentlessly protected from those plotting their destruction."[11]

For Margalit, however, the place that should be furthest from such easy emotion, Yad Vashem, the Shoah memorial in Israel, has, paradoxically, become an element of state kitsch. He cites a recently dedicated children's room, pitch dark with tape-recorded voices of children crying out for their mothers in Yiddish. As Margalit remarks, this kind of kitsch even a "kitschman of genius" like Elie Wiesel would find hard to surpass: "The real significance of this room is not its commemoration of the single most horrible event in the history of mankind--the systematic murder of two million children, Jewish and Gypsies, for being what they were and not for anything they had done. The children's room, rather, is meant to deliver a message to the visiting foreign statesman, who is rushed to Yad Vashem even before he has had time to leave off his luggage at his hotel, that all of us here in Israel are these children and that Hitler-Arafat is after us. This is the message for internal consumption as well. Talking of the P.L.O. in the same tone as one talks of Auschwitz is an important element in turning the Holocaust into kitsch."[12]

Margalit reports that with the outbreak of the Palestinian uprising, when criticism from within and outside Israel has reached its peak, the increased evocation of Shoah memories is noticeable. Included is a Shoah quiz show, shot in Poland, on which young Jews are asked questions relating to the massacre of Jews in Europe. For each correct answer two points are awarded. Applause is forbidden as being in bad taste. Margalit's conclusion: "Against the weapon of the Holocaust, the Palestinians are amateurs. True, some of them have adopted their own version of Holocaust kitsch, based on the revolting equation of the Israelis with Nazis and of themselves with Nazis' victims; but as soon as operation 'Holocaust Memory' is put into high gear by the Israeli authorities, with full-fledged sound-and-color production, the Palestinians cannot compete. The absence of the main actor and the stage queen, Begin and Golda, is certainly a loss for political kitsch, but a new star has risen, Benjamin Netanyahu ['Arafat is worse than Hitler.'], and prospects are now bright--nothing will make us cut the kitsch."[13]

Increasingly in Israel, the Shoah is seen in a similar light, as an event that is consciously manipulated by the state and it leadership. This is the theme of Boaz Evron, an Israeli writer and commentator, in his essay "The Holocaust: Learning the Wrong Lessons." For Evron, two terrible things happened to the Jewish people over the last half-century: the Shoah and the lessons learned from it. The ahistorical interpretations of the Shoah made deliberately or out of ignorance have become in Evron's mind a danger both to the Jewish people and to the State of Israel for the following reasons: The term "Holocaust" is rhetorical and ambiguous; it exists without historical reference and thus has become indefinite and movable, almost exempting one from understanding it. "The murder of the Jews in Europe," though not as galvanizing, more accurately reflected and locates a historical event in which there were murderers and those who were murdered. Such an even become worthy of historical investigation and is lifted from the mystical pseudo-religious. By analyzing the historical context, Evron finds different lessons to be drawn from the event than Shoah theologians do. For example, Evron points to the basic assumption that the Nazi policy of mass murder was directed almost exclusively against Jews. The facts speak differently: Gypsies and three million non-Jewish Poles were murdered, and millions of Russian prisoners of war and forced laborers were murdered as well. The enslavement and extermination of the Slav people was almost a possibility for the Nazis. For Evron, antisemitism served as "catalyst, as the focal point of the extermination system" that was destined to become a central and permanent institution of the Third Reich.[14]

Thus the Nazi murder of the Jews was unique only in preparing the world for the institutionalization of extermination. The argument presented as a corollary, that the Jews of Palestine were saved by Zionism, is also false: they were saved by the defeat of the Nazis at El Alamein and Stalingrad, which prevented the Nazis from conquering Palestine and exterminating the Jewish population. The lesson of the Shoah is therefore different: "The true guarantee against ideologically-based extermination is not military power and sovereignty but the eradication of ideologies which remove any human group from the family of humanity." For Evron, the solution lies in a common struggle aimed at overcoming national differences and barriers rather than increasing and heightening term, as strong trends within Israel and Zionist movement demand.[15]

There were many reasons why the historical presentation of the murder of the Jews in Europe was rejected for an ahistorical view summarized in the word "Holocaust." According to Evron, the Germans were interested in this because it limited, in a sense, their liability. Instead of focusing on the systemic and expanding possibilities of a system of extermination, a focus that might have kept alive the feelings of fear and suspicion after the War in Germany's neighbors, limiting the memory of the Jews and the Shoah enabled Germany to more easily reintegrate itself into the world of nations. The Western powers were also interested in this insofar as it allowed them to wipe the slate clean and begin to rebuild Germany as a barrier to Soviet expansion.[16]

The "Jewish monopolization" of the Nazi experience was also welcomed by Jewish leadership in Israel and in the Diaspora, as a way of strengthening German guilt, thus continuing and increasing the amount of compensation payments for survivors, and as a way of mobilizing world support, moral, political, military, and financial, for the Jewish state. For Evron, this new and creative policy of inducing moral guilt was a prime reason for the Eichmann trial. It shifted the tragedy out of the past and made it a basis for future preferential relationships. And as importantly, this policy became a blueprint for relations with most Western Christian states, especially the United States; they were to support Israel on the basis of guilt rather than self-interest.[17]

Evron sees the ramifications of this policy to be enormous. In the first place, it contravened an aim of the Zionist movement to normalize the status of the Jewish people and reduced Israel to the "level of an eternal beggar." Henceforth, Israel survives on the "six million credit" instead of, like any other country, on developing and marketing its energy and skills. Living off its past, Israel exists, like the Shoah, in an ahistorical context, thus avoiding economic and political confrontation in the real world. Paradoxically, a renewed feeling of isolation grows as the adulation of the survivor Israel increases. The policy also generates what Evron considers a moral blindness: because the world is out to get Israel in the present and in the future, any links with oppressive governments and any oppression of non-Jews within and around Israel can be justified.[18]

The Shoah can also be used as a powerful tool by Israel and Jewish leadership in the United States to organize and police the Jewish community. Diaspora Jews, for example, are made to feel guilty for not having done enough to prevent the Shoah; at the same time the message is conveyed that Israel is threatened with annihilation. The message is clear: unequivocal support for Israel prevents a second shoah. Evron sees the image of the Shoah past and Shoah future as so important to Israel and American Jewry that the reality of Israel's strength is submerged in myth:

> When you try to explain to American Jews that for many years to come we will be stronger than any possible combination, that Israel has not, in fact, been in danger of physical annihilation since the first cease-fire of the War of Independence in 1948, and that the average human and cultural level of Israeli society, even in its current deteriorated state, is still much higher than that of the surrounding Arab societies, and that this level rather than the quantity and sophistication of our arms constitutes our military advantage --you face resistance and outrage. And then you realize another fact: this image is needed by many American Jews in order for them to free themselves of their guilt regarding the Holocaust. Moreover, supporting Israel is necessary because of the loss of any other focal point to their Jewish identity. Thus, many of them resist the suggestion that the appropriate aim for Israel is to liberate itself from any dependency on outside ele- ments, even Jewish ones. They need to feel needed. They also need the "Israeli hero" as a social and emotional compensation in a society in which the Jew is not usually perceived as embodying the characteristics of the tough, manly fighter. Thus, the Israeli provides the American Jew with a double, contradictory image-- the virile superman, and the potential Holocaust victim--both of whose components are far from reality.[19]

The equation of Arab hatred of Israel with the Nazi hatred of Jews, for Evron, arises logically out of the ahistorical quality of the Shoah. The Nazis, who created an irrational hatred of the Jews so as to justify the system of mass extermination, are likened to the Arabs, who, according to Evron, have a quite rational reason for opposing Israel as a powerful enemy that has expelled and displaced over a million of their compatriots. The difference between an illiterate Palestinian refugee and a highly trained SS trooper is blurred beyond distinction, and the defense of the country in the Six-Day War and the Yom Kippur War becomes less an integral part of the sovereign political existence than a stage on which the destiny of the Jewish people is played out. Identifying Palestinians with Nazis, as the continuous reminder of the Shoah does, leads to hysterical responses rather than reasoned policy. These parallels have serious moral consequences as well. Because the choices presented to Israel are not realistic--only shoah or

victory--Israel becomes free of any moral re-strictions, because any nation
that is in danger of annihilation feels exempted from moral considerations
that might restrict its efforts to save itself. For Evron, this is the rationale
of people who argue that everything is permitted because the world wants
Israel's destruction. "They do not hesitate to recommend the most drastic
steps against the non-Jewish population in Israel. Although it is a serious
comparison to make, it is worth remembering that the basic Nazi claim
justifying the slaughter of Jews was the 'Jewish conspiracy' to destroy the
German nation." Evron concludes that Israeli and Jewish leadership, caught
up in an ahistorical world, threaten to become victims of their own propaganda. They draw on a bank account continuously reduced by withdrawals.
As the world moves on there are fewer who remember the Shoah, and those
who do, including the Jews, become tired of it as a nuisance and a reflection
of a reality that does not exist: "Thus the leadership, too, operates in the
world of myths and monsters created by its own hands. It has created this
world in order to maintain and perpetuate its rule. It is, however, no longer
able to understand what is happening in the real world, and what are the
historical processes in which the state is caught. Such a leadership, in the
unstable political and economic situation of Israel today, itself constitutes a
danger to the very existence of the state."[20]

III. Solidarity with the Palestinian People

With Lopate, Margalit and Evron we come full circle. In the beginning,
the Shoah necessitates empowerment; the misuse of the Shoah generates
doubt about the use of Jewish empowerment to close off dissent and oppress
another people and ultimately may even endanger empowerment itself.
Critique of the politicized use of the Shoah reasserts the dialectic of Shoah
and empowerment rescues the Shoah from becoming subservient to an
empowerment which takes on a life of its own. To a profound degree, the
reassertion of the dialectic of Shoah and empowerment returns us to the
original question first posed by Shoah theologians: the future of the Jewish
people. But if this question came to articulation in the miracu-lous victory
of the 1967 War, hence Shoah and empowerment, the question of the future
of the Jewish people today is raised within the confines of present history
and thus includes the Palestinian uprising and the aspirations of the Palestinian people. In sum, though enormously complex and with tremendous
ramifications, the dialectic of Shoah and empowerment must today broaden
to include a solidarity with the Palestinian people. Thus the step beyond the
impasse of Shoah theology and the critique of its politicized use lies in a
paradoxical embrace of those whom we as Jews have oppressed.

What does this solidarity with the Palestinian people mean today? What
are the foundational visions which may shape this concept of solidarity into
flesh and blood reality?

The first step, of course, is to abandon the two-rights understanding, as if the question of Jews and Palestinians is a symmetrical one. Whatever one wants to argue from the Jewish side vis-a-vis Jewish history--our difficult history in Europe which gave rise to Zionism and the culmination of that history in the Shoah, which provided the final impetus for the birth of the Jewish state--the effect for Palestinians has been brutal, even catastrophic. A. B. Yehoshua, the Jewish-Israeli novelist, writes that the "concept of historic right has no objective moral validity when applied to the return of the Jewish people to its land." Rather, as a committed Zionist, Yehoshua argues that the Jewish people have a "full moral right to seize part of Eretz Yisrael [the Land of Israel], or any other land, even by force," on the basis of a right he calls the survival right of the endangered. His underlying proposition is as follows: "A nation without a homeland has the right to take, even by force, part of the home-land of another nation, and to establish its sovereignty there." Thus Yehoshua, unlike most Jews, admits of what might be termed a "necessary theft," [a] "moral invasion," as it were. But to hold the Palestinians responsible for resisting that theft or to expect them to accept it is in Yehoshua's eyes ridiculous, as is the extension of that theft to the rest of historic Palestine, that is the possible annexation of the occupied territories. For Yehoshua, the basis for the Jewish right is the seizure of a part, and thus if Jews intend to extricate themselves from the "situation of a people without a homeland by turning another people into a nation without a homeland, our right to survival will turn to dust in our hands."[21]

Whatever one thinks of Yehoshua's foundational argument that the survival of the Jewish people is linked to a territorial sovereignty--a position that should be probed in a deep way by Jewish thinkers--his two-rights position moves well beyond the typical expression of Jewish innocence and Palestinian demonism. Though his book bears the English title Between Right and Right, his argument speaks of Jewish necessity, the dispersal of Palestinians, and the rights of Palestinians to resist. Thus the title might be better rendered as Between Jewish Necessity and Palestinian Rights to a Homeland. Accordingly, it could be that the formation of Israel was necessary in its historical moment and at the same time wrong vis-a-vis the Palestinian people. The original sin [sic-Ed.] was European antisemitism, not Palestinian resistance to a Jewish state. But even here, if one accepts Yehoshua's analysis of historical necessity in seizing only a part of the land, the framework he maintains is strictly separatist. That is, the necessity of survival, the formation of a Jewish state, is extended beyond the historical moment into a relentless future: to survive physically and culturally Jews must be separate in their own land for the remainder of world history. The moral invasion is to flee the fire and to build a new home among others who have fled the same fire. Those who fled the Jewish fire must re-build their own homes somewhere else.[22]

Here the "two state" position, while seemingly progressive, needs to be questioned within the framework of solidarity. The entire burden of proof is placed on the Palestinians. For example, the two-state position as argued by most Jews, including Yehoshua, places primary responsibility on the Palestinians to, among other things, demonstrate their ability to live peacefully with Israel, to renounce their fundamental claims of sovereignty over all of Palestine, to guarantee a demilitarized state with Israeli security positions within Palestine and the right of Israeli invasion if militarization occurs. At the same time, it also limits forever the size of Palestine to one-fifth its original land mass in the least fertile part of Palestine. Among other things, it assumes, at a foundational level, that Israelis should be afraid of Palestinians but Palestinians have nothing to fear from Israelis, a position that many Palestinians in their diaspora find surprising, if not untenable.[23]

Though a two-state solution may be the only practical possibility at the moment, it falls far short of the solidarity requisite to the crisis which confronts both sides. Most Jews, for instance, see the two-state solution as a way of ridding themselves of the Palestinian "problem" demographically and morally. Give them their state and Jews are free of a possible Palestinian majority, hence the preservation of the Jewish state; Jews are also morally cleansed of having expelled, beaten, tortured, and murdered Palestinians, thereby protecting the purity of the Jewish soul. The position is clear as Amos Oz, the Jewish-Israeli novelist describes it: granting a divorce between Jews and Palestinians.   The image is equally clear: separate Jewish and Palestinian states with a wall so high that Jews will never have to see another Palestinian. Palestinians will be banished from Jewish history.[24]

The desire to preserve, or rather reassert, Jewish innocence by banishing the victims of Jewish oppression is understandable and inadequate. It allows Jews to retreat from this confrontation with Palestinians and within themselves as if the bloodshed had not occurred. By allowing Jews to see themselves in their pre-state identity, they ignore the brutality of which Jews are capable, thus ignoring Jewish post-state reality.

That recent Jewish history is covered with blood through our contemporary oppression of Palestinians is a lesson absolutely necessary for Jews as a people. We cannot come to grips with our recent history unless we see the Palestinians now as intimate to our self-identity and capabilities as a people. That is, the victims of Jewish power are as intimate to us as we are to those who oppressed us. Confronting the Jewish abuse of power is impossible without the physical preservation of Palestine in our midst, and the prospects of Jewish healing both in its trauma of European mass murder and in its trauma of beating and expelling another people cannot be worked out alone.

Progressive proponents of the two-state solution seek to banish the bad Jewish conscience in a way that delays the future with the history Jews have created. Thus a genuine Jewish progressive position is dependent on moving beyond the State of Israel and the State of Palestine into a genuine vision of confederation which allows both autonomy and integration of Jews and Palestinians. Of course, this also leaves open the possibility of a Palestinian return to parts of Palestine that would be closed off in a two-state scenario. If genuine solidarity is to be gleaned, then the Palestinians have a right to be healed of their own trauma of displacement, thus allowing a new perspective on their own catastrophe. Only a Palestinian right to return can authenticate what the Palestinian educator, Muhammed Hallaj, has described as the interlocking destiny of Jews and Palestinians. In short, the argument for a reality of Jewish and Palestinian life together in historic Palestine moves beyond the typical Jewish concern for Jewish purity and innocence by envisioning a future which recovers the deepest ethical impulses of the Jewish people in confrontation with the reality of Jewish history.[25]

But arguing from the Jewish perspective does not in the least diminish the Palestinian recovery by placing it solely with the Jewish framework. The Palestinian future is for Palestinians authentic and self-generating. Their desire or refusal to live with Jews is of course their decision to make within the context of Palestinian history. Jewish life as interlocking with Palestinian life is an absolute necessity from the Jewish perspective, but is, in my view, entirely optional from the Palestinian perspective of living on the other side of Jewish power.

Solidarity with the Palestinian people moves beyond romanticization and demonization. Solidarity with the Jewish people in Europe was an ethical and practical necessity not because all Jews were beautiful but because Jews as a people were innocent. As documented by many Jewish historians, the Jewish ghettos had heroes, ordinary citizens, criminals, and collaborators. The behavior of Jews towards other Jews ran the gamut of great charity to unbridled brutality, and, of course, everything in between. And the Palestinians are no doubt similar in regard to their complexity, and, in this situation, their innocence. Hence, Jews often want it both ways: a retroactive demand of rescue of all Jews during the Shoah, coupled with no discussion of Jewish internal realities outside the framework of innocence. Similarly, they reject any connection between Jewish rescue and Jewish behavior just a decade after the Shoah, or even today, but find it surprisingly easy to take to task Palestinians with regard to the policies of the Palestine Liberation Organization, an example being the Palestinian reaction to Iraq's invasion of Kuwait, and anything that seems to compromise Palestinian innocence from a Jewish perspective. They also constantly link the Palestinian struggle for liberation with the policies of a future Palestinian state, as if the unknown future should determine the level of support for the current struggle. Thus, as Jews, we rightly shift the burden of proof to those who oppressed us, but, in a strange twist now continually shift the burden of proof to those whom we are oppressing.[26]

To accept this analysis is to radically change the Jewish perception of the Israeli-Palestinian conflict, from two rights to wrong and right; from aberration to continuity; from the need for "corrections" to a radical critical evaluation. As important, and as difficult, is the radical reevaluation of Jewish self-understanding these statements imply. Israel is not innocent, and neither are we: our claims on suffering are now forfeited. Our claim to chosenness, even in a secularized form, has become irritating rather than compelling. Israel is not redemptive; and neither is our empowerment. Instead, Israel, and for that matter the politicized use of the Shoah, is a burden to the Palestinian people and to the Jewish people as well. The question of Israel and the remembrance of the Shoah so central to Jewish identity have become something other than expected and so have we. Is it possible to see ourselves as a people organized to destroy another people without radically reevaluating who we have become as a people? And, if we have betrayed our suffering, and our empowerment is built on the blood of others, where are we to turn in order to reconstruct a way of being Jewish in which we can recognize our own faces and hearts and realize the deepest impulses of the Jewish people?

This is the task before us, one that will need the skills of politics, ethics and theology to successfully realize. In Emil Fackenheim's analysis of the imperatives of the Shoah in 1968, he emphasized the need for sheer survival of the Jewish people in order to face the questions of Jewish history and a possible Jewish future. Today, just [a little more than] two decades later, in a way that Fackenheim could not then and does not today understand, in a momentous inversion, the survival of the Palestinian people provides the possibility of a Jewish future. There is not doubt what the German Catholic theologian Johann Baptist Metz had in mind when he envisioned the future of Christians and Jews after the Shoah in these words: "We Christians can never go back behind Auschwitz: to go beyond Auschwitz, if we see clearly, is impossible for us by ourselves. It is possible only together with the victims of Auschwitz." In light of the Palestinian uprising, these words assume new meaning relative to the common journey of Jew and Palestinian. For Jews the challenge might be stated thusly: "We Jews can never go back behind empowerment; to go beyond empowerment, if we see clearly , is impossible for us by ourselves. It is possible only with the victims of our empowerment, the Palestinian people."[27]

IV. Toward a Jewish Theology of Liberation

The inclusion of the Palestinians in the historic drama of the Jewish people is to recognize our responsibility within empowerment and to realize that the test of a people's maturity and judgment is the ability to critically evaluate the history it has created. To seek empowerment after a history of victimization is natural and good; to create a new set of victims ultimately undermines that empowerment. Simply put, the destiny of Jew and Palestinian is intimately connected.

Though there are many strands of the Jewish tradition to be looked at in this regard, the most obvious and ancient is the theme of liberation. And while having political, economic and cultural dimensions, the theme of liberation has always been a basic theological question as well. The Israelites, in becoming a people, also chose a God who would be with them in their struggle for liberation. A crucial phase in this struggle and choice was an atheism toward theologies which held these diverse tribes in subjugation. Thus the Israelites said a profound "No" to political and religious ideologies which enforced injustice and a "Yes" to political and religious realities which led toward liberation. Of course, in the struggle for liberation new forms of oppression, both internal and external, appeared. The prophets were those who called attention to the tendency toward internal and external oppression. Social and political relations within and outside the nation of Israel were, according to the prophets, key to the question of the relation of the people to God.[28]

What is suggested here is not a return to the Biblical God as related in the Exodus and Sinai; Shoah theologians have correctly pointed out the new Sinai needed after the Shoah. But the need for a remembrance of Jewish suffering and for Jewish empowerment is hardly in a theological sense sufficient in and of itself. The triumph of a militant empowerment can only lead on the one hand to an angry and expansionist religious fundamentalism, as we have seen markedly in Israel, and on the other a continuing and militant alienation from the Jewish community by a majority of Jews. In short, the broken tension of suffering and empowerment is not only leading to the oppression of the Palestinian people; it is leading to a civil war within the Jewish community. The triumph of religious fundamentalism and alienation from the Jewish community may lead to the end of the Jewish tradition, or the development of a new Judaism almost unrecognizable to those born in the first generation after the Shoah.[29]

The theological challenge is therefore straightforward: Can the new Sinai called for by Shoah theologians move beyond militant Zionism and extreme alienation? The challenge in turn poses a further question: Can we in the Jewish community move toward a healing of our own wounds without binding the wounds of others, wounds that we have caused? Does not the task of Jewish theology rest in this challenge and question? And if we approach this challenge and question, mindful of our history and tradition, is it not here that the reality of liberation might take hold?

We know at least two roads, from the negative side, which will not yield a serious approach to liberation? the maintenance of our innocence and the proposition that Israel is redemptive. In fact, our experiences tell us something different. As it turns out, in the concrete reality rather than our wishful imaginings, where we as Jews have power we do most every-thing that has been done to us. Though the claim is that we were forced into things by our enemy [a claim made by most everyone who has power], the reality is something different. Historically vis-a-vis the Palestinian people, Israel has been and continues today to be expansionist and oppressive. Our innocence on this essential point, of course, does more than mask the facts; it helps preserve our sense of ourselves as victims which we are decidedly not today. A radical critique of Israel thus serves as a challenge to an essential part of Jewish identity, the perception of our-selves as victims. The sense of victimhood and innocence then reinforces the Jewish sense of powerlessness and isolation, even if we are more powerful than at any time in the last two thousand years, and, at least in the West, more accepted and integrated than ever before. In a strange twist, Shoah theology must state boldly that we as Jews are no longer innocent and in this way confront our own self-perception with the reality of our situation.[30]

At some point, and the sooner the better, Jews will also have to admit that Israel is not redemptive. A central aspect of Shoah theology and Jewish identity is tied to the dream of redemption as embodied by Israel, but the realities contradict the dream. As it turns out Israel is a state like any other; it has, for example, selfless public servants and corrupt political officials. Israel has corporations and prisons, white collar crime and prostitution. Aspiring to democracy, at least for its Jewish citizens, Israeli society, like most societies, has well-defined social and economic classes as well as a social order which exhibits widespread cultural and racial dis-crimination. Israeli occupation forces do essentially what all occupation forces do: they repress, displace, deport and torture the people whom they occupy. In one sense the discussion of Israel as a state, society, and occupy-ing force seems elementary, but Jewish discussion, especially within Shoah theology, rarely, if ever analyzes Israel in this way. Israel is a dream of redemption, but the reality is something different.[31]

At another level Jews within and outside of Israel know the other side of Israel. For years, before the latest influx of Soviet emigres forced to come to Israel, more Jews have left Israel than emigrated to it. The estimated number of Israelis in permanent residence in America and Canada, for example, is at least five hundred thousand and may approach one million people. Considering that the Jewish population of Israel is just over three million people, this is a large percentage of the Israeli population which has sought homes in other countries. And how many Jews from the United States have emigrated to Israel and stayed there? Despite the rhetoric the number is almost too small to mention: some fifty thousand Jews from the United States over more than four decades, a figure which does not include the number who have returned. Interestingly, of the four most prominent Shoah theologians, only one, Emil Fackenheim, lives in Israel, and this after his retirement. Shoah theologians are representative of the Jewish population at large: choosing to live outside of Israel. The point here is simple if it was not obfuscated by Jewish theology: Jewish people contradict the notion of Israel as redemptive with their bodies, which remain elsewhere. We do not as a people seek to live in what has become an isolated garrison state. Despite our theological ruminations, Jews, even after the Shoah, choose to live in Western democratic secular states as equal partners with non-Jews.

The addition of solidarity to the dynamics of Shoah and empowerment can only come by moving beyond innocence and redemption and therefore into a critical reevaluation of recent Jewish history and our own choices within it. But if our identity is bound up with the sense of innocence and redemption, even if we know differently, what is there on the other side? If we accept loss of innocence and understand that Israel is not redemptive, where and who are we as Jews? What, then, is our identity if it is no longer based on innocence and redemption?

The difficulties here are many and the reason we cling to this identity, despite all evidence to the contrary, lies within this difficulty. All of this has come upon us too suddenly: the Shoah, then Israel, then our realization that we are no longer victims and that Israel has become something other than we expected. In the larger sense, we have become something other than we expected or that our theology tells [us] we are. We might say that a new Jewish theology must begin with a celebration that we are no longer victims and a lament that we, like others, have created victims. That is, our call for redemption has become a form of domination over others and ourselves. We are weighed down by the burden of our history and our aspirations. Boldly stated, the memory of the Shoah and the State of Israel have become burdens to the Jewish people. The question is whether we are going to continue to labor under this burden and burden others with it, or choose another path: to see our suffering and the limits of our empowerment as a path of solidarity toward other struggling peoples, including and especially, those who labor under our power, the Palestinian people. Using our history of suffering and our new-found power as an opportunity for solidarity rather than as a blunt instrument of oppression, paradoxically opens up the possibility of healing the Jewish trauma of the Shoah.

Here lies before us the question of liberation, less in a final drama of messianic redemption than in a mature struggling with the limitations and beauty of life, with the suffering and hope of humanity and our small but significant contribution to the human future. Does the Shoah lead to a small garrison state, if you will an empowered ghetto, or to a difficult embrace of the world which rejected us? Hidden here is the explosive question of whether the world has changed, whether for instance Western Christians have been transformed from enemy to friend. But one suspects that though the behavior of Christians toward Jews has changed dramatically, the Jewish image of the Christian as enemy has hardly changed at all. Is this because if Jews recognize that Christians can transform themselves from enemy to friend, we might also have to admit that we have transformed ourselves from victim to oppressor? Do we seek to freeze the world at the moment of Shoah because it serves our purpose of remaining, at least in our own mind, victims and innocent? Does our present sense of chosenness revolve around this claim of ultimate victims, and does our perceived status in the world directly relate to this claim? To see ourselves always as victims, of course, perpetuates our brokenness and our isolation. Is this what we want to bequeath to our children? And if this ultimate victim status allows a blank check to Israeli power, will we have any tradition worth inheriting?[32]

Perhaps it would be better to simply admit that the experience of Shoah has led us to the conclusion that only a new form of Judaism, based on statehood and power, can help navigate Jewish survival in a hostile world. Surely then we must admit to the formation of a Constantinian Judaism which, like Constantinian Christianity, links religion and state power, where religion, granted its realm of freedom, agrees to bless the state and legitimate state power. Whether we want to admit it or not, Shoah theology has assumed this posture: it is a theology in service of the state. In Constantinian Judaism the religion continues and becomes even more publicly evident. Rabbis are produced in great number and the synagogues become more expensive and beautiful. Unfortunately, these elaborate synagogues, like the Medieval Cathedrals of Europe, sacrifice depth even as they gain their symbolic public importance. Judaism continues but the bottom, as it were, drops out: the ethical commands praised in prayer are in reality practiced less and less and more often transgressed. In fact transgression, rather than aberration, is woven into the structure of Jewish life. This is, the logic of Jewish state power in Israel is the elimination of Palestinians from Jewish life and therefore is embedded in the very structure of the state. If this logic is not critically confronted then it must be declared off-limits to critical discourse. To a large extent this has already occurred. Silence is assumed, then counselled. If silence is broken and reality spoken publicly, penalties can range from social ostracism to excommunication from the Jewish community.[33]

Yet Constantinian Judaism is always reminded through text and tradition that a Jewish ethical inheritance remains, and that those ethics are part of a covenant once accepted at Sinai. A corollary is that the covenant remains even in periods of the eclipse of God and that at these times it is even more urgent to seek out others beyond the Jewish community for solace and strength. The main thrust of the Jewish tradition in a sense becomes even clearer in light of the Shoah and Israel, that is the movement toward community and away from empire. The temptation of empire is a warning of dislocation and fragmentation and a reminder of the possibility of community.

The original Sinai seems to have embodied this temptation and possibility: leave empire [Egypt], form community [Sinai], tend back toward empire [Solomon], be reminded of community [prophets]. Thus the Israelites were called from empire to community and soon it was realized that the test was the people's tendency toward one or the other, and that somehow the question of God was intimately involved in this choice. Can we today place the realities of Shoah and Israel within the dialectics of community and empire? And might the question of God be related to this choice? Or put more subtly, is it possible to approach the question of God after the Shoah if we decide, light of our domination, to dominate another people? Or does the possibility of the question of God take on new form if after the Shoah and Israel we again choose community, especially with the Palestinian people? Thus the preservation of Palestinians in our midst involved the possibility of our healing, as related earlier, but also may allow us to approach the question of God in a different way. If in feminist parlance the personal is political, the political is also theological. There is a Jewish community, beyond a warrior God and an empty secularism, beyond the conquest of another people and a convenient silence, and that position is found in the pursuit of community.

Within the claims of innocence and redemption, within the tendency toward empire, there are voices who assert that community is the only way forward for the Jewish people, and that within this path the possibility of liberation arises. And strangely enough this voice was sometimes spoken within the ultimate empire, the death camps, much more clearly that it is today. Within Constantinian Judaism one hears, as a subversive witness, the voice of the Dutch Jew, Etty Hillesum, who, despite the possibility of escape, accompanied her own people to Westerbork and then Auschwitz. In Hillesum we find hope for a world beyond suffering, that indeed Jewish suffering might become a clarion call for community. In her March 21, 1941, diary entry, Hillesum writes of forgiveness as a way of refusing to hate even the enemy. Her solidarity with the Jewish people extends to those caught up in a system that dehumanizes and in effect murders the conquerors as well.

What a bizarre new landscape, so full of eerie fascination, yet one might also come to love again. We human beings cause monstrous conditions, but precisely because we cause them we soon learn to adapt ourselves to them. Only if we become such that we can no longer adapt ourselves, only if, deep inside, we rebel against every kind of evil, will we be able to put a stop to it. Aeroplanes, streaking down in flames, still have a weird fascination for us-even aesthetically-though we know, deep down, that human beings are being burnt alive. As long as that happens, while everything within us does not yet scream out in protest, so long will we find ways of adapting ourselves, and the horror will continue. Does that mean that I am never sad, that I never rebel, always acquiesce, and love life no matter what the circumstances?

No, far from it. I believe I know and share that many sorrows and sad circumstances that a human being can experience, but I do not cling to them, I do not prolong such moments of agony. They pass through me, like life itself, as a broad, eternal stream, they become part of that stream, and life continues. And as a result all my strength is preserved, does not become tagged on to futile sorrow or rebelliousness.

And finally: ought we not, from time to time, open ourselves up to cosmic sadness? One day I shall surely be able to say to Ilse Blumental, "Yes, life is beautiful, and I value it anew at the end of every day, even though I know that the sons of mothers, and you are one such mother, are being murdered in concentration camps. And you must be able to bear your sorrow: even if it seems to crush you, you will be able to stand up again, for human beings are so strong, and your sorrow must become an integral part of yourself, part of your body and soul, you mustn't run away from it, but bear it like an adult. Do not relieve your feelings through hatred, do not seek to be avenged on all German mothers, for they, too, sorrow at this very moment for their slain and murdered sons. Give yourself all the space and shelter in yourself that is its due, for if everyone bares his grief honestly and courageously, the sorrow that now fills the world will abate. But if you do not clear a decent shelter for your sorrow, and instead reserve most of the space inside you for hatred and thoughts of revenge-from which new sorrows will be born for others-then sorrow will never cease in this world and will multiply. And if you have given sorrow the space its gentle origins demand, then you may truly say: life is beautiful and so rich. So beautiful and so rich it makes you want to believe in God.[34]

Two years later on July 3, 1943, just months before her deportation to Auschwitz, Hillesum concluded with the hope:

All I wanted to say is this: The misery here is quite terrible; and yet late at night when the day has slunk away into the depths behind me, I often walk with a spring in my step along the barbed wire. And then time and again, it soars straight from my heart-I can't help it, that's just the way it is, like some elementary force-the feeling that life is glorious and magnificent, and that one day we shall be building a whole new world.[35]

Emil Fackenheim, whose seminal influence upon both post-Ausch-witz philosophical and theological thought speaks for itself, as always, raises issues profound in their implication in his essay included here. Preferring the term "unprecedented" to "unique" as regards the Shoah, he reminds us that, now, both philosophy and theology must be rethought in light of the historical fact of the Shoah[1], and, subsequent to it, the whole notion of missionizing the Jews on the part of Christians is "a theological obscenity." Then, too, the very idea of human nature must equally be rethought, now confronted with a humanity "infinitely deparavable." Lastly, in traditional Jewish terms, the Shoah took place in Galut [Exile], and is, therefore, an experience of "Galut-Judaism." The lesson: Galut has now come to its end; it is time for the Jew to take leave of his/her Exile and return to Zion. Hence, because of the Shoah, Fackenheim now supplies a new rationale, both philosophical and theological, for Zionism, yet echoing both Jewish tradition-al religious thought and the experience of Jewish history succeeding the Roman destruction of the Second Temple in the year 70.

THE HOLOCAUST: A SUMMING UP AFTER TWO DECADES OF REFLECTION

Emil L. Fackenheim

I. Preamble

My preamble consists of two quotations.   The first is from Peter Demetz, Postwar German Literature:

> In West Germany [where, according to the revised statute of limitations, concentration camp murderers who did not act from base motives can no longer be prosecuted] Celan's "Fugue of Death" has become a popular textbook piece, and one of the academic commentators admonishes the classroom teacher to stick to the text lest "student discussion deviate from the work of art to the persecution of the Jews."

My second text is taken from the Proceedings of the Nuremberg trials and consists of the interrogation of a Polish Auschwitz guard by the Russian prosecutor and reads as follows:

> Witness: Women carrying children were always sent with them to the crematorium. The children were then torn from their parents outside the crematorium and sent to the gas-chambers separately.   When the extermination of the Jews in the gas-chambers was at its height, orders were issued to the effect that the children were to be thrown into the crematorium furnaces or into the pit near the crematorium, without being gassed first.
> Smirnow [Russian prosecutor]:   How am I to understand this? Did they throw them into the fire alive, or did they kill them first?
> Witness? They threw them in alive. Their screams could be heard at the camp.
> Smirnov: Why did they do this?
> Witness: It is very difficult to say. We do not know whether they wanted to economize on gas, or if it was because there was not enough room in the gas-chambers.

"Holocaust" by Emil L. Fackenheim.   Reprinted with permission of Char Scribner's Sons, an imprint of Macmillan Publishing Company, from Contempor Jewish Religious Thought, by Arthur A. Cohen and Paul Mendes-Flohr, Editors. [c] 1 by Charles Scribner's Sons. [The Premable and Epilogue were added for Amy D. Cc [Editor], Agumentum e Silentio: Internationales Paul Celan Symposium, Berlin, Wal de Gruyter, 1987, pages 285-295.]

II. The Term "Holocaust"

"Holocaust" is the term currently most widely employed for the persecution of the Jewish people by Nazi Germany [1933-1945], first in Germany
itself and subsequently in Nazi-occupied Europe, culminating in "extermination" camps and resulting in the murder of nearly six million Jews.
However, "Shoa" ["total destruction"] would be more fitting since "Holocaust" connotes, in addition, "burnt sacrifice." It is true that, like ancient
Moloch-worshippers, German Nazis and their non-German henchmen at
Auschwitz threw children into the flames alive. It was not, however, their
own children, in acts of sacrifice, but those of Jews, in acts of murder.

III. The Holocaust and History

Is the Holocaust unique? The concept "unprecedented" is preferable as it
refers to the same facts but avoids not only well-known difficulties about
the concept "unique" but also the temptation of taking the event out of history
and thus "mystifying" it. [See the warnings voiced especially by Yehuda
Bauer.] To be sure, Auschwitz was "like another planet" ["Ka-tzetnik
135683," the pen name of the novelist Yechiel Dinur], i.e. a world of its own,
with laws, modes of behavior and even a language of its own. Even so, as
"unprecedented" rather than "unique" it is placed firmly into history.
Historians are obliged, so far as possible, to search for precedents; and
thoughtful people--by no means historians only--are obliged to ask if the
Holocaust itself may become a precedent for future processes, whether as
yet only possible or already actual. Manes Sperber has written: "encouraged by the way Hitler had practiced genocide without encountering
resistance, the Arabs [in 1948] surged in upon the nascent Israeli nation, to
exterminate it and make themselves its immediate heirs."

The most obvious recent precedent of the Holocaust is the Turkish
genocide of the Armenians in World War I. Like the Nazi genocide of the
Jews in World War II, this was [i] an attempt to destroy a whole people, [ii]
carried out under the cover of a war, [iii] with maximum secrecy and [iv]
with the victims being deported to isolated places prior to their murder, [v]
all this provoking few countermeasures or even verbal protests on the part
of the civilized world. Doubtless the Nazis both learned from, and were
encouraged by, the Armenian process.

But unlike the Armenian genocide the Holocaust was intended, planned
and executed as the "final solution" of a "problem." Thus whereas e.g. the
Armenians in Istanbul, the very heart of the Turkish Empire, were left
almost untouched, Nazi Germany, had she won the war or even man-aged to
prolong it a little, would have murdered every last Jew available. [North
American Indians have survived in reservations; Jewish reservations in a
victorious Nazi Empire are inconceivable.] Thus the Holocaust may be said

to belong, with other catastrophes, into the species "genocide." Within the species "intended, planned, and largely executed extermination," it is without precedent and, thus far at least, without sequel. It is--here the term really must be employed--unique.

Equally unique are the means without which this project could not have been planned or carried out. These include: [i] a scholastically precise definition of the victims; [ii] juridical procedures, enlisting the finest minds of the legal profession, aimed at the total elimination of the victims' rights; [iii] a technical apparatus including murder trains and gas chambers; [iv] most importantly, a veritable army not only of actual murderers but also of managers, army officers, railway conductors, entrepreneurs, and an endless list of others.

All these were required for the "how" of the "Final Solution." Its "why" required an army of historians, philosophers and theologians. The historians rewrote history. The philosophers refuted the idea that man-kind is human before it is "Aryan" or "non-Aryan." And the theologians were divided into Christians who made Jesus into an "Aryan," and neo-pagans who rejected Christianity itself as "non-Aryan." [Their differences were slight com-pared to their shared commitments." Such were the shock troops of this army. Equally necessary, however, was its remainder: historians, philoso-phers, and theologians who knew differently but betrayed their calling by holding their peace.

What was the "why" of the Holocaust? Even the shock troops never quite faced it, though having no reason or excuse for not doing so. As early as in 1936 Julius Streicher was on record, to the effect that "who fights the Jew fights the devil," and that "who masters the devil conquers heav-en." And this basest, most pornographic Nazi expressed only most succinctly the philosophy of the most authoritative one, to the effect that "if the Jew will be victorious" in his cosmic struggle with mankind, his "crown" will be the "funeral wreath of humanity, and this planet will, as it did millions of years ago, move through the ether devoid of human beings" [Hitler in Mein Kampf].

Planet Auschwitz was as good as Streicher's word. When the Third Reich was at the height of its power, the conquest of heaven seemed to lie in the apotheosis of the master race; even then, however, the "mas-tery" of the Jewish "devil" was a necessary condition of it. And when the Third Reich came crashing down and the apocalypse was at hand, "Planet Auschwitz" continued to operate till the end, and Hitler's last will and testament made the fight against the Jewish people mandatory for future generations. The "mastery" of the Jewish "devil," it seems, had become sufficient condition for the "conquest of heaven," if indeed not identical with it.

To be sure, this advent of salvation in the Auschwitz gas chambers was but for relatively few eyes to see. What could be heard by all, however, was the promise of it years earlier, when the streets of Germany resounded to the stormtroopers' hymn: "When Jewish blood spurts from our knives, our well-being will redouble."

Never in history has a state attempted to make a whole country--indeed, in this case, a whole continent--rein of every single member of a whole people, man, woman, and child. Never have attempts resembling the Holocaust even somewhat been pursued with methods so thorough and with such unswerving goal-directedness. It is difficult to imagine, and impossible to believe that, this having happened, world history can ever be the same. The Holocaust is not only an unprecedented event. It is also of an as yet unfathomable magnitude. It is world-historical.

IV. The Holocaust and Philosophy

As such it poses new problems for philosophical thought. To begin with reflections on historiography, if, by near-common philosophical consent, historically to explain an event is to show how it was possible then, to the philosopher, the Holocaust-historian emerges sooner or later as asserting the possibility of the Holocaust solely because it was actual--as moving in circles. This impasse, to be sure, is often evaded, most obviously when, as in many histories of World War II, the Holocaust is relegated to a few footnotes. An impasse is even explicitly denied when, as in Marxist ideological history, Nazism-equals-fascism-equals-the-last-stage-of-capitalism; or when, as in liberalistic ideological history, the Holocaust is flattened out into man's-inhumanity-to-man-especially-in-wartime. [For Arnold Toynbee, "what the Nazis did was nothing peculi-ar"]. The philosopher, however, must penetrate beyond these evasions and ideological distortions. And when he finds a solid historian state, correctly enough, that "the extermination grew out of the biologistic insanity of Nazi ideology, and for that reason is completely unlike the terrors of revolutions and wars of the past" [K. D. Bracher], he must ponder whether "biologistic insanity," in this case, has explanatory force, or is rather a metaphor, the chief meaning of which is that explanation has come to an end. And, as he does ponder this, the philosopher, and indeed the historian also, may well be led to wonder "whether even in a thousand years people will understand Hitler, Auschwitz, Maidanek and Treblinka better than we do now....Posterity may understand it even less than we do. [Isaac Deutscher].

Such questions turn philosophical thought from methodological to substantive issues, and above all to the subject of Man. Premodern philosophy was prepared to posit a permanent human "nature" that was uneffected by all historical change. More deeply immersed in the varieties and vicissitudes of history, modern philosophy generally has perceived, in abstraction from historical change, only a human "condition," and this was considered permanent only insofar as beyond it was the humanly impossible. At Auschwitz, however, "more was real than is possible" [Hans Jonas], and the impossible was done by some and suffered by others. Thus, prior to the Holocaust, the human condition, while including the necessity of dying, was seen as also including at least one inalienable freedom--that of each individual dying his own death [Martin Heidegger]. "With the administrative murder of millions" in the death camps, however, "death has become something that was never to be feared in this way before....The individual is robbed of the last and poorest that until then still remained his own. In the camps it was no longer the individual that died; he was made into a specimen" [Theodor Adorno].

As well as of dying, the Auschwitz administrators also manufactured a new way of living. Prior to the Holocaust no aspect of the human condition could make so strong a claim to permanency as the distinction between life and death, between still-being-here and being-no-more. The Holocaust, however, produced the Muselmann, the skin-and-bone walking corpse, or living dead, the vast "anonymous mass, continuously renewed and always identical, of non-men who march and labor in silence, the divine spark dead within them, already too empty really to suffer. One hesitates to call them living. One hesitates to call their death death" [Primo Levi]. The Muselmann may be called the most truly original contribution of the Third Reich to civilization.

From the new ways of being human--those of the victims--philo-sophical thought is turned to another new way of being human, that of the victimizers. Philosophy has all along been acquainted with the quasi-evil of sadism [a mere sickness], the semi-evil of moral weakness, the superficial evil of ignorance, and even-hardest to understand and therefore often ignored or denied--the "radical" or "demonic" evil that is done and celebrated for its own sake. Prior to the Holocaust, however, it was unacquainted with the "banal evil" [Hannah Arendt] practiced by dime-a-dozen individuals who, having been ordinary or even respected citizens, committed at Auschwitz crimes on a scale previously unimaginable, only to become, after it was all over, ordinary and respectable again--without showing signs of suffering sleepless nights.

The evil is banal by dint, not of course of the nature of the crimes but of the people that committed them: these, it is said, were made to do by the system what they did. This, however, is only half a philosophical thought, for who made the system--conceived, planned, created, perpetuated, escalated it--if not such as Himmler and Eichmann, Stangl and Hoess, to say nothing of the unknown-solder-become S.S. murderer? Already in difficulties with "radical" or "demonic" evil, philosophical thought is driven by the "banal" evil of the Holocaust from the operators to the system, and from the system back to the operators. In this circular movement, to be sure, "banal" evil, except for ceasing to be banal, does not become intelligible. Yet the thought-movement is not without result, far from it the Holocaust emerges as a world or, rather, as the anti-world par excellence. The human condition does not dwell in a vacuum. It always-already-is within a world, i.e., within a structured whole that [i] exists at all because it is geared to life and that [ii] is structured because it is governed by laws of life. [Innocent so long as they obey the law, the inhabitants of a world have a right to live, and forfeit it, if at all, only by an act of will--the breach of the law]. The Holocaust anti-world, while structured, to be sure, was governed by a law of death. For the victims--mostly Jews--existence itself was a capital crime--an unheard of proposition!--and the sole raison d'etre of the others was to mete out their punishment. In this world, the degradation, torture, and eventual murder of some human beings at the hands of others was not a by-product of, or means to, some higher, more ultimate purpose. They were its whole essence.

Modern philosophers, we have said previously, were able to conceive of a "human condition" because not all things were considered humanly possible. Even so, some of their number--possibly with modern history in mind-- have not hesitated to ascribe to Man a "perfectibility" that is "infinite." Auschwitz exacts a new concession from future philosophy: whether or not Man is infinitely perfectible he is in any case infinitely depravable. The Holocaust is not only a world-historical even. It is also a "watershed" [Franklin Littell], or "caesura" [Arthur Cohen] or "rupture" [Emil Facken- heim] in Man's history on earth.

V. The Holocaust and Theology

Is the Holocaust a rupture in the sight of theology? This question re- quires a separate inquiry. Theology, to be sure--at least if it is Jewish or Christian--is bound up with history. But it can be, and has been, argued that this is a Heilsgeschichte immune to all "merely secular" historical events. Thus for Franz Rosenzweig nothing crucial could happen for Jews between Sinai and the Messianic days. And for Karl Barth it was "always Good Friday after Easter," the implication being that the crucial saving event of Christianity has already occurred--and is unassailable ever after.

Is the Holocaust a rupture for Christianity? German Christians [and possibly Christians as a whole] "can no longer speak evangelically to Jews" [Dietrich Bonhoeffer]. They cannot "get behind Auschwitz, beyond it" if at all only "in company with the victims," and this only if they identify with the State of Israel, as being a Jewish "house against death" and the "last Jewish refuge" [Johann Baptist Metz]. Christians must relate "positively" to Jews, not "despite" Jewish non-acceptance of the Christ but "because" of it [H. H. Henrix, F. M. Marquardt, M. Stoehr]. Even to go only this far and no further with their theologians--it seems fitting in this context to cite Ger- man theologians only--is for Christians to recognize a post-Holocaust rupture in their faith, for the step demanded--renunciation of Christian missions-to-the-Jews, as such and in principle--is, within Christian history, without precedent. [Of the Christian theologians who find it necessary to go much further Roy Eckardt is, perhaps, the most theologically-oriented]. To

refuse even this one step--for Christians to stay with the idea of missions-
to-the-Jews in principle, even if suspending it altogether in practice--is
either to ignore the Holocaust or else sooner or later to reach some such
view as that missions-to-the-Jews "is the sole possibility of a genuine and
meaningful restitution [Wiedergutmachung] on the part of German Christendom" [Martin Wittenberg, a German Luther-an]. Can Christians view such a
stance as other than a theological obsceni-ty? The Jewish stance toward
Christian missionizing attempts directed at them, in any case, cannot be what
it once was. Prior to the Holocaust, Jews could respect such attempts,
though of course considering them misguided. After the Holocaust, they can
only view them as trying in one way what Hitler did in another.

It would seem, then, that for Christians Good Friday can no longer be
always after Easter. As for Jews, was the Holocaust a crucial event,
happen though it did between Sinai and the Messianic days? Franz Rosen-z-
weig's Jewish truth, it emerges in our time, was a truth not of Judaism but
of Galut-Judaism only. [Of this latter, his thought was the most profound
modern statement]. Galut-Judaism, however, has ceased to be tenable.

"Galut"--or "exile"--Judaism may be defined as follows:

[i] a Jew can appease or bribe, hide or flee from an enemy and, having
succeeded, can thank God for having been saved.

[ii] when in extremis such salvation is impossible--when death can be
staved off only though apostasy--he can still choose death, thus becoming a
martyr; and then he is secure in the knowledge that, while no Jew should
seek death, kiddush hashem [sanctifying God's name by dying for it] is the
"highest stage" of which he can be worthy [Maimonides].

[iii] Exile, though painful, is bearable, for it is meaningful--whether its
meaning is punishment for Jewish sins, vicarious suffering for the sins of
others, or whether it is simply inscrutable--a meaning known only to God.

[iv] Galut or exile will not last forever. If not he or his children's
children, so at any rate some Jews' distant offspring will live to see the
Messianic end.

These are the chief conditions and commitments of Galut-Judaism.
Existing in these conditions and armed by these commitments, a Jew in past
centuries was able to survive the poverty, deliberately engineered, of the
East European Ghetto; the slander, ideologically embellished and em-
broidered, of antisemitism in modern Germany and France; the medieval
expulsions; the Roman Emperor Hadrian's attempts once and for all to
extirpate the Jewish faith; and, of course, the fateful destruction of the
Jerusalem Temple in 70 C.E., to which Galut-Judaism was able to survive.
The Holocaust, however, already shown by us to be unprecedented simply as

an historical event, is unprecedented also as a threat to the Jewish faith--
and Galut-Judaism is unable to meet it.

[i] The Holocaust was not a gigantic pogrom from which one could hide
until the visitation of the drunken cossacks had passed. This enemy was
coldly sober, and systematic rather than haphazard: except for the lucky
few, there was no hiding.

[ii] The Holocaust was not a vast expulsion, with the necessity [but also
possibility] arising of, yet once again, resorting to wandering, with the
Torah as "portable fatherland" [Heinrich Heine]. Even when the Third
Reich was still satisfied with expelling Jews there was, except for the
fortunate or prescient, no place to go; and when the Reich became dissatisfied with mere expulsions, a place of refuge, had such been available, would
have been beyond reach.

[iii] The Holocaust was not an assault calling for bribing or appeasing
the enemy. This enemy was an "idealist" who could not be bribed; and he
remained unappeasable until the last Jew's death.

[iv] The Holocaust was not a challenge to Jewish martyrdom but, on the
contrary, an attempt to destroy it forever. Once Hadrian had decreed death
for Jews for the crime of practicing Judaism--and inspired the martyrdom
of such as Rabbi Akiba, which in turn inspired countless Jewish generations.
[According to legend, it was not lost even on his Roman executioner; unable to
forget Akiba's steadfastness he at length became a convert to Judaism.]
Hitler, who unlike Hadrian sought to destroy Jews but also, like Hadrian,
Judaism was too cunning to repeat the ancient emperor's folly. He decreed
death for Jews, not for a doing or even believing, but rather for being--for
the crime of possessing Jewish ancestors. Thus Jewish martyrdom was
made irrelevant. Moreover, no effort was spared to make it impossible as
well, and the supreme effort in this direction was the manufacture of
Muselmaenner. A martyr chooses to die; as regards the Muselmaenner, "one
hesitates to call them living; one hesitates to call their death death."

It cannot be stressed enough that, despite these unprecedented, super-
human efforts to murder Jewish martyrdom, countless, nameless Akibas
managed to sanctify God's name by choosing how to die, even though robbed
of the choice of whether to die: their memory must have a special sacredness to God and Man. Such memory is abused, however, if used to blot out,
to minimize, or even just divert attention from, the death of the children as
yet unable to choose, and the death of the Muselmaenner who could choose no
more.

That these four nova made Galut-Judaism untenable has found an ad-
mirable expression in an ancient Midrash that was originally meant to
expound it. In this Midrash God, at the beginning of the great exile initiated

by the destruction of the Temple in 70 C.E., exacts three oaths, one from the Gentiles and two from the Jews. The Gentiles are made to swear not to persecute the Jews, now stateless and helpless, excessively. The Jews are made to swear not to resist their persecutors, and not to "climb the wall," i.e. prematurely to return to Jerusalem.

But what, one must ask, if not Auschwitz, is "excessive persecution"? In response, some have said that the Jews broke their oath by climbing the wall, i.e. by committing the sin of Zionism, and that in consequence God at Auschwitz released the Gentiles from theirs. Any such attempt to save Galut-Judaism, however, reflects mere desperation, for it lapses into two blasphemies--toward the innocent children and the guiltless Muselmaenner, and toward a God who is pictured as deliberately callously, consigning them to their fate. There remains, therefore, only a bold and forthright taking leave from Galut-Judaism: it was the Gentiles who, at Auschwitz, broke their oath, and the Jews in consequence are released from theirs.

A "post-Galut-Judaism" Judaism is, unmistakably, in the making in our time. Its most obvious aspects are these, that "resisting" the persecutors and "climbing the wall" have become not only rights but also ineluctable duties. After the Holocaust, Jews owe antisemites [as well as, of course, their own children] the duty of not encouraging their murderous instincts by their own powerlessness. And after the absolute homelessness of the twelve Nazi years that were equal to a thousand, they owe the whole world [as well as, of course, their own children] the duty to say "no" to Jewish wandering, to return home, to rebuild a Jewish state.

These aspects of the Judaism-in-the-making are moral and political. Their inner source is spiritual and religious. In the Warsaw Ghetto Rabbi Yitzhak Nissenbaum, a famous and respected orthodox rabbi, made the statement--much quoted at the time by Jews of all persuasions in their desperate efforts to defend, preserve, hallow Jewish life against an enemy sworn to destroy it all--that this was not a time for kiddush hashem [martyrdom] but rather for kiddush ha-chayyim [the sanctification of life]. It is a time for kiddush ha-chayyim still. The Jewish people has passed through the Nazi anti-world of death; thereafter, by any standard, religious or secular, Jewish life ranks higher than Jewish death, even if it is for the sake of the divine name. This people has experienced exile in a form more horrendous than ever dreamt of by the apocalyptic imagination: thereafter, to have ended exile bespeaks a fidelity and a will-to-live that, taken together, give a new dimension to piety. The product of this fidelity--the Jewish state--is fragile still, and embattled wherever the world is hostile or does not understand. Yet Jews both religious and secular known in their hearts that Israel--the renewed people, the reborn language, the replanted land, the rebuilt city, the state itself--is a new and unique celebration of life. There are many reasons why Israel has become the center of the Jewish people in our time; not least is that it is indispensable to a future Judaism. If a

Jewish state had not arisen in the wake of the Holocaust, it would be a religious necessity--although, one fears, a political near-impossibility--to create it now.

VI. Epilogue: The Holocaust and Poetry

Theodor Adorno has written that to write poetry after Auschwitz is barbaric, presumably on the grounds that it presupposes stopping one's ears to the cries of the murdered children. Such poetry, like philosophy carrying on its business at the same price, is, to cite Adorno again, comparable to the music by which the SS customarily drowned out the cries of their victims. Subsequently Adorno mitigated the harshness of his statement about writing poetry after Auschwitz. However, so far as I know, he never withdrew it.

But what about writing poetry about Auschwitz? To cite Adorno yet again, the "metaphysical capacity," once confronting Auschwitz and self-exposed to it, is "paralyzed." What is a poetry that is self-exposed to Auschwitz, and therefore self-paralyzed? And what is its role in, and effect upon, the writing of future poetry?

I confess I do not know. I do not even know the effect upon the future reading of poetry--of a poetry written long before Auschwitz became part of our world. There is no greater poem in the German language that Goethe's "Wandering Nachtlied." Few poems have so timeless, spaceless a validity. It reads as follows:

> Uber allen Gipfeln
> Ist Ruh.
> In allen Wipfeln
> Spurest Du
> Kaum einen Hauch.
> Die Vogelein schweigen im Walde.
> Warte nur, balde.
> Ruhest Due auch.

> On the peaks of all mountains-
> Tranquility.
> On all treetops
> You feel
> Barely a breath.
> The birds in the forest are silent.
> Hush, soon for you too-
> Tranquility.

[The translation is mind.--ELF]

Under no circumstances can we allow this poem to be destroyed for us by the Holocaust. But can we read it now as before, i.e., partake of its spaceless, timeless quality? The mountain peaks and treetops looked at by Goethe are the same that were looked at by the murderers of Buchenwald. Doubtless not a few of them were of aesthetic cast of mind and steeped in German poetry. Possibly some of them may have read Goethe's poem of an evening, so as to regain tranquility after a hard day's work, and strength for the work of the day to come. For us to read Goethe's poem as timeless and spaceless would be comparable to the music by which the SS customarily drowned out the cries of their victims.

For Irving Greenberg, "voluntary covenant" begins with the self-limitation of God and, therefore, the participation of humanity in creating a "perfect" world. Rabbinic tradition essentially reinterpreted the Torahitic covenant with God, especially after the destruction of the Second Temple in the year 70 C.E. Now, in light of the Shoah, that covenant with God can no longer be morally commanded. Jewish have now become "senior partners" in this covenantal relationship by, realistically, voluntarily recommitting themselves to covenant with God as evidenced, for example, by the recreation of the State of Israel after the Shoah, and must now assume total responsibility for their actions and behavior.

VOLUNTARY COVENANT[1]

Irving Greenberg

I. Redemption, Human Freedom and the Covenant

The central teaching of Judaism is redemption. Yahadut teaches that the world and the life which emerges within it are grounded in the infinite source of life and energy which we call God. As the continuum of life unfolds, the emerging life becomes more and more God-like--more and more valuable, more and more responsive to others, more and more free. Animals have soul qualities, but humans reach the level of being an image of God[2]--the highest level of holiness except for the Divine itself.

The intrinsic nature of God is beneficent, giving and pulsing with life. Therefore, the life which is growing in the ground of the Divine will continue to grow until all of its possibilities will be fully realized and perfected.[3]

However, the present condition of the world does not appropriately support the fullness of the image of God. There is poverty, sickness, oppression, and degradation. Death itself is the ultimate denial of life and its dignity. But reality is not neutral; it is rooted in a loving transcendent God who cares. Therefore, it cannot remain indefinitely oppressive and valueless. Some day all this will be corrected--the world will become the paradise it was meant to be. Even death will be overcome so that life/holiness will be fully upheld. In this messianic time, death will be defeated not only prospectively, but retrospectively through resurrection. Only then will the divine nature underlying reality be truly manifest.

Judaism makes an even more remarkable statement. God respects human freedom. Although God yearns for this messianic consummation and promises that it will be, God will not force humans to be perfect. By a process of voluntary self-limitation [covenant], God allows humanity to participate in the process of creating a perfect world. Underlying this process is the concept, the reality, of covenant. God's first covenant is with humanity as a whole. Never again will God bring total destruction on the world even if it is evil. Total destruction is so intimidating that is incompatible with human freedom and dignity. The divine acceptance of humanity's flawed quality allows humans the margin to go on even if evil wins out temporarily. Yet the Divine remains committed to, and yearning for, the attainment of the final perfection. Therefore, God does not surrender the capacity to punish or reward. God only yields the right to force and overwhelm the human.

From the Divine perspective, the great danger in the grant of freedom is that humans may exercise their freedom by settling for a reality which is less than the final perfection. Given the limits of reality, the power of inertia, the force which oppressors maintain, there is real danger that some status quo, far short of the final perfection, will triumph. God is caught between the freedom given to humans and the ultimate dignity which God wishes to be the possession of all humans. Yet forcing the final freedom is not the way to have people become free.[4]

This logic leads God to a second covenant with Abraham and the Jewish people. This Jewish covenant makes possible reconciliation of the conflict between the Divine respect for human dignity and respect for human freedom. God first singles out Abraham; later the entire Jewish people accepts this covenant. They promise that they will testify, model a way and teach the world the goal of final perfection. The Jews will not settle for less; they will not fully join humanity until the redemption comes. Instead they will challenge; they will testify "not yet;" they will debunk all absolutes because there are not but God. The Divine promise is that this is not a totally quixotic mission--redemption will come to be. The divine promise is that God will be Israel's God throughout the way; that as long as this people carries on this purpose and keeps its Divine connection, it will remain alive to carry it out. Knowing that the Jews will permanently represent that party of final redemption, the Divine is willing to release all of humanity to exercise its freedom. Thus, the Jewish covenant is a blessing for all the families of the earth and is part of a covenant with all humanity. "....if you will obey Me faithfully and keep My covenant then you will be My treasured possession of all the nations. Indeed all the earth is mine but you will be a kingdom of priests [i.e. ministering to all nations, connecting them to the Divine] and a holy nation to Me."[5]

Respect for human freedom means that Israel too must make concessions to reality. The Way of Judaism upholds the principles of the ultimate human condition--to the extent that it is possible now. Jews are commanded to treat others with as much justice and kindness as present parameters allow--and a bit more. Thus the halakhah, although it is the way to perfection, makes many compromises along the way--from eating meat at the ritual pole to slavery, war and the status of women at the ethical pole.[6] These concessions are part of the process of redemption. They will be overcome ultimately but, on the way, they are affirmed. Any covenant that respects freedom must allow for process.

Because redemption will not be achieved in one generation, the Torah is not only a covenant between God and Israel, but also a covenant between generations. It is offered to those "present here standing with us today before the Loving God, our Lord and also to the one who is not here with us today."[7] By taking us its task, each generation joins the past and carries on, until the day that the hopes of all will be fulfilled. If one generation rejects the covenant or fails to pass it on to the next generation, then the effort of all the preceding and future generations is lost as well. Each generation knows that it is not operating in a vacuum; what precedes it makes its work possible, just as its successors will make or break its own mission. Thus, the covenant is binding not just because it is juridical--that is, commanded--but because others continually accept its goal and become bound to its process.

However, there is a catch again--a Divine Catch-22 as it were. If Israel's freedom is respected, then there is a danger that Jewry will sell out along the way. The Jews are only human; they were not chosen because of superior, innate goodness any more than they were because of any numerical greatness.[8] Therefore, who shall be witness to the witnesses? What guarantee is there that Israel will not yield to moral fatigue along this endless way?

Preventive mechanisms operate on both sides of the covenant. On the Divine side, God is more 'active' with Israel, holding the people to the standard by a visible process of reward and punishment designed to teach the people to uphold the covenant. This is the theme not only of the Pentateuch [viz., rain and long life are rewards for obedience] but also of the historical books of the Bible.[9] On the human side, since Israel may waver, some element of coercion or enforced loyalty is necessary to take up the moments of moral slackness. The covenant is sealed into Jewish physical existence, and thus is experienced in part as 'involuntary'.

The great symbol of the involuntary covenant is circumcision; once the covenant is carried in the flesh, it is hard for the Jew to assimilate, i.e., to 'pass' as an uncovenanted one. The Jews journeying to redemption may be compared to Ulysses about to pass the Sirens. Knowing that the Sirens' music is beautiful and indeed irresistible, waiting to hear it yet knowing that to draw near the sound is to inexorably smash the ship and scuttle the voyage. Ulysses has himself lashed to the mast. No matter how seductive the music, nor overwhelming the urge to go to the Sirens and live [or die!] with them, he cannot do so because he is bound without escape. Circumcision is the physical mark that prevents Israel's escape into the mass of humanity. Even when the spirit is weak, the flesh forces some willing or unwilling testimony, imposed at an age when the child cannot accept or reject circumcision is a powerful symbolic statement that all Jews[10] are bound by birth and stand for the covenant whether or not they are in the mood to witness, or are spiritually heroic enough to actually practice the higher level of behavior which faithfulness demands.

This is far from a perfect solution to the problem. Circumcision is not an absolute barrier, and with enough effort Israel may succeed in overcoming this obstacle to assimilation. In addition, if the covenant is only a burden then it will become hateful. And Jewish behavior may become so deviant from the covenant as to outweigh and contradict the verbal or symbolic testimony. Instead of bearing witness, Jews could disgrace and degrade the Divine Name and make the covenantal testimony non-credible. Nevertheless, since the covenant is carried in the flesh, and the existence of the people is, in itself, a statement of Divine Presence and concern, then every Jew--even one who sins or whose behavior is not up to par--carries the message.

Other dynamic aspects of the covenant model are central to Jewish history and religion. From this concept also stems the Jewish vision of God as pedagogue--teaching Torah to Israel and the world. If goodness cannot be imposed by power, then humankind must be educated toward perfection. Teaching becomes the special role and concern of God. Indeed the special covenant with Abraham and the revelation at Sinai are part of the process of teaching humanity. For teaching purposes, God is the ultimate model. The imitation of God becomes the basis of ethics.[11]

The Jewish tradition also asserts that the covenant binds God. The Divine is not merely the source of the Torah but is also bound by the covenant's terms. Form this principle stems the Jewish tradition of arguing, indeed going to trial, with God. The task of the religious person is not only to obey God, but to represent the human claims in the covenant. A teacher and/or a parent, however warm or responsive, cannot truly enable the student/child to grow unless he/she is prepared to be available in some committed way as a reliable and consistent model. Thus Divine acceptance of human freedom becomes irrevocable--unless the covenant itself is revoked. Since humans are limited, the final perfection will come slowly, and only through partnership of humans and God. Of course, once God is bound then God too becomes dependent on the partner, Israel, for the final achievement of the goal. As this implication emerged in history, it was initially resisted both by Prophets and Rabbis who feared that God's ultimate power would be undermined by such a view.

The Divine is saddled with an erratic covenantal partner. God must ask repeatedly--every time the Jews fail--is the game worth the candle? Is this partner too frail a reed on which to lean? Is Israel too weak or incorrigible to carry this burden through history? The logic of respect for freedom is to accept the Jews' limitations, but the urge to change partners is strong. The temptation to shift is expressed in Exodus 32:40 when God struggles with the idea of wiping out Israel and starting again with Moses. Before the initial covenant, the Divine exercised this tactic by wiping out humanity with the Flood and starting again with Noah. In the Biblical stage of the covenant, after every catastrophe, Jews asked themselves whether the Divine has lost patience. Was God upholding the covenant by punishing Israel or was God rejecting Israel as the covenantal partner?

The dynamics of these interacting aspects of the covenant model account for the pattern of the unfolding of much of Jewish religious history and development. My contention is that the concept of covenant has been transformed as it has unfolded under crisis, that we are living in such a moment of crisis and transformation now, and that there are possible models of past response that we can apply to the present.[12]

II. The Covenant in History

A. The First Destruction and Exile

Since Judaism affirms that the final perfection will take place in history, Jewish triumph and Jewish liberation tend to raise the credibility and persuasiveness of the redemptive hope and the covenant itself. Indeed the core event of the covenant and of Jewish religious history is the Exodus, the paradigm of God's redemptive action. Yet great tragedies or defeats shake the confidence in the coming of the final redemption. The persuasiveness of imperfection and evil overwhelm the frail evidence of redemption [the memory of the Exodus]. When the First Temple was destroyed, the very sanctuary of God had been violated, a seemingly impossible feat as long as the Divine Presence was there. But because the prophets perceived that Israel's sinfulness justified the Destruction, the catastrophe proved not that God abandoned them--or that other gods triumphed over God--but that God was punishing the Jews for their failure to live up to the covenant. The punishment was educational, a way of conditioning the Jews that obedience to the covenant benefits them. And, like circumcision, punishment 'forces' Israel to live up to the covenant.[13]

However, a deeper crisis grew out of the intensity of the Destruction. Possession of the Land was the symbol and guarantor of the validity of the covenant--yet the Jews were forced from the Holy Land. Then the covenant itself might have been forfeit! If the evil of the Israelites had so angered God, might not God have totally rejected the Israelites? In a sense, the Destruction was a test of what the covenant idea itself implied. Was it a utilitarian or functional covenant in which the Divine Partner had now decided to cut losses or was it fundamental to God's being, a plan that could not forfeit? The classic expression of this issue is found in Hosea and the story of Gomer, the unfaithful wife. In Hosea's experience, the Divine instruction to claim back the heart-breaking adulterous wife overrides the halakhic rule to divorce her. Similarly, after the rage, the hurt, the jealousy, the wrestling with rejection, comes God's anguished affirmation: "How shall I give you up, Ephraim? How can I surrender you, Israel?"[14] The prophets come to see that the Divine love was so total as to override laws and logic--and any notion of Divine limited liability in the covenant.

Ezekiel [37:11] gives a similar report. Jews were saying: "Our bones are dried up, and our hope is lost; we are cut off." The implication that the

Jews are dead grows out of the fear of forfeiting the covenantal promise of eternal existence for this people. The prophetic answer that God will not abandon the covenant no matter how many times the Jews break it was decisive on this score. "Yet for all that, when they are in the lands of their enemies, I do not reject them, nor do I abhor them to finish them off and thus to break My covenant with them, for I am the Loving God, their Lord." These consoling words at the conclusion of the curses [Leviticus 26:44] became so normative that the concept of a Divine rejection of the covenant was ruled out in later Jewish writings. The punishment-for-sins theory became dominant in prophetic literature, the only trace of an alternative theory of destruction being Isaiah's theme of Israel as a suffering servant, i.e., suffering for the sins of others.

B. The Second Destruction and the Unfolding of the Covenant

The crisis of the Destruction of the Second Temple was even greater. The wound was so deep that it could not be healed without a transformation of the relationship within the covenant.[15] Christian Jews concluded the covenant was broken. Jesus' life therefore ushered in a New Covenant and his followers left the Jewish community. The Sadducees and others insisted that the covenant was unchanged and the Temple had to be rebuilt so that the traditional covenant channels of worship, grace, and forgiveness could be reopened. The Rabbis, however, concluded that fundamentally the covenant was a pedagogical model. God, as master pedagogue, had raised Israel to a new point: in the Destruction was a call to Jews to a new level of covenantal relationship. God had 'constricted' or imposed self-limitation to allow the Jews to take on true partnership in the covenant.[16] While the word shutafut, partnership, appears nowhere in the Bible, it is a motif in Rabbinic literature.

Many other conclusions follow. The Second Destruction means the end of prophecy; direct revelation is inappropriate in a world where God is not manifest. Yet even as the Divine Presence becomes more hidden, it becomes more present; the widening ritual contact with the Divine goes hand in hand with the increased hiding. The synagogues which are more 'secular' than the 'sacramental' Temple are located everywhere. They take over the central role in Jewish cult that was formerly invested in only one location, the Holy Temple in Jerusalem where there was a uniquely manifest Divine Presence. The Rabbinic emphasis on Talmud Torah and on Jewish learning bespeaks the internalization of religious awareness and understanding which is needed to perceive the hidden Divine Presence. This level of perception is appropriate and necessary for a more mature partner in the covenant. An enormous expansion of halakhic models in living follows, an expansion described by scholars as the application of Temple holiness standards to daily, more secular, settings. Blessings and ritual purifications articulate the presence of the hidden Divine everywhere and sensitize the practitioner to 'see' that Presence. In the same way, the Rabbis stress that when one performs acts of kindness, the Shechinah [Indwelling Presence of God-- Ed.] is present. The Divine Presence is there when one visits the sick, or makes love, or when one is modest, or when one honors the aged.[17] Other actions: arrogance[18], sexual immorality[19], or perversion of justice obscure or remove the Divine Presence.[20]

The interpretation of the Destruction as a call to greater responsibility in the covenant underscores the role of God as teacher, what Maimonides later described as the pedagogical model in the tradition. Talmud Torah, i.e. study, becomes the central religious act: "Talmud Torah equals all the others [mitzvot]."[21] The holiday of the giving of the Torah, observed in the Pentateuch, is articulated in the Torah She B'al Peh [Oral Law]. The Rabbis' liturgy for Shavuot [Festival of Weeks--Ed.] constitutes a symbolic renewal of the covenant at Sinai. Learning becomes equivalent to the Biblical ritual acts; for example, the study and recitation of sacrifices is equal [in efficacy] to the act of bringing the sacrifices.[22] God portrayed repeatedly as learning and teaching Torah: "In the first three hours [of the day] the Holy One Blessed be He sits and studies Torah....what does God do in the fourth quarter of the day? Sits and teaches Torah in the house of the Rabbis."[23] Learning becomes a form of imitating God.[24]

Without using the formal term of 'Revelation', a term not really in their vocabulary, the Rabbis interpret the Destruction as revealing both the new role of God and the new responsibilities of Israel in the covenant. But the shift from manifest intervention to hidden Presence brings out further implications of the covenant model about which the Rabbis feel ambivalent. Punishment are somewhat mechanical forms of pedagogy. In a sense, they also operate as external reinforcement, much as external Revelation operates. This was less problematic in an age when sparing the rod was considered pedagogy. But still, the best pedagogy would seem to be one that elicits internal response by the pupil--a system in which the teacher serves as model rather than enforcer.[25] Explaining the Destruction as Divine punishment for sins is not as adequate an explanation as before. This remains the dominant explanation, in part because it is also an important defense against the claim that the Destruction is a rejection of Israel as covenant partner. However, there is a significant expansion of an alternate interpretation. The Divine Presence does not so much punish Israel in the Destruction as its suffers alongside Israel.[26] The Divine does not so much punish Israel with Exile as it goes into Exile with Israel: "Where [Israel] went into Exile, the Shechinah when with them....to Egypt....to Babylon...."[27]

Finally, if the Shechinah is hidden, then awareness of the Presence will be more dependent on Jewish actions. The Rabbis were both attracted and concerned by this implication: "You are My witnesses," says the Loving God, "and I am Lord. [Isaiah 43:12]. The Rabbis comment on this verse: "When you are My witnesses, I am the Lord; when you are not My witnesses,

I am not, as it were, Lord."[28] "When Israelites do God's will, they add strength to the Mighty on High....when the Israelites do not do God's will, they weaken, as it were, the great strength of the One who lifts them up...."[29]

C. New Roles in the Covenant

Out of the Rabbinic understanding of the Destruction of the Temple came a fundamental transformation of roles in the covenant. The promise and goal remained the same--God and Israel. The Divine Presence became at once more shielded and more present; the Jews' role became more active. God's will was no longer revealed through prophets, ongoing messengers carrying out Divine instructions, but rather through the judgments of the Rabbis. These judgments grew out of the past record of instruction [i.e. the Scriptures and salient precedents][30] which Rabbinic wisdom then applied to the present situation.[31] Since individual judgments differed, decisions were reached by majority rulings. Such de-cisions were considered authoritative, and equivalent to a word from God. Hence, formulation of the blessing concerning God, "Who sanctifies us in His commandments and commanded us to...." is recited even over Rabbinic injunctions. True, the Rabbis offered a Biblical justification for such an application of the blessing: God "commanded us" by instructing us to listen "to the judge [Rabbi] who will be in those days" [Deuteronomy 13:9-11].[32] While this can be understood mechanically, at a deeper level the Rabbis were asserting the authority of the covenantal way. The generations that follow must have the authority to apply and adapt the covenant in their days or we will not reach the final goal. If one accepts the goal, then every future judge's ruling has the authority of the One whose commandments initiated the way.

Still, the Rabbis were modest in their ideology. They saw themselves as inferior in authority, not empowered to judge the Torah or revise it according to their lights. Their authority is rather as the continuers of the way. Nonetheless, they did not shrink from the responsibility to bring the Torah and the Jewish people through the next stage on the way to Redemption. Thus, they interpreted the law of the rebellious son[33] as theoretical, not actual[34]. They restricted the process of capital punishment so narrowly that two Rabbis said that with one more twist they could prevent any capital punishment from ever being applied.[35] They permitted a woman to testify to her own husband's death lest she otherwise be "an-chored," unable to ever marry again. They improved the terms of divorce and the financial protection for women in marriage beyond those in the Torah.[36] In truth, they even suspended the laws of the Torah, although they did not believe that they had the authority to repeal them. After the Second Destruction, the ordeal of the sotah, the wife suspected of unfaithfulness, was set aside by Rabbi Yohanan ben Zakkai on the grounds that there were so many cheaters that the ordeal was no longer effective. I suggest that this is a halakhic consequence of the loss of the manifest Divine force. The sacramental efficacy of Divine power evident in the Temple [i.e. the swelling of the faithless woman's belly] was no longer available.[37]

The mixture of authority and modesty of the Rabbis is also consistent with the unfolding of the covenant model. For the Rabbis, Scriptural commandments had primacy of place because they set the ultimate goal: Scriptures are the foundation of authority for everything that follows. Furthermore, while God was perceived as self-limiting, God was still commanding and active; Scriptures, with their record of an earlier more intense role for God, retained primacy. Although the prophet Samuel was manifestly more noble, more learned, more 'miraculous' in power than earlier judges, the need to proceed through history gave "Jeftah in his generation [as much authority] as Samuel in his."[38] By extension, the Rabbis had all the authority they needed. Indeed, the decisions of the Rabbinic Court were studied and used in the Heavenly Court.[39] An erroneous setting of the calendar, or, according to some, even an erroneous interpretation of the Torah, is still accepted on High.[40] Since the covenant is the way to final perfection, the Torah had to take into account the flaws and limits of human beings.[41] Thus there is room for addition, extension, and perfection of the Torah. In our generation, Rabbi Joseph B. Soloveitchik expressed the ultimate logic of this position: the scholar is co-creator of Torah, just as by their actions, human beings become co-creators of the universe.[42]

The Rabbis had a powerful sense of both the continuity and discontinuity in their role. The classic expression of this dialectic is the Rabbinic tale of Moses in Rabbi Akiva's Yeshiva. When Moses came to visit, he could not understand the Torah that was being taught there. He grew faint, presumably from embarrassment and grief that his teaching had been left behind. Then, when a student asked from whence Akiva's teaching is known, and was told: It is tradition from Moses at Sinai, Moses is calmed and consoled. We cannot dismiss this text with Mordecai Kaplan's patro-nizing view that the Rabbis were so ignorant of method that they undertook radical revisions in an unselfconscious way. Nor need we accept the traditionalist view that everything to be said in the future was already said at Sinai. Rather, the Akiva story is parallel to the Talmudic passage that "whatever a tried and true student [talmid vatik] will some day innovate was already told to Moses at Sinai."[43] There is conscious recognition of novum in the aphorism, but the new is in fact fully continuous and identified with what Moses was given at Sinai. The novum too is part of the process of the covenant. As part of the way to perfection, a new ruling has all the authority of the covenant with which it is identified and whose goals it seeks to realize. Kaplan has reversed the truth and dismissed the Rabbis as intellectual 'yokels' who have no consciousness of method because of the modern tendency to underestimate the past.[44] The Rabbis understand well that they are developers and conservers at the same time. Development is not the same as revision, reform, or rejection.

Another analogy may shed some light on this view. In the New Testament's Gospel of Matthew, which is written in a Hebrew Christian setting, contemporaneous with the emergence of the post-Destruction Rabbinic view, Jesus says in the Sermon on the Mount: "I am not come to destroy [the Law and the Prophets] but to fulfill [them] for verily I say unto you, 'til heaven and earth pass, one jot or one tittle shall in no wise pass from the law, 'til all be fulfilled."[45] Yet in the very same speech, he calls for going beyond previous standards. We know that the Hebrew Christians also operated out of a covenantal model. They believed that the new covenant was the unfolding of the old. The Destruction convinced them that the new covenant succeeded the old. Although it led them out of the Jewish community, they were being very Jewish in their thinking in applying the model of the revelation message in their historical event.

The unfolding of the covenant involved a transformation of the partner people and their observance, but not a repudiation of the covenant as it had been up them. One should not push the parallel between Rabbinic and Hebrew Christian views too far because in one key, decisive way they parted company. Convinced by the Destruction of the Temple and the failure of subsequent attempted rebellions, especially the messianic Bar Kochba revolt, the Christians decided that a New Covenant had been born. The Rabbis, however, concluded that the covenant had been renewed; the was rebirth, not new birth.[46]

D. The Renewal of the Covenant

The claims of the Rabbinic interpretation of the covenant is articulated in a classic Talmudic passage which, despite its notoriety, had been taken too lightly. In it, the Rabbis hint at a second acceptance of the Torah.

> "They stood at the bottom of the mountain" [Exodus 19:17]. Said Rav Avdimi bar Chama bar Chasa: this teaches that [coming out of Egypt] the Holy One Blessed be He clapped the mountain over them like a tub and said: If you accept my Torah, good; if not, this will be your burial place. Said Rav Acha bar Yaacov: from this we can derive a legal "out" from the Torah [i.e. if we fail to observe it we can plead that this covenant was taken under coercion and is not legally binding--See Rashi, loc. cit.]. Said Rava: nevertheless [it is binding] for they accepted it again in the days of Ahashuerus, as it is written, "the Jews established and took upon themselves" [Esther 9:27], i.e. they [re]established what they had already taken upon themselves.[47]

Why is the Sinai Covenant acceptance labeled 'coerced' in this passage? Tosafot [Talmudic commentaries--Ed.] is disturbed by this view and points to other, seemingly voluntary acceptance of the Torah found in the Pentateuch such as the Israelite response "we will do and we will listen" [na'aseh v'nishma] and the covenant ceremony on Mounts Gerizim and Eyval.[48] Rabbeinu Tam suggests that at Sinai the Jews were pressured by the awesomeness of the Revelation--that "because it comes by Divine Speech [i.e. Revelation] therefore it is coerced, but in Ahasuerus' time they accepted it out of their own will [mi-da'atam--literally of their own mind or judgment] out of love of the miracle.[49] But is not appreciation of a miracle also coercive? I would suggest that the Talmud understood that the Covenant of Sinai was not coercive when it was given, as witness the Israelite affirmation "we will do and we will listen," etc. However, living after the Destruction, after the Divine ceased manifest interventions, in retrospect, the overt Divine salvation which backs the Sinai offer of covenant is perceived as coercive, if for no other reason that the gratitude in the heart of the saved ones obligates them to accept. The miracle of Purim is not coercive because unlike the Exodus miracles, it is hidden. Purim occurs after the Destruction of the Temple. The name of God is nowhere mentioned in the Book of Esther. The Purim miracle of salvation from genocide can be explained away as natural, achieved by imperfect humans using morally arguable methods. The recognition of the hidden Divine hand in all this is the insight which shows the Jews have come of age. They have reaccepted the covenant of Sinai on the 'new' terms, knowing that destruction can take place, that the sea will not split for them, that the Divine has self-limited and they have additional responsibilities.

If we take the Talmudic story to its ultimate logic, it is even bolder; it says that were Jews living only from the covenantal acceptance at Sinai, the Torah would not be fully binding after the Destruction. Post-Destruction Jews are living under the command of the Torah by dint of the reacceptance of the Torah at Purim time. The covenant of Purim is also a covenant of redemption, but it is built around a core event that is brought about by a more hidden Divine Presence acting in partnership with human messengers. Yet the covenant of Purim does not replace Sinai; it renews it.

Later the Talmud completes the circle of interpretation in an extended comparison of Moses imposing the covenantal oath on Israel to the oath taken by a litigant in a legal case. The Talmud says:

> We know that the commandments are binding on those who stood at Sinai; from whence do we know that future generations and future converts [are bound]? Scripture tells us [not only with you do I establish this covenant....but] with those who are not here with us today [Deuteronomy 29:1-4].

Thus the Talmud holds that the covenant is open, is offered to all who choose to join in it in the future, and is binding on them by that acceptance. Then the Talmud asks:

From whence do we derive that commandments which will be innovated in the future such as reading the Megillah [are binding]? Scripture tells us "[the Jews] established and took upon themselves" [Esther 9:27]. they [re]established what they had already taken upon themselves.[50]

In this passage, the authority of Rabbinic ordinance is based on the reaccepted covenant, the Purim renewal of the redemptive way. The authority of the Rabbis ultimately stems from their role in taking up the covenant and leading the way on this portion of the covenantal journey to redemption.

E. The Authority of the Rabbis

If the authority of Rabbinic ordinance stems from its role in carrying out the covenant further, then it is as binding as anything in written Scripture to anyone who accepts the covenant and its goals. Indeed, insofar as a Rabbinic law may move us closer to the covenantal goals, it may be more binding than Scripture. When Rabbinic law goes beyond the Torah law and brings us closer to the ultimate goal of the woman also being in the image of God, i.e., of infinite value/equal/unique, its authority becomes even more compelling than its predecessor sources.

This view is a change in my own thinking, and is contrary to two classical modern theological responses. Under the impact of modern values, various nineteenth century thinkers, seeking to clean up the halakhah and to bring it closer to the contemporary state of moral, intellectual and ethical judgments, tried to distinguish between Scriptural and Rabbinic ordinances. Scripture contained the universalist, prophetic Judaism; Rabbinic tradition was the later set of accretions--a literature in which legalism, particularism, and ritualism had run riot. In this same spirit, many secularists, especially Zionists such as Ben Gurion, tried to recover the pristine Biblical Judaism and to reject the Rabbinic, Diaspora traditions. These views fail to take history seriously. Ironically, despite their surface humanism, they end up glorifying God and failing to grasp the extraordinary shift in the covenantal partnership which is represented in Rabbinic Judaism. Implicit in these views is a loss of hope that the covenantal mechanism can respond to the crisis of modernization. Thus many Re-formers felt impelled to reject law and legal process in order to assert the freedom needed to clean up moral problems in the tradition, as well as to develop new models and values for the new conditions. Ironically enough, despite their present-mindedness, they missed the radical openness of the covenant to further events in history. After all, Jeremiah spoke of a new [renewed] covenant and of a day when people would swear not by the God who brought up Israel out of the land of Egypt but of the God active in a later redemption.[51] This same blind spot blocked Reformers from considering Zionism favorably, yet the later redemption of which Jeremiah spoke was that of bringing Israel back to the land of its ancestors. Thus the Enlightenment thinkers failed to recognize the transfer from the Divine to the human realm of religious function and of leadership in developing the law which was at the heart of the Rabbinic vision and achievement. Yet this increased role for human beings in the covenant constitutes an empowerment and a bestowal of dignity which is the true goal of modern culture.

This is also contrary to the other classic position which evolved under modern influence. In defense against rapid change and reform, Orthodoxy developed an ideology denying that any development or change ever took place in the halakhah. In further defense against change, there has been a strong tendency to deny any overall goal or telos to the Torah by halakhah by rejecting any attempt at a rationale of mitzvot and by eliminating the study of Bible and philosophy. Instead, Orthodox ideology offered a juridical view of the covenant. The Law is commanding and binding because God ordered it. Human judgment itself must be sacrificed wher-ever it comes into conflict with the authority of the tradition. In the extreme version, the Rabbis are seen as "tape recorders," replaying words that were in truth said thousands of years ago. In the more moderate forms, the Rabbis are glossators, footnoters, judges who can expand or underscore existing patterns but whose authority must remain that of epigones. The range of the process is per-ceived as having been further restricted by later decisions such as the closing of the Talmud or the acceptance of the Shulkhan Arukh as the universal authority. While there is support for this view in the ahistorical tendencies of later Rabbinic Judaism, I submit that this is essentially a lockjaw view of the tradition caused by the traumatic infection of moder-nization. This view is particularly inappropriate because it denigrates the Rabbis' achievement, and occurs in an age where another unfolding of the covenant is taking place. The final irony is that the divisions between Orthodox, Conservative, Reform, and Reconstructionist [or at least between Orthodox on the one hand and the latter three, on the other] appear to be at a peak at a moment when they are all being challenged, and even by-passed, by a new covenantal transformation.

III. The Age of the Voluntary Covenant

A. The Shattering of the Covenant

When the Nazis came to power, they began a devastating assault on the Jewish people. As other nations and peoples failed to resist, the attack broadened. An unprecedented decision was taken to kill every last Jew in the world--for the crime of being. In 1941 the phase of mass murder began.

As the attack developed, the Nazis unleashed all-out violence against the covenant as well. The values and affirmations of the covenant were totally opposed, indeed reversed, even as the covenant people were killed. Jewish holy days were violated with roundups, Aktionen, selections and evil decrees.

The Warsaw Ghetto was enclosed on Yom Kippur, 1940. Deportations from Warsaw to Treblinka death camp at the rate of 6,000, then 10,000 a day were begun on Tisha B'Av, 1942. The final destruction of the Ghetto was scheduled for Passover, 1943. Public prayer was prohibited in Warsaw in 1940. Keeping the Sabbath became impossible because forced labor was required on that day. Education was forbidden; newspapers were closed; libraries confiscated.

The assault on Jewish life and values became total. Einsatzgruppen [shooting squads] were deemed too slow, too costly, too problematic. The search for cheaper, swifter killing methods led to use of Zyklon B gas, an insecticide, in the Auschwitz gas chambers. To bring the cost down, the amount of gas used was cut in half the summer of 1944. This doubled the time of agonizing death, a death marked by asphyxiation, with damage to the centers of respiration, accompanied by feelings of fear, dizziness, and vomiting. Jews were impressed into service to round up other Jews for transport. The alternative was death or being sent themselves. Parents were pitted against children and children against parents for survival. A food ration of 800 calories per day was established in the ghettos, in a climate where working people need 3,000 calories per day. But the amount of food needed to supply even the official caloric standard was never delivered. Kosher slaughter was banned.

The degree of success of this attack constitutes a fundamental contradiction to the covenant of life and redemption. In Kovno, pregnancy was prohibited on pain of death. In Treblinka and Auschwitz, children were automatically selected for gassing upon arrival [except for some twins and others selected for medical experimentation]. The Jewish covenant pledges that human life is of infinite value. As the killing frenzy intensified, thousands of Jewish children were thrown directly into the crematoria or burning pits in Auschwitz to economize on gas. Still another time, the gas chambers were full of adults, so several thousand children were gathered and burned alive. This sonderkommando prisoner testified about this as follows:

> When one of the SS sort of had pity upon the children, he would take a child and beat the head against a stone before putting it on the pile of fire and wood, so that the child lost consciousness. However, the regular way they did it was by just throwing the children onto the pile. They would put a sheet of wood there, then sprinkle the whole thing with petrol, then wood again, and petrol and wood and petrol--and then they placed the children there. Then the whole was lighted.[52]

"Could there be a more total despair than that generated by the evil of children witnessing the murder of other children....being absolutely aware that they face the identical fate....there is now a Godforsakenness of Jewish children that is the final horror."[53] Does not despair triumph over hope in such a moment?

Since there can be no covenant without the covenant people, is not the covenant shattered in this event? In Elie Wiesel's words: "The Jewish people entered into a covenant with God. We were to protect His Torah, and He in turn assumes responsibility for Israel's presence in the world ....Well, it seems, for the first time in history, this very covenant is broken."[54] Or as Jacob Glatstein put it: "We received the Torah at Sinai/and in Lublin we gave it back/Dead men don't praise God/The Torah was given to the Living."[55] In response to the Destruction of the Temple the Talmudic Rabbis said: "Mi Kamocha ba'ilmim HaShem?" ["Who is like You among the silent, O God?"] instead of "Mi Kamocha ba'elim HaShem?" ["Who is like You among the mighty, O God"][56] Today would they not say what Glatstein said?

By every logical standard, Wiesel and Glatstein are right. The crisis of covenant runs deep; one must consider the possibility that it is over. Had the Shoah stood alone, would not affirmations of the covenant of redemption appear to be mockery or illusion?

A. Roy Eckardt was pointed to yet another dimension of the crisis. In retrospect, the Divine assignment to the Jews was untenable. In the covenant, Jews were called as witness to the world for God and for a final perfection. In light of the Shoah, it is obvious that this role opened the Jews to a murderous fury from which there was no escape. Yet the Divine could not or would not save them from this fate. Therefore, morally speaking, God must repent of the covenant, i.e. do teshuvah for having given His chosen people a task that was unbearable cruel and dangerous without having provided for their protection.[57] Morally speaking, then, God can have no claims on the Jews by dint of the covenant.

The fundamental shift in the nature of the covenant can be put yet another way. It can no longer be commanded. Covenantally speaking, one cannot order another to step forward to die. One can give an order like this to an enemy, but in moral relationships, one cannot demand the giving up of the other's life. One can ask such a sacrifice, but one cannot order it. To use another image of Elie Wiesel's: When God gave us a mission, that was all right. But God failed to tell us that it was a suicide mission.[58] One cannot order another to go on a suicide mission. Out of shared values, one can only ask for volunteers. Similarly, God can no longer enforce or educate for the covenant by punishment. The most horrifying of the curses and punishments threatened in the Torah for failing to live up to the covenant pale by comparison with what was done in the Shoah. All Jews now know that by being Jewish they expose not only themselves but their children and even grandchildren to ultimate danger and agony.[59] No Divine punishment can enforce the covenant, for there is no risked punishment so terrible that it can match the punishment risked by continuing faithfulness to the covenant. If the Jews keep the covenant after the Shoah, then it can no longer be for the reason that it is commanded or because it is enforced by reward or punishment.

B. The Assumption of Covenant

But do the Jews keep the covenant? There were a significant number of suicides among survivors who so despaired that could not live on without their lost loves, lost families, lost faith. Still others converted or ran away from the Jews to assimilate and pass among the Gentiles and so tried to shake off the danger and pain of being a Jew. But the overwhelming majority of survivors, far from yielding to despair, rebuilt Jewish lives and took part in the assumption of power by the Jewish people. For many of them, refusal to go anywhere but Israel meant years of waiting in DP camps, or a miserable risky trip in crowded, leaky, and unseaworthy boats to Israel or internment in refugee camps in Cyprus and Mauritius. Was there ever faith like this faith?

The Jewish people overwhelmingly chose to recreate Jewish life, to go on with Jewish testimony after the Shoah. What is the decision to have children but an incredible statement of hope, of unbroken will to redemption, of belief that the world was still to be perfected--so that it is worth bringing a child into this world. When there was no hope, as in Kovno or Warsaw in 1943-44, the birth rate dropped precipitously to a ratio of less than 1 to 40 deaths. Logically, assimilated Jews should have gone even further with assimilation once they heard about the Shoah for thus they could try to rid themselves of the dangers of being Jewish. Instead, hundreds of thousands of them opted to become more Jewish. Committed Jews have responded by the largest outpouring of charity and concern for other Jews in history. Observant, learned Jews have recreated yeshivot and Torah study so that today more people study Torah/Talmud full time than ever before in Jewish history, and that includes the Golden Age of Spain and the heyday of East European Jewry.

By every right, the Jews should have questioned or rejected the covenant. If the crisis of the First Destruction was whether God had rejected the covenant, then the crisis that opens the third stage of the covenant is whether the Jewish people would reject the covenant. In fact, the bulk of the Jews, observant and non-observant alike, acted to recreate the greatest Biblical symbol validating the covenant, the State of Israel. "The reborn State of Israel is the fundamental act of life and meaning of the Jewish people after Auschwitz....The most bitterly secular atheist involved in Israel's upbuilding is the front line of the Messianic life force struggling to give renewed testimony to the Exodus as ultimate reality."[60]

What then happened to the covenant? I submit that its authority was broken[61] but the Jewish people, released from its obligations, chose voluntarily to take it on again. We are living in the age of the renewal of the covenant. God was no longer in a position to command, but the Jewish people was so in love with the dream of redemption that it volunteered to carry on its mission.

When the Jewish people accepted the covenant, they had no way to measure what the cost might be. The Midrash repeatedly praises the Israelites' response to the offer of the covenant, "We will do and we will listen,"[62] as amazing. As the cost of faithfulness increased, the Jews might have withdrawn and cut their losses. In fact, in this era, their faithfulness proved unlimited. Their commitment transcended all advantages of utilitarian considerations. They had committed their very being.[63]

In Solovietchik's words, the covenant turned out to be a covenant of being, not doing.[64] The purpose of the Jewish covenant is to realize the total possibility of being. It is not like a utilitarian contract designed to achieve limited ends where, if the advantage is lost, the agreement is dropped. The Jewish covenant is a commitment, out of faith, to achieve a final perfection of being. Faith sees the risks but knows that without the risks the goal can never be realized. Covenanted living, like marriage or having children, is an open ended commitment, for the risks are great and one never knows what pain, suffering, danger or loneliness one is taking on. Faith in the final perfection involves seeing what is, but also what could be, precisely because life is rooted in the ground of the Divine and we do have a promise of redemption. Out of this faith comes the courage to commit.

The crisis of the Shoah was that not in their wildest dreams did Jews imagine that this kind of pain and destruction was the price of the covenant. Nor did they realize that the covenant might unfold to the point where God would ask them to take full responsibility and unlimited risks for it. Yet, in the ultimate test of the Jews' faithfulness to the covenant, the Jewish people, regardless of ritual observance level, responded with a reacceptance of the covenant, out of free will and love. For some, it was love of God; for others, love of the covenant and the goal; for others, love of the people or of the memories of the covenantal way. In truth, it hardly matters because the three are inseparable in walking the covenantal way.[65]

If the covenant is not over, then what does the Shoah reveal about the nature of the covenant? What is the message to us when the Divine Presence was in Auschwitz, suffering, burning, starving, yet despite the most desperate pleas, failing to stop the Shoah?

The Divine Presence need not speak through prophets or Rabbis. The Presence speaks for itself. If the message of the Destruction of the Temple was that the Jews were called to greater partnership and responsibility in the covenant, then the Shoah is an even more drastic call for total Jewish responsibility for the covenant. If after the Temple's de-struction,

Israel moved from junior participant to true partner in the covenant, then after the Shoah, the Jewish people is called upon to become the senior partner in action. In effect, God was saying to humans: You stop the Shoah. You bring the redemption. You act to ensure that it will never again occur. I will be with you totally in whatever you do, wherever you go, whatever happens, but you must do it. And the Jewish people heard this call and responded by taking responsibility and creating the State of Israel. Thereby, the people took power into its own hands to stop another Shoah as best it could.

The decision to create a Jewish state is also a decision to create a society and social reality in which Jews and Jewish values direct the fundamental decisions. For two thousand years, the Jewish witness to the world could only operate on the verbal level, indirectly, influencing the forces which moved the world such as Christianity, Islam, Western culture. Now Jewish actions can directly affect the historical destiny of the world. Now Jews can construct a society that can affect others by example. Israel, as a Jewish-run reality, can exemplify the joint process of human liberation and redemption. For example, Israel represents an agricultural society that utilizes limited resources, transforming desert into fertile, productive land, thus offering the way for the world to overcome poverty and hunger. Israel serves as a model of an open, educational society taking a population from pre-modern poverty and passivity and creating from it a people that assumes responsibility and increases its dignity without losing is past and its values. This is what Israel has done in part with its Oriental Jewish migration. Both these models are particularly significant for the Third World where the bulk of humanity struggles with the problems of poverty, fatalism and renewal of social institutions.

Of course, the politics of oil and world rivalries have isolated Israel and reduced its influence. Also, Israel itself is far from perfect and has only partially succeeded in these models. However, these limitations are congruent with the shift from powerlessness and ideal existence to exercise of power and the conquest of reality. Reality is recalcitrant and flawed, and all triumphs are partial and equivocal. It is also true that many Israelis accept the call to prevent another Shoah, but do not accept the commitment to create a redemptive model society. In a situation of voluntary covenant, there cannot be one goal imposed from above. Rather those who accept the calling must persuade and influence the others to take part in the process.

The Jewish tradition itself has been less helpful than it could be because traditionalists have not fully taken up the challenge of the new covenantal role for Israel. Religious leaders have spent must energy trying to rebuild the pre-Destruction reality rather than sanctifying the new every day. Sometimes people say that they would respond if only they were to receive clear prophetic instruction.[66] But the revelation of our lifetime is so veiled and ambiguous that there is little certainty and few clear, unassailable responses. This very lack of clarity is consistent with the voluntary nature of the covenant and the new maturity of the people Israel. Anything clearer might be coercive. The redemption will become obvious only retrospectively when the Jewish people recognize it as such. Jews must take a more active role in discerning the covenant's presence and in realizing its goals. Then will the Jewish people truly have come of age in the covenant.

C. Was the Shoah Necessary?

The recognition that consciousness of the voluntary covenant grows out of the experience of the Shoah may lead to misunderstanding. This insight may be interpreted as an affirmation of the Shoah.[67] Some have argued: Without the catastrophe, there would have been no State of Israel. Therefore, the Shoah is a necessary sacrifice or blood-letting that paves the way for redemption. Similarly, some may think that since the matura
tion of the covenant comes out of the Shoah, the disaster was necessary. Some may also believe that this unfolding of the covenant is an explanation of why the Shoah happened or even some rationale for it. I reject these possibilities.

There can be no rationale for the Shoah. If anyone offers such, you may be sure that the explanation has domesticated or denatured the Shoah. The explanation is no explanation but rather some plausible tale about a sanitized and selected version of the Shoah which has little to do with reality.[68] There can be no historical or sociological or military explanations of how the Shoah actually operated and what factors enabled the Nazis to carry out the mass murder so successfully. Such explanations are necessary if for no other reason that the need to prevent a recurrence. But that is a far cry from explaining the 'why' or the essence of the event.

The same must be said about the development of the voluntary covenant. In retrospect, the voluntary stage is implicit in the covenantal model from the very beginning. Once God self-limits out of respect for human dignity, once human free will is accepted, the ultimate logic is a voluntary covenant. As Soloveitchik writes: "The very validity of the covenant rests upon the Juridic-Halakhic principle of free negotiations, mutual assumption of duties, and full recognition of the equal rights of both concerned with the covenant."[69] The full dignity of the human partner can only emerge when that partner takes full responsibility. Any state less than that is encouragement to dependence out of weakness. Residual punishment is coercive and erodes the moral insight of the human partner. In a voluntary covenant, there is a deeper dependence--that of relationship, love, self-expectations based on the model of the other--but it is a dependence out of strength. The ultimate logic of parenting is to raise children to meet life's challenges, but to sustain them with a continuing presence and model, not with continual interference or rescue from problems. Further analysis suggests that in every covenantal relationship, the part-ners must ultimately choose between equality and force. True love can only exist when the imbalance of power has been overcome by redistribution of power, or, in God's case, by a binding renunciation of using the imbalance.[70]

This redistribution of power was the underlying thrust behind modern culture's empowering of the human being. In retrospect, this is what Zionism sought to do to the Jewish covenant starting in the nineteenth century. Thus there were positive reasons and forces operating before the Shoah to bring Jews and humanity a higher level of responsibility for redemption, just as there were 'secularizing' trends preceding the Destruction of the Temple. Nevertheless, most traditionalists and modernists failed to see this new dynamic of power as operating within the covenantal framework. Many concluded that the true purpose of modern culture was to reject the covenant or slay the covenantal partner for the sake of human liberation. In significant measure, this misconstruction is directly implicated in the emergence of pathological forms of total human power unleashed in the modern forces which reach a climax in the Shoah itself. In a counterpart error which was the mirror image of that of modern total secularists, religious groups interpreted the covenant to demand human subservience or passivity and opposed the emergence of the new level of human responsibility. However, now that the Shoah has occurred, it is no longer possible to delay the emergence of the new level.

There is no good in the Shoah, only a tragedy which forces us to face up to an issue and a responsibility which was long coming. The Jewish response to the Shoah, as to the Destruction of the Temple, is the act that crystallizes and energizes this transition. The Shoah is not a necessary quid pro quo for anything. It is the shock that almost destroys the covenant. It continues to degrade God and educate humans to savagery and destruction. However, thanks to the power of human love and faith that will not yield the dream of redemption, the Shoah can be fought, and perhaps its effects can be overcome in history. This is the struggle that is now going on.

IV. Implications of the Voluntary Covenant

A. The Promise of Pluralism

The total assault on Judaism and on the Jewish people was an attempt to stamp out the covenant, the witness, and, ultimately, the pres-ence of God who is the Ground of life and the covenantal hope. Therefore, the very existence of the Jewish people is a fundamental statement that the covenant is ongoing. The survival of the Jewish people in a world full of enemies, where the model of the Shoah is circulating, is in itself testimony to the existence of a hidden God whose awesome, if invisible, force is evidenced in the ongoing life of the Jewish people.[71] The renewal of Jewish living through having children, and restoring human dignity constitute the creation of images of God.[72] These images point to the God of whom they are the image; they are the best, most indelible testimony to God in a world where total evil has triumphed in recent times. Such witness could not be given without profound wells of faith and hope to draw upon the individual Jews who live this way. Finally, the Jewish people, by recreating the State of Israel and rebuilding the land, has given the witness which shows the world that God lives and the covenantal hope is not in vain. All Jews who elect to live as Jews makes these statements whatever their self-definition and official behavior.[73]

It makes no essential difference if the Jews involved consciously articulate the covenantal hope or express a belief in God who is the Ground of the covenant. The witness is given by their actions. Actions speak louder than words. People who profess God but gas men, women, and children or burn them alive are atheists whatever their words may be. People who profess to be atheists or to be without hope yet who actively uphold the covenant, even at the cost of their lives, betray their true position by their actions. If anything, their denials only add to the hiddenness of the Divine. Therefore, their theological language is the appropriate one for this time, more appropriate than those who go on speaking as if God were visible and fully performing under the previous terms of the covenant.

In the age of voluntary covenant, every person who steps forward to live as a Jew can be compared to a covert insofar as a convert, one who voluntarily opts to be a Jew, must make certain commitments and express certain beliefs. Then the classic conversion ceremony may guide us to contemporary Jews' proper affirmations. Through the conversion pro-cess, the convert testifies that although the Jews are driven, tormented, and persecuted to this very day, the convert still wants to be a Jew, that is, wants to offer the testimony of hope anyway. The convert learns the unity of God and the denial of idolatry; the analogue in our time is the affirmation of God's presence which is witnessed by Jewish existence itself.

The convert must affirm some of the weighty commandments/obligations of a Jew and some of the lighter ones. In this generation, all who opt to live as Jews automatically state their readiness for martyrdom, not only for themselves but for their children and grandchil-dren as well. There can be no 'weightier' commitment than this. A decision to live in Israel, and to a lesser extent a commitment to support it, constitute acceptance of the mitzvah to witness, to build a redeeming social reality, even to bring the Messiah. The appropriate range of 'lighter' commandments/obligations to be undertaken can be explored or debated between the denominations. But morally speaking, the simple observance of all of the classical mitzvot can hardly be the only option offered under the covenantal definition.[74]

While the covenant is now voluntary, birth into it remains an important statement. By being born a Jew, a person summons up all the associations and statements implicit in Jewish existence, including the Jewish testimony to a God who cares. One may opt out by refusing to live as a visible Jew, by trying to escape the fate of a Jew, by trying to deny. However, if one chooses to continue living as a Jew, one makes all the fundamental affirmations implicit in Jewish existence. This is true even if one does not use the officially articulated ways of making one's statements such as bearing witness to creation through Shabbat [Sabbath] observance or expressing the Messianic hope through prayers such as Aleinu.

As long as the covenant was involuntary, it could be imposed from above in a unitary way. This corresponds with the image and role of revelation in the Biblical period, which includes unequivocal command and visible reward and punishment for obedience and disobedience. With the shift in covenantal relationship which characterizes the Rabbinic era, the revelation becomes more hidden, more subject to pluralist interpretation. Focus on reward and punishment shifts from the worldly toward the other-worldly hidden realm.

In the new era, the voluntary covenant is the theological base of a genuine pluralism. Pluralism is not a matter of tolerance made necessary by living in a non-Jewish reality, nor is it pity for one who does not know any better. It is a recognition that all Jews have chosen to make the fundamental Jewish statement at great personal risk and cost. The present denominations are paths for the covenant-minded all leading toward the final goal. The controversy between them will not be whether God has commanded these ways. Conservative, Reform and secular Jews can freely concede the dimensions of past commandments, but insist nevertheless that these are no longer effective or optimal ways of achieving the goals. Orthodox Jews, even the ultra-right who uphold every past observance or minhag [custom], will recognize that their commitment to observe the entire tradition constitutes a voluntary acceptance, one which can be modeled but cannot be demanded of all. Thus, they can be faithful to the full authority of the halakhah, accepting the challenge of modeling it and making it credible and persuasive to Klal Yisrael, while respecting the incredible other types of commitment and contributions which other Jews are making. Such an admission would only confirm the phenomenology of Jewish life as it is now being lived. It would be morally and humanly liberating without yielding the hope of moving Klal Yisrael into the classic paths of halakhah. Of course, the psychology of Orthodoxy currently will not be receptive to this approach, but such an obstacle is not a problem of principle or integrity. Rather, it is a function of human limitations, community and political needs, all of which can be dealt with tactically.

It would be unreasonable and, considering the varieties of religious experience and sociological circumstance, unwise to expect total religious unity. There can still be ongoing controversies and policy differences between the denominations. But the members of all the groups have committed their total being to be witness to the covenant by living as Jews. The recognition of this overarching unity enables us to adjudge these controversies as being "for the sake of Heaven."[75]   In the Talmud, the school of Shammai and the school of Hillel often gave diametrically opposite rulings. Yet they affirmed that both views are "the words of the living God,"[76] precisely because they recognized the underlying unit of their common assumptions about the nature of God and Revelation. The unity which was destroyed in the modern period is restored in the common recognition of the voluntary covenant.

Groups can go on judging and trying to persuade each other to change, but the criteria for resolution of the conflict will be the ability to reach the goals of the covenant, including contemporary effectiveness and transmissibility. Orthodoxy might concede that a particular practice is not effective today. However, they continue to accept it as binding out of respect for past generations and their role in the covenant. Out of the sense that this generation is only a way station on the long covenantal road, they can accept temporary ineffectiveness of a practice in one moment in order to have the resource available in another. The definition of being Orthodox might be accepting the models of the past as binding out of recognition of the incredible, Divine power in them, and being bound by the process of the covenant, a process seen as inseparable from is goals and content. Then the differences with non-Orthodox Jews are tactical, and others' faithfulness to God and to the covenant can be admitted without undermining Orthodox affirmations. Once the validity of the others is recognized, the shortcomings or faults in the halakhic system can be admitted, and, to the extent possible, corrected. As long as the legitimacy of the others is not recognized, many problems will be denied and possible solutions rejected on the grounds that to change would give aid and comfort to the "enemy."

By the same token, Reform, Conservative, and secular Jews would waive the modernist criteria that justify their positions. This means that every part of the tradition may present itself for serious consideration to be judged by the same criteria of consistency with the covenant, transmissibility and effectiveness. Any new approaches developed by these Movements will also be reviewed by the same criteria. Some changes may be judged as concessions legitimated by the need to successfully negotiate the covenantal paths, and they are subject to repeal or redirection if the situation changes. New paths or models may be as sacred or more sacred that then inherited ones if they are deemed closer to the covenantal values or more effective in attaining them. It follows from this, however, that both reform and tradition are aligned along a continuum of attempts to live by the covenant. Reform behavior is not antinomian, but is distinguished from traditional Judaism by the giving of different weights to different covenantal values. The increased "heavier" role of women in Reform is an affirmation of the covenantal promise of redemption and ultimate dignity for women as well as men, rather than a rejection of the commandments or roles for males in tradition. Feminist corrections of the halakhah are an attempt to move more urgently toward the covenantal goal of humankind being in the image of God, which implies equality for women, rather than a rejection of the concept of obligation or of the traditional feminine positive roles.[77]

Once disagreements take place within the bounds of the common risk and dream of Jewish existence, the groups might take on or set aside a common practice for the sake of unity, beyond the merits of the practice itself. Each group would be committed to use all its resources and meth-ods to reach out and enable the others to live in good conscience with the same model or at least not to disrupt or shatter the others' ways where they differ. At least all groups would recognize the element of risk and creativity in trying to be faithful to the covenant at a moment when new roles and new institutions are emerging. Since whatever models of service are offered tend to be projec-tions of past experience, there is a tendency in transition times to offer the familiar even when something new or original may be needed. At moments of transformation there is the risk of a faithfulness that misdirects, even as there is a risk of excessive novelty and betrayal of the tried and true methods of the covenant. Each group should welcome the insights and criticisms of the others as necessary correctives, sources of perspective in a fluid and unformed situation in which all want to do the right thing but fear falling short.

B. Human Co-Creativity in the Covenant

Although obedience is the natural response in an involuntary cove-nant, nevertheless the principle of mutual obligation stimulated the Jews to engage in controversies with God throughout history. The greater the degree of human partnership, the more frequent and profound is the role of humans in challenging God to live up to the covenant. In an age of voluntary covenant, humans have all the more right and obligation to represent the covenantal goals and values to God. Humans must take responsibility, both for the goals and the consistency of the means with the goals. Since humans are being called to take full responsibility in action for the reali-zation of the covenant, they cannot escape the responsibility to judge the means and methods available to pursue the goals. Those who are entrusted with a task, and who take full responsibility for its realization, must be allowed discre-tion to achieve the goal. This delegation of authority is all the more justified in light of the Jewish faithfulness to the covenant, exemplified by the voluntary reassumption of the covenant in this generation despite the obvious risks involved.

The urgency of closing any gap between the covenantal methods and goals is greater in light of the overwhelming countertestimony of evil in this generation. The credibility of the covenant is so weakened and so precari-ously balanced that any internal element that disrupts or contravenes its affirmations must be eliminated. So savage was the attack on the image of God that the counter response of reaffirmation must be extraordinary. Any models or behavior patterns within the tradition that demean the image of

God must be cleansed and corrected at once. The hope of breakthrough toward perfection is higher in a generation which feels the obligation to match the extraordinary outburst of evil with a countervailing upsurge of good. Therefore, there is motivation and sufficient authority even among the Orthodox to correct the tradition or move it toward its own goals of perfection. The authority to change grows out of loyalty to the tradition and to the covenantal goals.

Part of the response must be to identify covenantal values and make judgments on the relative weight to be assigned to each. In the past, it has been argued that any judgment in conflict with established tradition is improper. Since the word of God is self-validating, change, by definition, must be based on appeal to outside criteria and is therefore invalid. With increased human responsibility and greater hiddenness of God and of Revelation, the exercise of judgment not only by Rabbis but by a wider variety of people becomes urgent. One cannot pass the buck to tradition. The responsibility for getting to the final perfection is squarely on this generation. It must exercise the responsibility with humility and self-criticism, but faithfulness requires that judgments be made.

Since the State of Israel is the central vehicle of Jewish power, self-defense and redemption-building, its needs should be given greater religious weight, perhaps rated as a matter of life or death. Some will object that this runs the risk of idolatry vis-a-vis the state. Both tradi-tionalist and liberal Jews might conclude that the danger of idolatry is the overriding concern. Other traditionalist and liberal Jews might pursue a policy stressing the State's needs while taking action to avoid idolatry. Either decision would be good, particularly as it grows out of a wrestling with the actual situation, rather than out of the routine party lines of conflicting forces in modernity and tradition. The treatment of women, of the handicapped, and of Gentiles in the tradition are other examples where Jewish utopian values are in conflict with the present reality. These value concessions to reality must now be challenged even if we agree that they are Divinely normative. The challenge, the defense, and the final resolution should not follow present party lines, but should explore the best ways of advancing the covenantal goals. Indeed, side by side experiments may be the right prescription until we sort out the best ways. In an experimental situation, either a more traditional or more innovative modus operandi becomes a creative and helpful foil for the other position, so that pluralism becomes a source of strength.

C. Messianic Time

Classically great destruction so challenges the affirmations of the covenant that it creates an urgent anticipation of a countervailing achievement of redemption. Nothing less can restore the credibility of the way. An event as massively devaluing as the Shoah needs an event of Messianic proportions to restore the balance. Voluntarily taking up the covenant, then, means taking up the challenge of Messianic breakthroughs. The expectation of great redemption is further nurtured by the incredible nature of the creation of Israel, which is heralded in the tradition as the harbinger and necessary condition for the Messianic fulfillment.

Why, then, has this generation hesitated to speak in Messianic terms? Partly it is due to the need to speak modestly after such a triumph of evil; partly the hesitation is due to the triumph of modernity and its rational, limiting style which has a chilling effect on Messianic expectations.[78] And why has the Messianic principle, when applied, been such a poor guide to action? The invocation of Messianic associations for David Ben Gurion was essentially a political trick to gain new immigrant votes for the very people who were proceeding to strip the Sephardim of their traditional values and give them the short end of the social stick. In the case of the Gush Emunim, the Messianic models have led to a devaluation of security and other realistic considerations and sometimes to a down-grading of the dignity of Arab concerns and needs on the West Bank.

I submit that these ills grow out of a failure to grasp the nature of the Messianic in the era of voluntary covenant. A Messiah who is triumphant and does it all for Israel would be utterly inappropriate in such an age. The arrival of such a Messiah would be morally outrageous, for the Messiah would have come at the wrong time. As Elie Wiesel has written, if any Messiah is going to redeem us by Divine strength, then the time to have come was during the Shoah. Any Messiah who could have come and redeemed us, and did not do so then but chooses to come now is a moral monster. Wiesel is right: it is too late for the Messiah to come.[79] Therefore we will have to bring the Messiah. Bringing the Messiah is the crowning response to the Divine call for humans to take full responsibility in the covenant. A Messiah who needs to be brought can only be partial, flawed, hidden[80]. Such a model of the Messiah may dampen the dangerous tendency to exercise utopianism, not to mention anti-nomianism, implicit in the end-time. At the same time, the model assigns new urgency to achievements of justice and peace, to coming closer to vegetarianism[81] and the full dignity of other humans, to witnessing more openly and more universally even as we prepare to become one with the world.

D. Responding

In a situation of fundamentalist transformation, playing it safe is tempting, but dangerous. The familiarity of the response gives consolation and a false sense of security in a bewildering vortex of change. However, there is a real risk of acting like the Sadducees at the Destruction of the Temple. Upholding the familiar, insisting that it is the only authoritative way, may leave one totally invested in recreating the status quo. When the status quo does not return, exhaustion and death of the spirit follow.

The alternative is to incorporate the new events and the new situation, first into understanding and then into the covenantal way. This process may lead to mistaken judgments ranging from premature Messianism to present-mindedness to loss of a coherent sense of the past. Taking action is risky; not taking action is risky. The appropriate response is to act, with anxiety, with conflict, with fear, but to act nonetheless. The first step is to incorporate the new event into the traditional way of life and into Jewish memory. Yom HaShoah and Yom HaAtzmaut [Israel Independence Day] must become central holy days of the Jewish calendar. Their 'secular' nature and grass roots origin are appropriate to the new era of holiness in which humans take responsibility for sanctifi-cation and redemption. The ambiguity of the days, and the fact that their sanctity is open to challenge, is an expression of the hiddenness of the Divine in the new era.

Many other commandments emerge from the new reality. The model-/mitzvah of pilgrimage both to the scenes of the Shoah and to Israel, and the telling of the tale in secular settings including film, books and other media are the new secular liturgical acts. A range of acts of justice and restored dignity, which flow from these events ["You were slaves, you were in ghettos, you were in camps, therefore you....you were freed, you were outsiders and taken to the Promised Land, therefore you...."], are the ethical counterparts of this liturgical development. Both types of acts are part of the expansion of the covenantal round of life to incorporate the new experiences. The accounts of these events and the lives and the models that grow out of them constitute a new Scripture and a new Talmud.[82]

The redemption event of this era, Israel, the Scriptures which are being written, the spiritual leadership of this new age will be even more secular, more 'naturalistic,' more flawed than in the Rabbinic Era, as is appropriate given the greater hiddenness of God. Every act of life be-comes potentially holy, the locus of the hidden Divine Presence. Not only are special days such as Shabbat and prohibition of work ways of sanctification, but work itself properly done is a religious act. Work as the expression of the commandment lashevet [to settle the world]--work as the creation of an infrastructure for human dignity, work as the exercise of the human capacity for power and control which are part of the image of God--will become a halakhically holy enterprise.[83] Thus, every day and not just one out of seven can become a holy day.

The holiness of sexuality can be expressed not only the prohibition or in mikveh [ritual immersion], but in the acts of love themselves. Sexuality as communication, as the revelation of the image of God in me, as the discovery of the image of God in the other, as affirmation of the pleasure of life, as a joyous vehicle of creating life becomes the continual expression of holiness. The Torah commands the Jewish people: "Kedo-shim   tih'yu" [Be holy!].[84] In a classic commentary, Nachmanides defines holiness above and beyond specific ethical and ritual commandments as fulfillment of the

Talmudic dictum, "kadesh atzmecha b'mutar lach" [Sanctify yourself in the areas which are permitted][85], go beyond the letter of the law and exercise restraint in those areas which are permitted.[86] The concept of secular sanctification suggests that holiness in the permitted is achieved not only by extending prohibition, but by directing action and spirit toward the covenantal goal.

Much of the expression of holiness can be accomplished using the existing models of b'rachah [blessing], selection, and sharing. Some of this expansion may come from heightened consciousness and developing inner attitudes and perceptions of holiness. Thus the voluntary covenantal model reaches a climax. In such moments, it begins to approximate Jeremiah's promise of a new covenant written on the heart.[87] However, this renewed covenant does not reject law or form, nor does it repudiate or supersede the original covenant. The voluntary covenant is built on the involuntary covenant; it continues and moves toward the final goal.

Contemporary Jews will have to explore the liturgical sources and models that can nurture a holiness that is at once more subtle and more elusive. The great covenantal symbol, circumcision, reflects the involuntary nature of the covenant. It also 'excludes' women and makes their representative function relatively less central.[88] In the new era, the symbol of the voluntary covenant may well be the revival, side by side with circumcision, of the brit bayn habetarim, the covenant between the pieces.[89] This was the original covenant ceremony, the conversion ritual of Abraham, the first non-Jew to become a Jew. He entered this covenant voluntarily before he became circumcised and permanently marked. Women can enter into the covenant between the pieces equally with men. This ceremony symbolizes that in the era of voluntary covenant, all are bound equally, i.e. all have voluntarily committed themselves to this incredible and dangerous task.[90]

Modern history has shown that democracies can ask for and elicit more total sacrifices from their citizens than even the great tyrannies can dare demand of their people. This encourages us to hope that the age of voluntary covenant will be marked by more encompassing religious life, greater commitment to justice, and an overall higher level of spiritual achievement by the Jewish people. The age has already started with unprecedented spiritual heroism in the response to the Shoah. One may pray that we be worthy--and that the best is yet to come.[91]

Peter J. Haas would have us shift our focus from Divine involvement and/or intervention in the Shoah to humanity's absence of thinking about God and its replacement by "secular, scientific" thinking which allowed such evil to happen. For him, the proper arena is not that of God's involvement-- which would have required miraculous intervention on a consistent basis-- but, rather, what were the factors and, therefore, implications which led to the empowering of that evil which the Shoah embodies. He, too, raises concern as to the "uniqueness" debate vis-a-vis the Shoah--which he regards as "dangerous" in its theological implications--as well as the inherent danger of reducing the Shoah to a banal expression of recurrent evil.[1]

AUSCHWITZ: RE-ENVISIONING THE ROLE OF GOD

Peter J. Haas

I. Introduction: The Question of Theodicy

For any theologian who contemplates its horror, the Shoah must raise anew the question of theodicy, of the nature of evil in a universe [allegedly] ruled over by a Benevolent Creator God. The absence of any Divine intervention to save the victims of the Nazi fury forces us to ask about the nature, and even relevance, of such a God in the modern, technology-driven world. There have been, of course, a number of attempts by theologians to deal with just these questions. None, at least so far, has found a way of both maintaining the goodness and omnipotence of God while at the same time preserving the utter evil of the Shoah. In the following, I wish to argue that such theologies are bound to fail to convince modern people precisely because they rely on traditional [that is, medieval] concepts about the nature of such a Creator God, and, specifically, how such a God is assumed to interact with the human world.[2]   In particular, all envision a God that is active physically in the world. I will suggest in what follows that a more helpful model for dealing with theodicy in the "post-modern" world is to conceive of God's presence being made active discursively or semiotically. Viewed in this way, the Shoah, rather than making the concept of God meaningless, in fact does the opposite: makes God that much more necessary and urgent.

This shift of focus immediately changes how we must frame the question of theodicy. In what follows, I shall be asking not so much why God did not intervene, but how it was that such evil came to be conceived and then empowered. As I shall discuss more fully later on, the idea that we, as moderns, can expect God to interrupt human affairs so as to abort impending evil is not only naive but unworkable. Once the stage has been set for an evil to occur, the most predictable outcome in this world of ours is for that evil to occur. So the question that should occupy us is how people came to adopt evil as a reasoned course of action, rather than why it is that God does not intervene in the process of evil already underway.

In fact, I want to argue that it is precisely the absence of God from the decision-making discourse that may help us to account for such evil as the Shoah.[3] My contention will be that it was only when God was removed as an active force in the shaping of Western thinking that Auschwitz becomes conceivable. In this sense I agree with Elie Wiesel when he claims that the Shoah represents a problem not so much in Judaism as it does in Christendom. It was within Western civilization, after all, that the evil was conceived, discursivized, organized, and managed. And while it is true that much of the intellectual background of the Nazi anti-Jewish thinking was drawn from Christian tradition, and while it is also true that for the most part organized Christian institutions did little or nothing to aid Jewish victims, I think it is wrong to conclude that the Shoah was a "Christian" event. Quite the opposite: it represents, to my mind, the eclipse of Christianity [or more broadly, of religion] as a source of morality in the West. It seems quite clear, at least in retrospect, that during the Shoah most Christian institutions acted as pure secular organizations, despite their claims to the contrary. They, in effect, abandoned the moral field to the scientists, engineers, and bureaucrats of the secular Nazi ideology. God had, in effect, ceased to function as a meaning-generating concept for the bulk of European civilization despite the continuity of Christian bureaucratic institutions. To be sure there were still believing Christians in Europe who never accepted the Nazi version of things and who at times even risked life and limb to defy them. But Christianity as an organizing moral force of a civilization was dead. The secular Nazi ethic won the ability to shape the course of things to come by default. While this loss of God's presence is more of a problem within Christendom than in Judaism, it nonetheless raises important theological issues even for Jews.

My argument shall be in the following that if we continue to allow our future to be governed by the principles of the secular, scientific world, we open ourselves to the same boundless possibilities that opened the way for the Nazi exploitation of the situation in Germany. While reference to God or religious principles is no guarantee in and of itself of righteousness or moral propriety, it at least gives us a language within which to carry on a moral discourse. It gives us control over what we will be willing as a people to tolerate . This lesson it seems to me is an important one for us to bring forth from the Shoah.

II. The 'Sitz im Leben' of Shoah Studies

Before explaining my thesis in detail, let me situate my thoughts in their context. My reflections find their place in what might be termed the "third generation" of Shoah studies. The "first generation" includes by and large the studies done up into the sixties. At that time, there was little work done on trying to interpret or account for the Shoah in any other than the most mechanical ways. The interest was on documenting what had occurred. In the decades immediately following the Shoah, the theological questions it raised rarely entered academic discourse. Shoah studies was in the main the specialized area of a few isolated scholars.

A noticeable shift occurred in the late sixties, signalling the begin-ning of the "second generation" of Shoah studies. It was in fact at about this time that the term "Holocaust" came into general usage. One important academic harbinger of this change was the publication of the first edition of Raul Hilberg's magisterial study The Destruction of European Jewry.[4] This

study showed that enough data had been achieved for the Shoah to be examined "as a whole" and so take its place in the academy. It was also at this
time that the first major post-Auschwitz Jewish theology appeared, in the
form of a collection of essays by Richard Rubenstein entitled After Auschwitz.[5] In fact, Rubenstein's essays were not so much a theology as a claim
that in the wake of Auschwitz there was no need for theology, since Auschwitz made it clear that the idea of God is dead. Along with Hilberg, Rubenstein helped set the academic agenda of Shoah studies for the next twenty
years. After Hilberg, the historical task was to carry forward the work of
showing how the Nazis conceived, and more importantly controlled, their vast
empire of evil. After Rubenstein, the theological task was to reappropriate
God, to show that God was somehow still alive and worthy of Jewish
respect after the Shoah. The major Jewish "Shoah theologians" I shall
discuss shortly all fit more or less into this period.

What I am calling the "third generation" of Shoah studies is just now
coming into focus. In his recent book, The Holocaust in History, Michael
Marrus argues, I believe correctly, that in the last few years, there was
evident a growing interest in using our knowledge of the Shoah as a jumping
off place for addressing the larger humanistic questions of the modern age.[6]
That is, the field of Shoah studies has reached a level of maturity in which
the task is no longer the accumulation of additional data, but rather reflections on the data already at hand, and the integration of the Shoah into overall
discourse of modern consciousness. As Marrus' book also indicates, this
generation is likely to be characterized as well by a reappraisal of some of
the conclusions reached in the past.

It seems to me that two general approaches to the interpretation of the
Shoah have taken shape up to this point, each with its own implications for
how one might approach the theological problems generated by the Shoah.
The first treats the Shoah as an utterly unique event; one that was so evil
that it forms its own category. The second alternative view sees the Shoah
as an example of the cruelty that is implicit in human nature, and of the
power of technology to make the exercise of that cruelty possible to an
unprecedented extent. On this view, the Shoah, while surely different in
degree from other past [and present] atrocities is not to be understood as
fundamentally different in kind. Each of these positions, as I have said,
establishes fundamentally different perspectives from which to approach the
theological questions.

The first view, that the Shoah is unique, is the assumption of most
Jewish [and, for that matter, Christian] "Shoah theologians." It is, of
course, precisely this view that stands behind Rubenstein's claim that the
Shoah points to the death of God. For Rubenstein, this means that after
Auschwitz, we are forced to face up to the fact that the older concept of God
as an active agent in our world can no longer work: It is dead.[7] We must

prepare ourselves to get along in a world without God, relying on the support of the human community for survival.

While not all Jewish theologians have drawn from the unprecedented character of the Shoah the extreme conclusion that Rubenstein has, they have all acknowledged that to some extent the conceptions of God and history that flourished before the Shoah are no longer functional. Arthur Cohen, for example, calls the Shoah a "caesura" in human experience, such that we are forced in its wake to bring all our previous assumptions into question: no theology, no understanding of history, no view of the nature of the human being can remain unquestioned in the shadow of Auschwitz.[8] Emil Fackenheim has likened the Shoah to Sinai, a world-shaking theoph-any from which new foundational elements of Jewish existence emerge [in this case, the imperative to survive, although I am not sure how really unprecedented that is].[9]

The problem here is that if the Shoah is really that much of a break with the past, then nothing of the past is really relevant anymore, including traditional Judaism. Nothing, as it were, emerges from the black hole of Cohen's caesura. Or to use Fackenheim's more troublesome metaphor, if the Shoah is really "Sinaitic" in implication, then we must wonder if the first Sinai has been rescinded or superseded in whole or in part, and if in part, which part. Fackenheim wants to treat the Shoah Sinai was an addendum to the original Sinai, but that I think begs the question.[10] In all events, I find this whole range of responses dangerous. If the Shoah is really unique, then there is the possibility that it really has no bearing on the rest of human history. It becomes, in essence, an event that stands by itself in a splendid isolation, and so incapable of teaching any lessons applicable to normal history.

The second view, that the Shoah is not ontologically or essentially different from other acts of human cruelty, is a minority position among Jewish theologians. The reason is that this view renders the Shoah somehow trivial, robbing it of any special power to make us rethink the human situation. This attitude toward the Shoah might be summed up in Hannah Arendt's famous phrase, "the banality of evil."[11] Evil, in other words, is just one of those things. I think Arendt had a much different and suggestive meaning in mind, and I shall get back to that in due course. But this popular reading of her saying I think captures the implication of this view of the mass-murder of Jews in Europe. In the end, it is just one more event in the dreary history of humankind.

Since the two positions sketched above encompass the logical possibilities for categorizing the Shoah, the fact that neither approach has been able to sustain a viable theology calls for some reevaluation. My argument, to restate matters, is that the problem lies not in these two approaches, but in the common assumption underlying both. In each case, the theological response has been framed around the question of why God did not intervene. I want to argue, as I have said, that a more fruitful approach is to ask how evil comes to be empowered in the first place. But before pursuing my own argument, a closer look at the results of more traditional theological reflection will be helpful.

It has been a stable element of Western theology that the term "good" reflects an objective reality and that that objective reality is [or is established by] an infinitely powerful creator God. One corollary of this conviction is that evil can in the end not prevail against those cared for by God. Since this creator God is all-knowing and all-powerful, evil can only exist with the acquiescence of this God, and, since this God is also assumed to be perfectly good, it follows directly that this God cannot by nature abide the untrammeled assertion of evil. What appears to us as evil must, therefore, be either [1] deserved, that is just, punishment, [2] part of a larger divine plan that we cannot fully discern or appreciate, or [3] illusory.

There have been theological responses to the Shoah built on this scheme, but they are all disappointing. Some are, in fact, downright pernicious, such as the view that the Shoah was simply a just punishment for Jewish sins.[12] From a Jewish perspective, these attempts to account for the Shoah are simply unworkable. If indeed the child hung by piano wire as described in Elie Wiesel's Night is receiving his just punishment by a good and powerful God, then the terms "good" and "powerful" take on new and horrid meanings.[13] This, is not I think a theology with which to we can live.

Not all responses constructed in terms of this traditional matrix of assumptions are this naive, however. A somewhat more sophisticated response is that of the conservative Christian theologian David Rausch who at least sees in the Shoah a reflection of human evil and a charge to people not to be complacent in the face of evil.[14] The most sophisticated response in this key is that of the Jewish Orthodox thinker Eliezer Berkovits.[15] For Berkovits, there is still a traditional Judaic theological system than can comprehend the Shoah, that of El Mistater, the "hiding God." There are times, this theology claims, that the good and powerful God of the universe detaches the Divine self from the world. In a cosmic sense, this Divine distancing has to be seen as a gift, allowing for the full expression of human freedom and initiative. At those times, of course, evil is also free to be unleashed and horrors like the Shoah can occur. Nonetheless, this theological strategy holds, the Divine is never permanently withdrawn, but will eventually reassert its presence and then in some way balance the evil that was done in its "absence." Thus the argument has been made, for example, that the Divine Face was "hidden" during the early part of this century, allowing the Shoah to proceed unhindered. But subsequently the involvement of God again became apparent in the revitalization of Judaism and especially in the birth of the State of Israel.

Although this approach has some advantages--it takes the evil of the Shoah seriously [It really took place in the absence of the Divine], and it preserves the conviction that God is ultimately is ultimately good and caring--it is not without its problems. There is first of all the question of God's hiding. As I said, this is done to grant humans freedom of action. Horrors like the Shoah, it is said, are simply the price we must pay for freedom. An analogy, I suppose, is to let little children get hurt doing something dangerous so that they can learn by experience. While this makes a certain amount of sense, I think it can be pushed too far. After all, a parent can hardly be expected to let his or her child shoot a neighbor's child in order to teach the danger of handguns. Certainly the slaugh-ter of 11 million people by the Nazis, and the deaths of maybe 35-40 million others in the war altogether, is a brutal way for God to arrange a lesson on the evils of Jew-hatred. It is hard to imagine how we should be expected to face this God again after the Shoah, knowing that it was "allowed" by a Divine act designed to teach people a lesson.

Of course, this strategy has taken that into account. The Divine does eventually reappear in human affairs, and works to achieve some counter-balancing. I guess the analogy would be the parent who, after allowing a child to get hurt or inflict pain on another, steps in to make matters better, taking everyone out for ice cream or whatever. But this does not quite work in the case of the Shoah. First of all, while the resurgence of the Jewish community and the establishment of the State of Israel are surely related to the Shoah [and what in contemporary Jewish life is not?], it is simply incorrect historically to say that the State of Israel is a result of the Shoah, and it is awkward morally to say that it makes up for or compensates [even somewhat] for the suffering of the victims. Nor would this notion of Divine recompense square well with the whole point of the process of hester panim, the hiding of the Divine face. If the point is to allow people to suffer and learn from their freedom, then the idea that God will eventually return and make everything comes out okay in the end seems out of character. A consistent application of this theology, it seems to me, would be to allow the Shoah to happen, to let its lessons be learned or not as the case may be, and then let history follow whatever course it will.

In the end, then, these more traditional theological responses to the Shoah turn out to be asking good questions but to be fashioning poor an-swers. The problem is to determine what alternatives to the traditional axioms are available. In essence, anyone who is dissatisfied with the above is left with the alternative of eliminating one or more of the basic premises of Western theology on which the above is based. That is, one must assume that God is not all-knowing, not all-powerful, or not good. Let us look briefly at the results of accepting each of these options.

The first option, that God is not all-knowing, creates interesting prob-lems. While it might be possible to sustain a theology that holds that God is unaware of all the mundane and essentially trivial details of everyday affairs, it is a much more cosmic claim to say that God was unconscious of the Shoah. If the Deity is susceptible to this kind of unawareness, the we are basically left with an otiose [ineffective, useless, superfluous--Editor] God that has no reliable role in human destiny except maybe in the broadest sense. Nonetheless, this is certainly one way of accounting for the Shoah.

A second possibility is to claim that the creator-God may be omniscient but not all-powerful. Since this seems to be somewhat self-contradictory--if the Deity could create the world, this Deity should be able to control it as well!--this option seems the most problematic. It has a long history in Judaism, however, especially in mystic circles. The Lurianic Kabbalah of the sixteenth century, and its modern-day heirs in Hasidism, claim that while God was omnipotent at Creation, the ability of God to intervene in the Creation has become limited due to a cosmic accident. Evil is a result of this Divine catastrophe and will remain potent until the Divine power is restored through a process called tikkun. While powerful in its symbolism, this view cannot finally reconcile the claim that, on the one hand the Creator-God was omniscient and omnipotent, and on the other hand, that this God was the victim of an unforeseen accident.

One modern attempt to bridge this gap, by making the limitations of Divine power in effect a voluntary or self-imposed move on the part of God, is that of Eliezer Berkovits. We have already discussed his views above and pointed out some of the problems implicit in them.

The third option that God is not good can be easily dismissed. There would be no theological or moral point in worshipping such a deity.

In their classic forms, then, none of these theories is without its problems. It is difficult to see why we should worship, much less have faith in, a God who admittedly has only limited ability to respond to our needs. True the Kabbalists developed a scheme for getting around this through their particular devotions and practices leading to tikkun. But without this Kabbalistic technology of manipulating the flow of forces through the sefirot, we are left in a rather hopeless position. We acknowledge God's weakness without any countervailing power to overcome that deficiency. Given our own undeniable technological prowess, it is hard to see how a religion based on such a weak and unreliable God can compete for allegiance.

III. Re-Focusing on Evil

I am struck by the failure of all of these approaches to come up with an explanation of the Shoah theophany that makes helpful sense. This suggests to me that the question has to be posed in a different way. It is for this reason that I have chosen to focus not on the failure of God to intervene, but on the nature or source of the evil.

This rephrasing of the question allows me to avoid one of the major difficulties of reflections up to now, namely the assumption that somehow we must account for the lack of God's intervention in the Shoah. It is as if we are perfectly ready to accept the presence of evil but expect that it will always be addressed by God in miraculous ways. This seems to me to be a false premise. We are generally not prepared to assume that God will routinely intervene miraculously in individual human affairs. If I am flying an aircraft which I have failed to fill with sufficient fuel, the plane will crash. This is a simply law of physics. None of us would either [1] expect a Divine miracle to occur, such as a giant hand grabbing the plane and guiding it to a safe landing, or [2] feel that God needed to be blamed or justified for the ensuing and totally foreseeable crash. Acts have consequences and we are perfectly willing to accept that without calling all our theological assumptions into question.

It may be possible to look at the Shoah in the same way, only writ large. The Shoah was, at one level, "only" a series of individual decisions and acts, coordinated to be sure by a bureaucracy, but nonetheless individual acts which as a rule had precisely the outcome anybody would normally expect that they would. A Divine frustration of the Shoah would have involved innumerable miracles: perfectly good equipment that inexplicably would not function in certain cases, trains loaded at point A but arriving empty at point B, resurrections, etc. We expect none of these to occur in our daily routines, and there seems no good reason therefore to expect them at other times. Otherwise the Shoah would have turned into a series of miraculous interventions, utterly outside the range of human experience or thought, followed by a the sudden reassertion of normal physical and historical processes. I think we are being unrealistic to expect that. I grant that the Shoah was unusual in the depth and intensity of its evil, but it does not follow from this that we must demand that the laws of history, physics, etc. come to an end on this account.

On the other hand, it is abundantly clear from the Shoah [as it is from all history], that people exercise considerable initiative over the events of the world. It is, of course, true that the unforeseen or uncontrollable will happen; our influence is not perfect. But by and large the direction of political and economic affairs seems to follow along the channels laid down by human leaders. Certainly on a scale such as that of the Shoah, we seem to be able to shape and sustain an overall dynamic. So our consideration of the meaning of God's absence in the Shoah has to take place in the awareness that in the normal run of things, the force shaping events is human initiative and that God rarely if ever appears directly to reshape entirely what people have wrought. Otherwise the study of history and economics would be meaningless.

The result of these considerations is not necessarily to remove God from the picture entirely, but it is to make the human factor in the creation of evil the center of attention and to diminish our expectation that God must always [by nature, as it were] intervene. God may be benevolent and active in history in some way, but we ought to expect our deeds to bear their natural consequences and build our theologies on that. If we still have pretty good control over events, something every manager takes for granted, then we must be prepared to rephrase how it is that God does interact with this world.

I want to argue, then, that Western culture--and especially modern Western notions of ethics--has developed the unprecedented possibility of empowering and institutionalizing evil. In essence, I wish to argue that the loss of a traditional religious-based ethic, and the emergence of a secular, "scientific" ethic made the conception, and more important, the justification [in moral terms], of the Shoah possible. The Shoah represents, then, a kind of quantum leap in the human ability to institutionalize evil and so, while unique in some sense, is overwhelmingly relevant to us today.

IV. The Nature of Evil

Let me begin by considering the nature of evil as evidenced in the Shoah. I start by returning to Hannah Arendt's haunting phrase "the banality of evil" because I think she had in mind something along the lines of what I wish to propose here. I think her phrase can be taken to mean a number of different things and that it has often been taken in a way that Arendt herself may not have had in mind. Usually the phrase has been understood, because of its context in the Eichmann trial, to be referring to Eichmann more or less personally. That is, that for Eichmann [and others], doing evil had become banal, a matter of unreflective routine. The phrase has a much more powerful message if we take it to mean that evil itself had become banal.[16] That is, for the perpetrators of the Shoah, the evil they were doing was no longer regarded as bad, or at least no longer regarded as worthy of reflection. That is to say, that evil had lost its sting, becoming ordinary and even routine, and so not a matter requiring further reflection.

It is, in fact, precisely this view which I find evidenced in the literature of the Shoah: the casual carrying out of terrible acts of human cruelty day after day by people who in other ways seems perfectly normal and loving. It was certainly not that such people had no conscience; they indicate again and again in their diaries and memoirs that they did. To be sure there were those who knew what they were doing, recognized its evil for what it was and nonetheless enjoyed what they were doing. But I have been struck again and again in reading through diaries by the ordinariness and at times human decency and sensitivity of the authors who in other areas were out-and-out accomplices in mass murder. Somehow, for these people, the evil in which they were engaged had become sanitized, robbed of its horror.

I believe we can account for this neutering of evil in terms of a routine phenomenon in moral discourse. It is a commonplace in moral philosophy that actions take on a moral meaning only within the context of the specific act and how that act and its context are described. That is, as the description of an act changes, so might our moral evaluation of that act. A killing in a parking lot may appear to us to be a clear-cut case of murder. But if we subsequently learn that the alleged killer was in fact attacked and that he or she shot the "victim" in self-defense, what at first may have struck us as a vicious murder may now seem quite justifiable. In fact, as we add considerations and complications to the story, we can manipulate our hearers to react in certain foreseeable ways. When confronted with a particular situation, then, with all its details and interconnections, conclusions as to what "really" happened and judgments as to the rightness or wrongness of certain actions turn out to be much more complicated that they may have at first appeared. We have all certainly experienced this feature of moral reflection. We can come to know so much about a situation that it is often hard in the end to say who is really at fault, and even what real wrong was committed altogether.

This observation about moral thinking has something significant to tell us about the Shoah. It tells us, I think, that it is possible in theory for the Nazi authorities so to describe the situation that the common audience could come to see the grossest acts of evil as serving a greater good and so justifiable. That is, through appeals to history, science, theology or whatever, the moral meaning of Nazi-inspired atrocities was blurred beyond recognition for the participants. Caught in the descriptive web of Nazi discourse [or what I call in my book "the Nazi ethic"], everyday people simply thought they were doing the right thing. The evilness of their acts was no longer descriptively obvious.

That certain segments of Nazi society should have been immune to this sort of linguistic sleight of hand goes without saying. People constantly exhibit the ability to dissent from the popular ideas of the day. That is why the silence of the Christian community [and the legal and medical professions, to name some other obvious examples] is so striking. But for most people, it seems, the values of the Nazi ethic were simply accepted, and the ensuing evil was quite simply rendered banal, in this second sense.

Before moving on, let me pause to take an example out of our own national experience in Vietnam, for I think this reflects something of a similar dynamic at work. In the context of the war, good clean-cut American young people did commit atrocities on Vietnamese civilians. Rarely was this done, I suspect out of sheer sadism. Often the soldiers were acting out of fear or out of a belief that what they were doing was a necessary evil for winning the war. It is thinkable that at least on some occasions, our soldiers acted out of a sense of higher ideals and within what they thought were the parameters of Western morality. They were facing a savage enemy, the enemy posed not only an immediate threat to their lives and health, but also more indirectly to their country. Both the context of warfare and the context of legitimate self-defense provides a framework in which inflicting death on others is regarded as permissible [if not laudatory] in our received ethic. We can let slide for now the question of whether the soldiers' understanding of the nature of the threat was correct or even warranted. At issue for our received Western morality is the perception of the perpetrator, that is whether or not the moral agent was motivated by proper intentions. If the agent is convinced that a certain situation morally justifies a certain course of action, then that agent, as we generally, regard matters, is required to follow that course of action.

Because the distinction between what people think is required and what an ethic should require is important to my argument, I shall make a verbal distinction between the two. To this end, I will use the word "ethics" and its derivatives to denote the rationalizing process of the actor as she or he makes a decision as to what to do in a particular situation. My claim is that such a decision is ethical provided that the agent has considered general rules of moral behavior, has used moral arguments to arrive at a decision and sees himself or herself as acting in accord with the demands of morality as understood to apply at the moment. I reserve the word "morality" to apply to a more universal judgment as to the overall rightness or wrongness of the act, seen as it were from an outside, neutral position. That is, I use ethics to describe the inner dynamics of the decision to act one way or another, and morality to judge the character of that decision according to a theoretically constructed standard. My argument will be that many perpetrators, and even bystanders, of the Shoah may have been acting ethically in that they at the time saw themselves serving some higher good which seemed to them to be morally justified. This does not preclude the possibility that we might now find the acts morally reprehensible. All I mean to say is that from the point of view of the moral agent, all we can expect is for the individual to act according to what he or she deems to be the moral requirement at the moment. We may well decide in hindsight that the action was wrong or violated the spirit of morality. My claim, then, concerns not the content of the moral life per se, but rather the status of the decision.

If these remarks are correct, then it suggests how we might deal analytically with the evil of the Shoah and how that evil might be related to God. It first of all makes it possible for us to continue to regard the perpetrators [or at least a good proportion of them] as still operating within the parameters of an ethic. That is, we can treat the Shoah as part of the flow of human events rather than as some sort of unconnected anomaly. Second, still within our universe, the above model allows us to account for Nazi activity in a way other than that it simply was evil for evil's sake. Rather it makes it possible for us to view the perpetrators as what they probably were: more or less ordinary people living in a perverse universe but considering their actions and doing what they thought was the appropriate thing to do given the circumstances. Viewed in this way, the Shoah has a powerful and urgent message for us still today.

It speaks to us today because the above model bears close correspondence to how we experience our own internal moral dialogue. This is not to imply that we are all like Nazis. But it is to say that we have all faced the task of doing something we really would rather not have to do but feel compelled to do for reasons of profession, business, state or some other "greater good." Diaries and other evidences of the Shoah suggest, as I have said, that similar human factors operated in the Shoah.

Let me emphasize before moving on that I do not wish to say that all ethics are equally the same. I recognize that the Nazi ethic established itself, people thought within it in the normal way humans think. I want to shift concern from how the Nazis and their supporters could be such perverse people to the question of how it is that perverse ethics can so establish themselves that ordinary people will regard them as self-evident and then operate in good conscience within them.

This way of framing the problem, I think, leaves us with a sense of both our own power and our own helplessness. In terms of power, it means that human society has the capacity, through the formation of rhetoric, to establish the evaluative discourse within which most people will form their ethical judgments. What Nazism shows us is that the human understanding of right and wrong is not innate and changeless [as the ancients might have supposed], and that this understanding is not strictly rational as so much of Western philosophy has asserted. Rather, human understanding is rooted in how people in groups define and evaluate matters in public. This then is a powerful tool left in our hands. The content of right and wrong, good and evil, are forged by human minds given the materials of our own societies and civilizations. An ethic such as that of the Nazis not only can exist and did exist, but is very capable of existing again. We know now that intelligent, mature people, with access to sophisticated technologies can forge an ethical discourse to their own liking.

This is also, of course, the basis of our feeling of helplessness as well. In effect, the very affirmation of human power to produce such an ethic at the very same time denies that God ought to function as some sort of cosmic umpire who will step in at the appropriate time. We can become trapped in the very web of ethical rhetoric that we spin. In fact, I would argue that is what happened in Nazi-occupied Europe. Perpetrators and bystanders eventually become victims [in some sense] of the juggernaut that they had helped to set into motion. To be sure, some of these musings-after-the-fact may be self-serving. But many also indicate pain, anguish, and guilt; too late perhaps but real nonetheless. There can be no question that the Nazis and their collaborators have had to pay a heavy price for their entanglement in the Shoah even if they were not its official victims. The rhetoric captured even its inventors.

V. The Nazi Ethic

To recapitulate the argument up to this point, I have argued that in considering the relationship of God to the Shoah, we seem to hit a dead end if we focus exclusively on the question of why God did not intervene. A more fruitful approach, given the assumption that God generally will not intervene except in the unusual case of a miracle, is to ask how is it that such evil comes about initially. We have also at this point talked about the ability of people to create ethical systems that create accepted definitions of good and evil. The claim is that the Shoah can be accounted for on the basis of these ideas. Nazi Germany created an ethic that defined the killing of Jews [and others] as good. Absent any counter-ethic, and given the usual absence of miraculous Divine intervention in the flow of history, the inevitable happened. To help us understand the origin of evil in the world, then, it will be helpful to examine exactly how the Nazi ethic came into being and how it was able to co-opt other ethics. This will give us a clearer picture of the dynamics at work.

In the case of the Shoah, we have a fairly good idea of the intellectual background of its ethic.[17] This ethic drew largely on three intellectual currents that had become acceptable in German [and European] society in general during the late nineteenth and early twentieth centuries. These are racial antisemitism, social Darwinism, and fascism. I will argue below that the combination of these three strains of thought--one social, one scientific, and one political--created a worldview which could, and did, support an ethic of genocide. I want to discuss this intellectual confluence first. I then need to turn back to the question of what this means for our understanding of God's relationship to the world. I will argue since none of these premises are based on a notion or vision of God, the resulting ethic in effect left no place for God to operate and so made anything [or everything] possible. As I said at the beginning of this essay, this is one of the most striking lessons of the Shoah.

The social strain of thought has to do with anti-Judaism. This is the one thread in the Nazi ethic that has a clear grounding in religion, although by the nineteenth century it had become more or less secularized.[18] The pariah-status according to Jews has a long history in the West, going back to Roman times. This attitude became a stable of Western civilization with the advent and spread of Christianity. Thus by the dawn of the Enlightenment, there was a long-standing and powerful critique of Jews and Judaism built into the social structures of Europe. So powerful was this tradition that it continued into the Enlightenment period, even though the intellectual hegemony of the

Christian churches had been broken. Thus Jews still found themselves to be outsiders in large parts of central Europe into the nineteenth and twentieth centuries, although this social exclusion was now based on scientific or secular grounds, not on theological ones. That is, Jews were no longer outcasts because of their religio-mythic crime of decide or because of their failure to acknowledge the truth of Catholic or Lutheran doctrine. Rather, Jews were outsiders now because they were seen as racial or national aliens, people incapable of assimilating into and contributing to true Western civilization. We can already see this change in attitude in the latter part of the eighteenth century when Wilhelm Dohm could argue for extending civic rights to Jews on the grounds that given a chance, Jews could indeed become productive members of German society.[19]   His unspoken assumption was that Jewish differentiation was a function of social and cultural forces, not theological ones.

Gradually this social exclusion, freed of its religious mooring, became attached to a much different sort of warrant: scientific racism. By the nineteenth century, European colonial expansion had brought West-erners face to face with societies in Asia and Africa. These cultures were regard-ed as clearly more primitive than those of Europe. On the one hand, this evaluation was used to justify Western colonial paternalism over the "be-nighted" natives. It became the "white man's burden" to bring civilization to these masses. On the other hand, the discovery of primitive societies raised the question of why Europe was so much more advanced. What had kept these other areas from attaining the same scientific and cultural achieve-ments as the Europeans? An answer gradually emerged from nineteenth century science. Research in genetics and physical anthropology convinced many scientists that the human species was not homogeneous, but was made up of a number of different sub-species. Each such sub-group had its specific genetic make-up and so its particular abilities. These abilities manifested themselves in the diverse areas of human culture developed by the population in question: language, literature, social organization, art, etc. Thus the relative primitiveness of native societies in Africa or Asia could be accounted for on the basis of racial endowments of the group; its innate "civilizing" ability. In all cases, the level of civilization achieved by a race reflected the limits of its abilities; inferior cultures indicated underlying limits within the genetic group, the race.

This conviction in fact stands behind a number of philosophical and scientific initiatives undertaken in the nineteenth century.[20]   These studies not only took the idea of racial diversity seriously, but tended through their results to ratify these assumptions in the popular mind. One good example is the "science" of phrenology, the measurement of the proportions of the human skull. This field emerged out of the simple deduction that if dif-ferent human populations were in fact different races, and if each race had different genetic endowments, then these should be apparent not only in such hard-to-measure traits as language, literature and culture, but also in quantifiable areas like bone size.   The skull was seen as an especially promising source of data since it houses the brain.   Thus a complex scientific and pseudo-scientific sub-culture emerged which measured skulls, tabulated different ratios, looked at nose size and compiled impressive piles of data meant to document the existence and relative advance of various racial types.

While natural scientists concentrated on these matters, social scientists concentrated on the cultural attainments of the world's diverse racial groups. For a number of reasons, the most promising cultural traits for this kind of study were taken to be language and literature.   Thus racial theorists appropriated the results of philology, the study of language, to illustrate their theories.   In essence, the idea was that by charting out how languages are related to each other, one could see how the underlying racial groups of speakers are related to each other.   A good example of how intertwined philology and scientific racism became is the case of the "discovery" of the Indo-European family of languages.   Philologists by the nineteenth century had sufficiently developed the study of linguistics to be able to create a taxonomy which showed the relationship of a number of diverse European and sub-continental languages.   Thus a category of Germanic languages incorporating German, Dutch, and Swedish, for example, could be contrasted to a category of Romance languages such as French and Italian.   These, in turn, could be associated with each other over against Indian languages, and both conglomerates could be combined over against completely unrelated languages such as those of the Semitic family [Arabic, Hebrew, etc.].   If languages represent racial groups, it followed, then the filial relations apparent in language should reveal the filial relations among the relevant racial populations.   It is just this logic which gave rise to the hypothesis of an ancient Aryan racial group, i.e. the group that "produced" and carried forward the ancient Indo-European language.

The results of all this was raised to the status of a philosophical truth through an appropriation of the writings of the great German philosopher G. W. F. Hegel.   Hegel's contribution to nineteenth-century thought was to articulate a theory of historical evolution.   In his view, human culture over time traces out a kind of progression in which the spirit of truth is seen gradually to reveal itself.   Primitive cultures simply reflect an earlier stage in this progressive self-revelation of the Spirit.   On the basis of this philosophy of history, each contemporary civilization can be located at its proper point on the continuum of human cultural evolution, and so its level of civilization is accurately developed.

What made Hegel's ideas attractive was that they seemed to parallel the results of scientific investigations that assumed that human abilities had evolved.   This meant that a primitive culture reflected a population that was innately and objectively less developed.   Thus, for example, a Hottentot might be taught to speak proper English and to dress like a country squire, but underneath he would still be finally a Hottentot, and that ultimate bedrock of character would always finally make itself known. Thus the differences among diverse populations is real, objective and scientifically verifiable. The relevance for us here is, of course, that Jews, having their own culture, religion, language and facial types, must represent just such a race, and insofar was they are deemed inferior socially and culturally, so, it follows, must they be understood to be innately inferior as well.

It is against this background that the second stream of thought takes on immense importance. I am talking here of a certain view of what we might call social Darwinism. While the nineteenth century scientific view of race clearly established superior and inferior peoples, it did not pass moral judgments on these differences. It was simply a way to create a scientific taxonomy of the diversity of human cultures. But social Darwinism, by positing a scenario in which these races were in conflict, and within which it was the natural order of things for the stronger [and presumably therefore better] to dominate if not destroy the inferior, set the stage for a program of race with its own unique ethic.

It should be noted at the outset that the conclusions reached by the social Darwinist were only distantly related to the scientific work of Charles Darwin himself. Darwin had set out to explain how different species of animals had come to predominate in certain areas while other species of the same genus dominated in other areas. His conclusion was that there was a certain natural variety in any genus, and that those individuals and their offspring that had characteristics that best fit a particular environmental niche would over time come to dominate that niche. In another region, of course, a different pattern of environmental characteristics would be present, and so a different set of characteristics in the population would be selected, so that over the course of generations, we could talk of the emergence of two different species of the same genus.

Social Darwinists began with this basic scheme but added stipulations that radically changed its character. First of all they applied the process of natural selection [or "survival of the fittest" as it became known] not to genetic characteristics but to societies or cultures. In short, they claimed that societies or cultures which were "superior" were naturally destined to dominate or even oust those that were inferior.

It is, of course, quite a jump to go from the process of genetic selection to social conflict. More ominous was the [mis]appropriation of the basic mechanism of "survival of the fittest." For Darwin, this was basically a matter of statistical probability. Individuals better suited to the environment would stand a better change of surviving and of having off-spring that would survive, thus gradually changing the genetic pool. The social Darwinists took the struggle entirely literally. In their view, social groups were in constant physical conflict over who could inhabit a certain ecological niche.

The law of nature was that the superior group had to win, and the inferior group must either become subservient or die out. To anticipate where this argument is heading, it was from this a short jump to the assumption that the dominant group had a moral obligation to survive and in the process to eliminate its inferior rivals.

The latent ethical imperative of social Darwinism comes to the surface when it is combined with the scientific racism we discussed above. This combination yields an ethic in which the human genus is understood to be composed of diverse and unequal species that are engaged in an inevitable conflict over who will dominate available resources. It is also the case that for the proper working out of the Spirit, the superior group has, as it were, a moral obligation to win out and dominate or eliminate its rivals. Social conflict of this kind thus is really a matter of literal social life or death.[21] The old medieval theological view of the just war was now resurrected as it were, as a natural struggled to be fought with any means possible to ensure the survival of the superior group.

All that is lacking now for the full ethic of the Nazi worldview to take shape is a theory of how this metaphysical struggle between good and evil is to be translated into politically usable terms. This last component is provided by the political theory of fascism. This theory provides a political program for formulating institutions in light of these modern "insights" into the forces of history. One of the foundational assumptions of this theory is that there is a fundamental distinction between what was called "the nation" and "the state." In technical terms, the nation was the genetic pool or population that is represented in a particular culture. Thus in Europe, the Italians, French, Germans, Slavs, etc., all represent different nations. Their national identity comes out in a variety of expressions: language, law, art, literature, social customs, etc. The state, on the other hand, is a political organization, a government and its various social and cultural institutions. The idea of fascist political theory was for each nation [i.e. genetic or cultural group] to have its own political expression in a state of its own: Italy for Italians, France for the French, Germany for Germans, etc. On the one hand, this could be seen as merely a pragmatic tool for insuring cultural survival--a nation dominated by the institutions of a foreign state might not be allowed to express its national culture fully or freely. There is a more ominous side to this theory, however, when it is combined with the racial conflict theories of social Darwinism. What emerges is a scenario in which diverse races, each organized into a political state, are engaged in a natural struggle for the survival of the fittest. Political tension between states thus takes on a new meaning, and the need to subdue rivals becomes a cosmic moral imperative. Every state, by its very existence, is now seen to be a threat to, and a target of, every other nation [or state] in Europe.

The question, of course, is how is the state to embody and express authentically the real interests of its underlying racial group, its nation. It is at this point that the theories of fascism come into play. The basic idea here is that the state is to be the institutional manifestation of the nation. To achieve this, the state must be governed by a single voice, that of the folk as a corporation. The problem, of course, is how to do this. Democracy might seem an obvious answer to us, but from the point of view of many nineteenth and early twentieth century nationalists, it appeared to be the exact opposite. After all, the point of democracy is to recognize and legitimate a variety of voices and constituencies. The parliaments of European democracies seemed to be in essence arenas within which different national and ideological interests fought things out and learned to compromise their own principles. Indeed, many of the parties in the parliaments had acknowledgedly non-statist interests in mind: socialism, for example, or regional autonomy. So democracy was seen as in fact a form of government that explicitly undercut the creation of a single national voice in the political arena. Fascist thought, therefore, led quite natur-ally to the idea that the state could be an authentic expression of the underlying nation only if power and initiative were lodged in one individual at the top who was in touch with the character of the folk and could be its sole spokesperson. This person, in essence a dictator, could then form the institutions and laws of the state to reflect in a straightforward and uncompromised fashion the will of the nation.

This notion of politics, combined with the thesis of history as the arena of a natural struggle among the nations for the survival of the fittest, leads directly into the ethic of the Shoah. For any particular nation, the assumption is the highest good is its own survival. This survival must be defended again and again on the stage of history. Further any surrounding nation [or race] must be seen as at least a potential enemy. Every neighboring nation must either dominate you or be dominated by you. So the ultimate good for any nation is to struggle as hard as it can to dominate its potential rivals.

The alternative, according to the ironclad laws of nature, is extinction. The state now has an important role to fulfill. Its job is not so much to protect individual rights as to defend the nation in the "Darwinian" struggle for survival. In this sense, the defense institutions of the state stand at the center of its raison d'etre: the army, police, internal security forces, etc. Conversely, any foreign group that resides within the boundaries of the state must ipso facto be suspect. This includes not only groups of other obvious nationalities, but even people of the state's nation-ality who have become recruited to other non-national causes, that is, ideologies which question the authority of the state or question the assumption that the highest moral good is the defense by the state of its national or racial interests. Thus political movements such as communism [or international socialism] and religious groups such as the Roman Catholic Church with its international character, or Jehovah's Witness with its allegiance to God placed above allegiance to state, all were seen as natural enemies of the proper fascist state.

In light of the above considerations, it does not take much imagination to see how the Nazis could come to see the Jews as mortal enemies, despite the small number of Jews in Germany, or why the Nazis were so intent on purging Jews from all vital organs of the state, and then finally from the state itself; why there was such dread of international communism, which was seen as linked in some way with the "Jewish race" [so-called "Jewish Bolshevism"]; and how, as the war began to turn against Germany, the "war against the Jews" [to use Lucy Dawidowicz's powerful phrase] became almost hysterically urgent.

Nor, I think, is it hard to see how others could be persuaded to go along with the Nazi program, at least to some extent, given the wide range of scientific, philosophical and historical arguments on which they could draw to validate their interpretation of events. In a country as adrift as was Weimar Germany in many ways, in a country that was mired in a sense of malaise, the appeal of a clear, logical, scientific explanation that also offered a plan to reverse matters should hardly be surprising. And above all, and this is my point, once accepted the general truth of the above interpretation of the human predicament, one could more or less tolerate the Nazi war against the Jews with a clear conscience. In the long run, its serves a higher natural good and so is ethically right as a program. True, it may entail certain injustices or sufferings when applied on an individual level, but so does almost any government program. Resistance was short-circuited further by the fact that to resist meant to posit an alternative view of the world, one that had to deny the entire historical, scientific and philosophical legacy on which the Nazi ethic was based. This few individuals were willing, or able, to do with any degree of self-assurance. That professional organizations could not see the possibility of an alternate ethic, especially professional organizations in fields like medicine and law, and even more so theology, is a more serious problem.

VI. The Role of God, Religion, and Religious Ethics

I now wish to return to the original question concerning the role of God in all this. One of the striking features of the intellectual complex that stands behind the Nazi ideology is its thoroughly secular character. To be sure, it drew its satanic images of the Jew from a massive repertoire of defamations promulgated by the Church. It is even true that many of the early anti-Jewish measures of the Nazis [e.g. yellow badges, ghettos] had been initiated by the Church in the Middle Ages [to include in an indirect way the concern with race in the form of the Spanish Inquisition's concern with limpieza de sangre, purity of blood]. Nonetheless, the ideology framed by the Nazis was not a religious system. It claimed, correctly, to be secular and scientific. This is, I think, an important point because it makes the Nazi ethic self-referential in a way that is normally not true of religious ethics. Let me explain.

Although religion and religious ethics are notoriously hard concepts to define, there seems to be a general consensus that one common feature of all religions is their referral at some point to a sacred source of authority. Thus, to take but one example, Little and Twiss in Comparative Religious Ethics define religion in part as "a set of beliefs, attitudes, and practices based on a notion of sacred authority...."[22] John P. Reeder's analysis of Judaic and Christian ethics begins at a similar point, claiming that both traditions have in common a sense that a transhuman source causes and legitimates the moral order.[23] It is this transhuman or sacred source that is one distinguishing feature of Jewish and Christian ethics as opposed to a purely secular ethic.

A second distinguishing feature, it seems to me, is the aspect of tradition. By this I mean a sense that the articulation of the ethic must be in some way consistent with what the ethic is understood always to have been. In Western religious ethics, the notion that an ethic is timeless is an important ingredient in ethical discourse. This is not to say that religious ethics do not change, nor is it to say that religious ethics do not reflect their time and place. It is to say, however, that in formulating ethical arguments within a Western religious context, we are concerned with the relationship between what we propose to do now and what has been the accepted norm for our religion in the past. We in general respect the past and want to be able to claim that our own standards are consistent with it. In real terms this does not limit our present options, but it is a feature of ethical discourse   or rhetoric which, I am now proposing, is of some importance. This importance lies in the fact that it provides some sort of accepted standard by which to judge the acceptability of proposed change.

It is the lack of these features, I wish to argue, that allowed the Nazi ethic to reach the extremes that it did. In the first place, it could make no reference to a source of morality beyond the physical processes of nature. That is, for the Nazi ethic, the question of right and wrong was reduced to the question of mechanics: how to exploit the laws of nature to certain predetermined ends. Such a question, of course, can be part of any ethical discourse. The problem is that in the Nazi ethic there does not appear to be any room for appeal or consideration beyond this. Once the question of how best to harness the forces of nature has been asked, there remains only the question of specific tactics. Broader reflections on rightness or goodness are ruled out a priori.[24] Ethical discourse, in short, has been reduced to a kind of social science in which the sole value is the physical survival of one side or the other at any cost.

In the second place, there is a lack of historical or social depth in the Nazi ethic, and thus no internal way to achieve perspective on newly-emerging claims. The Nazi ethic, as I have tried to show above, was based on the popular scientific insights of the day. This is, of course, what gave their ethic its aura of truth. But we also know that scientific theories, and more generally the paradigm out of which theories grow, are always to be regarded as hypothetical and ephemeral.[25]   Scientific theories are proposed in a sense precisely to be tested and surpassed. They are poor foundations for a permanent and trustworthy ethic. We know that the self-evident truths of yesterday are the quaint curiosities of today, and we ought to be just as sure that the self-evident truths of today hold no pro-mise of eternal validity.[26]   But the perspective to achieve that sort of skepticism comes only from historical experience. It is only through knowing the past, or at least being forced to confront its values seriously, that we can break the hold of today's self-evident truths.   This is the service provided by traditional religious rhetoric. It may not force us to continue in the conclusions reached in the past, but it at least forces us to consider how more recent proposals might be an improvement or an advance. The problem with a purely secular, scientific ethic is that there is no room for such a perspective; people are in a sense ethically obligated to conform to the apparent demands of the most up-to-date hypothesis. The end result is that in this type of ethic, there can be no appeal made to a source of legitimation beyond what people see as their own immediate good.

In many ways the argument I am making here is similar to the one made by Alasdair MacIntyre in After Virtue. In his ground-breaking study of the state of contemporary moral philosophy, MacIntyre argues that in essence much of what passes for ethics today is merely a sort of Weberian utilitarianism. By this he meant that one of the paradigmatic "characters" of the modern world is the manager and that the hallmark of the manager is competence and efficiency in getting the required job done.[27] This is, as it were, the telos of the manager, and he displays his virtue by fulfilling the telos effectively.   The problem, of course, is that in such a case, the worthwhileness of the mission, or the cost of the means needed to accomplish the job are not fully comprehended by ethical discourse. The larger issues of right and wrong are lost to view in the narrow focus needed by the manager.[28]

The point is that with the breakdown of any overarching sense of what the human species is and the loss of any perspective on what the proper telos of our deeds might be, ethical thinking has become focused and contextualized. MacIntyre labels this essentially emotivist ethic Weberian because it is Weber who demonstrated most forcefully how one's social role, that is, what one is expected to be or to accomplish, determines one's values. Without an ethic that allows the individual to transcend reflectively his or her social role of the moment, any ethical choice that must be made will perforce be based on whatever theories of the world are then current. In other words, the manager will be able in his or her mind to justify the actions or decisions in question only in reference to the organizational context in which the action or decision takes place.

This narrowing of the base of moral decisions need not be restricted to merely managerial positions in an organization. MacIntyre shows that even major ethical theories of the last several centuries need to be understood in context. What sound like universal descriptions of the moral enterprise are in fact little more than culturally-bound articulations of certain positions which have been expressed as though they were universal truths. Emotivism, to take but one of his examples, is best not understood as a universal ever-applicable theory of the nature of ethics, but is a particular position staked out at a certain time to address a single issue. The problem of misunder-standing begins when, like the bureaucrat's justification, it is abstracted out of its particular institutional or dialogical context and made out to be a universal theory for the definition of all ethical deliberation everywhere and at all times.

It is my contention here that the Nazi ethic is a prime example of where this loss of transcendence in ethical discourse can lead. The Nazi policy toward the Jews, we now know, did not appear full-blown in 1933. Rather, the details of the Nazi policy underwent a long period of incubation and refinement during which time the specific policies, procedures and institu-tions of their ethic were gradually shaped. It in fact seems that it was not really until the Wansee Conference of January, 1942, that the ultimate policy of extermination through gassing was fully articulated. Up to that point, the policy developed by fits and starts, depending on bureau-cratic infighting, conditions in Germany, the progress of the war and so forth.[29]

To summarize, then, the myriad decisions that were made to plan and then carry out the Shoah on a day-to-day basis were made within a bureau-cratic context and, as MacIntyre makes clear, reflect the rather narrow world of the bureaucrat. There was, of course, an attempt to frame the decisions of the bureaucracy in terms of larger ethical principles, and it was these that were supplied by the trends listed above, namely Jew-hatred, Social Darwinism, and fascism. These provided the secular rationale, or rather the secular discourse, for expressing what the bureaucrats had already chosen to do within the constraints of their own positions.

The Nazi ethic then really justifies in universal and scientific terms the particular needs of its own bureaucracy. The values that emerge are based on what the organizational process has already determined to be necessary. The reason that such a bureaucratic discourse could drive the ethical think-ing of the entire country, to include its professionals and its religious institutions, is that no [effective] counter-discourse seems to have been available. It was precisely this lack of a more religious, traditional ethic, I maintain, that made the Shoah possible. The bureau-cracy under Hitler simply developed policies it felt were necessary to carry forward its mission. Since no higher system of ethical values seems to have been available for judging the mission, the needs of the bureaucracy become by default the community's ethic.

Within this context, the activity of the Nazis and their collaborators makes a certain amount of sense. These people retained their moral sensitivity and their sense of duty to a higher good. What changed, simply, is the nature or the description of that higher good. The content of the older ethic, based on God, was replaced by an ethic defined by bureaucratic need and buttressed by the supposed rational neutrality of science. People could devote themselves to this new ethic with good conscience, feeling that they were still fulfilling their moral duty and serving a higher good. This I think helps account for the apparent devotion so many Germans and others displayed toward their gruesome tasks. They were not moral cripples, they were normal, well-intentioned people who could, and did, do their jobs with dedication and devotion and return home at night to be average husbands and fathers. This is I think why Hannah Arendt resorted to the notion of the banality of evil. Within this ethic, people were simply doing their jobs. The evil we now see was for them not regarded as evil. Had they so regarded it, I contend, they would not have done it so consistently without challenge or revolt. People simply do not do, on the whole, what they really regard to be evil. That seems to me to be part of what it means to call something evil. Rather, by relying on an ethic that was purely contemporary and scientific, people lost sight of the real evil they were doing.

If this view of matters is correct, then a number of conclusions would been to follow. One is that acting ethically is a matter of form rather than content. That is, people can consider themselves to be acting in a good, commendable way regardless of the actual content of their ethic. This is what confounded the Nazis and their cohorts. They thought they were doing the right thing and in many cases at the end of the war were surprised to find that the Americans and British far from being impressed with the German deeds were repulsed. Many Nazis seem to have gone to their graves [or are still alive today] never having fully realized the enormity of the evil they did. The point is that just because one is dedicated to a cause and can call upon scientific and ideological warrants does not mean that they system of behavior is itself moral. It simply means that the behavior is able to be expressed in ethical form.

The second conclusion is that secular theories cannot be relied upon to generate a trustworthy ethic. The scientific [or pseudo-scientific] theories adopted by the Nazis misled them frightfully. They and their followers may have thought they were acting according to the dictates of history and nature. In fact they became the prisoners of a bureaucratic dynamic that I think eventually got out of control In some sense, the Nazi state ended up becoming a prisoner of its own system. They became pawns of the monster they themselves unleashed. Rather than bringing themselves and their country to a new level of security and respect, which was after all the stated goal, they brought their country to the exact opposite. Their reliance on science and political theory betrayed them. The betrayal was possible because the Nazis had no way of knowing when they were being led astray; they had no outside marker or standard by which to fix their position.

A third conclusion has to do with the power of this kind of system of meaning. After all, it engulfed not only the party ideologues, but also people who should have known better, who did in theory at least have an alternate ethic which should have governed their perspective on matters. Most obvious were the professions: doctors, lawyers, professors, etc. These people we would expect to be committed to a set of views that would or should preclude the Nazi ethic. Doctors, for example, ought to have seen through the notion that Jews were a different race analogous to different species in the natural world. After all, the species of the natural world have distinct genetic traits, which is untrue of Jews. Yet doctors not only participated in the Nazi racial warfare, but in fact in many cases were its leaders. And despite the fact that doctors as a matter of professional commitment should be dedicated to relieving human suffering, all too many took the opportunity of the <u>Shoah</u> to perform hideous experiments on unwilling human subjects. As a group they allowed their own professional ethics to be completely overridden.

The same can be said of lawyers. Here again is a group who we would expect would be especially sensitive to the rule of law, and to the impartial application of the law. This group should be especially sensitive to the claim of human rights and due process. However, quite to the contrary, lawyers ended up serving a system that denied just these principles. The reason was strikingly simple. Once the law was so written so as to deprive Jews as a class of human rights, the lawyers could proceed to treat Jews as non-humans and still uphold the highest values of "the law." Like the physicians, they allowed themselves to be reduced to mere practitioners of whatever the law happened to be, not questioning if that was right or wrong. They allowed their moral competence to be restricted to the narrow limits of their professional conduct.

The group that offers the biggest surprise in this regard is the Christian theologians. Here is a group clearly dedicated to a vision of the world diametrically opposed to the Nazi view of matters. This group would also seem to be the least likely to allow itself without further reflection to be reduced to mere functionaries. Their job after all is to think ethics and to challenge the powers that be after the model of the Biblical prophets. That this group too became entirely coopted is one of the big disappointments of the <u>Shoah.</u>

Exactly what we are to make of the impotence of the Christian theologians is hard to know. For one thing, I think, it reflects the very intellectual shift that made Naziism possible in the first place, namely the displacement of religion by science in the mid-nineteenth century. The Nazi ethic, with its scientific and rationalistic basis was able to gain ascendancy precisely because there was no stiff opposition. The religious worldview had withered away under the impact of scientific advance, Church obscurantism, and Higher Criticism.[30] The Church [whether Catholic or Lutheran] continued to exist as an institution, clearly had ceased to function as a moral or intellectual force.   Its practitioners no longer were truly dedicated to its own indigenous ethic. They too could become servants of the new Nazi ethic and could learn to fulfill their own religious functions within the universe of discourse fashioned by the Nazi system. They certainly proved incapable, as an estate, of bringing to bear against the development of Nazi Europe any alternative voice, much less a sustained critique.

What this tells us is how easy it is for religion to descend into idolatry. In effect, even the churches in Nazi Germany took their epistemological cues from the secular culture proposed by the Nazis. The bulk of church theology and theologians who supported Hitler did not point to a realm of meaning or moral significance beyond the Nazi construct of the Aryan race. Christianity had been reduced to a series of civil religions, each celebrating the sacredness of its own nationality and none [even the multi-national Catholic Church] arguing from a more global or universal position. The reason I think that the Church men [and women] themselves found the secular ideologies overwhelmingly persuasive.

VII. Summary and Conclusion

My argument can no be summarized as follows: [1] people establish systems of values on the basis of their understanding of good and evil, [2] these values then serve as a basis for persuading masses of people to pursue certain courses of action and to avoid others, [3] that history shows that once people set a certain chain of events into motion, all we can expect is for the natural consequence of that chain of events to occur, i.e., we cannot expect God miraculously to intervene to bail us out. From this it follows that [4] even the worst atrocities can be supported by an ethic if that ethic is able to define genocide or torture convincingly as good for the circumstances at hand.   The point, to restate my thesis, is that focusing attention on why God did nor did not perform miracles removes the responsibility from where it really belongs, on the human agents who subscribe to the ethic and then act in accordance with its precepts.

I do not mean to be naive on this point. Religious people have committed their fair share of horrors and atrocities. It is by now a well-rehearsed fact they almost every anti-Jewish measure instituted by the Nazis during their early years had its precedent in the Church's treatment of the Jews: yellow badges, ghettos, expulsions, etc. The mere appropriation of religious symbolism or the invocation of religious rhetoric does not in and of itself guarantee anything. But the acceptance of a religious worldview that demands that people look beyond the temporal thought of the day does offer a stance by which secular ideologies or bureaucratic convenience can at least be confronted and, if necessary, critiqued. It offers the possibility of a moral vision that transcends, or at least is different than, that of the prevailing political ideology of the day. It seems to be that if we do not allow that sort of view into our moral discourse, then we really have no basis for expecting people to counter the next "shoah" on moral grounds. There simply will be no Archimedean grounds upon which to exercise such moral leverage. The Shoah stands in stark testimony to the fact that if no longer moral vision is present, if religious rhetoric is not allowed to offer a voice over against secular purposes and ideologies, then anything is indeed possible.

Bernard Maza's essay, unique to this collection, is an attempt by an Orthodox Jew and Rabbi to deal with both the Shoah and an interpretation of the Jewish Religious Tradition which sees the "hand of God" in all things and events. For Maza, the Biblical prophet Ezekiel holds the key to a correct understanding of the Shoah, especially Chapter 20, verses 32 and 33, along with Ecclesiastes Chapter 1, verse 5. The Almighty used the Shoah as a means whereby an errant Israel, falling away from its true destiny of commitment to Torah, might be brought back to its responsibilities. The "birth pangs of the Messiah," as evidenced by the rebirth of the State of Israel as a result of the Shoah, now becomes the beginning of Redemption for Jews the world over. Difficult and problematic as this position is for non-Orthodox Jews to accept, it does remain true to Orthodox Judaism, and, likewise, attempts to address the horrors of the Shoah from that vantage point.

WHY?

Bernard Maza

In my book With Fury Poured Out: A Torah Perspective on the Holo-caust[1], I explained "why the Shoah?" In this essay I will lay out before the reader a brief review of the explanation: How did I arrived at the explanation? What aspect of "why" did I explain and what aspect of "why" did I not explain? Why I explained what I did and why I did not explain what I did not? And, since the explanation bears upon the future of the Jewish people, how does the developing history of the Jewish people since the writing of the manuscript conform to the explanation?

I. The Rising and Setting of the Sun

King Solomon said in Ecclesiastes, "The sun rises and the sun sets".[2] The Talmud declares that sentence to be a prophecy. The Torah always will have a central source from which it spreads to the world. It may be a central place like the Bais Hamikdash, the Holy Temple. Or it may be a person who teaches Torah from wherever he may be, like Samuel who travelled from city to city teaching the words of the Almighty wherever he went.

When destiny decrees that the Torah will pass from that central course, "the sun rises" first in a new central source before "the sun sets" in its passing central source. In the words of the Talmud, "when Rabbi Akiva was dying, Rebbi was born. When Rebbi was going to die Rav Yehudah was born....before the sun of Eli was extinguished the sun of Samuel shone."

This was true through all of history. The noted historian Solomon Grayzel writes in his History of the Jews:

> One of the most remarkable facts in the history of the Jews is that they have never been without a central leader-ship....Even before the one center realized that it was destined to give up the leadership of the scattered Jewish people, the next was developing the ability to resume where the former was leaving off.

This was true in all Jewish history. But every intelligent human analysis of Jewish history in the twentieth century pointed to the certainty that the prophecy was soon to lose its truth. In every country of major Jewish settlement, Torah was in steep decline.

The citadel of Torah in the twentieth century, the light of Torah to the world, was Eastern Europe--Poland and its neighboring countries: Hungary, Rumania, and the Baltic States. In the early part of the twentieth century came disturbing signs that the youth were leaving their parents' values and their way-of-life. They were pursuing Socialism and Zionism and rejecting Torah. At first the pace of the change was slow. But as the twentieth century progressed the rate of Jewish youth leaving the Torah life was accelerating. Their parents, the Rabbis, the established community tried desperately to stem the onrushing tide. But by the decade of the 1930's, the elders were overwhelmed. The youth were leaving the Torah at an increased rate. The outlook for the future of Torah in Eastern Europe was dark. The sun of Torah was setting in its source.

In the Soviet Union, since the Communist Revolution of 1917, there was spiritual desolation. There was no Jewish education or Jewish anything permitted. And there was a willing Jewish youth to help the Communist Revolution accomplish its designs. In the 1930's in the Soviet Union, where there was once world-renowned Torah scholars and millions of Torah-true Jews, there was nothing except an almost invisible fossilized remnant of the old generation.

In the early twentieth century, millions of Jews left Eastern Europe to come to the inviting shores of America. Most of them were Torah-observant, and they established a vibrant Jewish community in the United States. There were many synagogues, mikvaot[3], yeshivas[4] and kosher establishments. But in spite of their dedication they were losing their children. The Jewish youth loved America. They rejected their parents' way of life as "European" and they scorned their Torah values as "old-fashioned." They were leaving their parents' life-style in droves. In the United States in the 1930's, very few of the youth walked in step with their parents.

In Palestine, for thousands of years, even after the destruction of the Holy Temple and Exile of the Jews from the Holy Land, there was always brave Torah-true Jews who settled in the Yishuv, the settlement. They guarded the holiness of the land with dedication. But early in the twentieth century, Zionism of a secular-nationalistic persuasion inspired the youth of Europe. They led the aliyah, immigration, of Jews to Palestine, bringing hundreds of thousands of non-Torah observant Jews to Palestine, greatly outnumbering the Torah-minded Jews. Nowhere was the sun of Torah rising. The prophecy of King Solomon seemed to be coming to an end.

The Talmud tells of the gathering of the people of Israel at Mount Sinai to receive the Torah. The Torah states, "And they stood underneath the mountain." The Talmud [B.T. Sabbath 88a] comments:

> Said Rav Avdimi, the son of Chama, this teaches us that the Holy One, Blessed be He, tilted the mountain over them like unto a barrel and said, 'If you accept the Torah good! And if you do not, there shall be your burial place!'

And the Talmud says:

> Said Rabbi Simeon, the son of Lakish, 'What is the meaning of the passage, 'And it was evening and it was morning that sixth day'? It teaches us that the Holy One, Blessed be He, made a condition with all that He created and said to them, 'If the people of Israel accept the Torah which will be given on the sixth day of [the month of--Ed.] Sivan, good! And if not, I shall return the world to the state of void and emptiness!'

The Talmud teaches us that the existence of the Jewish people and of the world is dependent upon the fulfillment of the Torah, which is the plan of the Almighty for the conduct of the world. The people of Israel are the bearers of the Torah. When the Jewish people accept and fulfill their function, the Almighty blesses the world with prosperity and peace. Would the Jewish people not fulfill their function and not accept and carry the Torah, the Almighty might discontinue the existence of His creation.

In the twentieth century, the sun of Torah was setting all over the world. What was going to happen to the Torah? To the Jewish people? To the world?

Since the destruction of the Holy Temple, and for all of the centuries of Exile which followed, the people of Israel have recited the following prayer in their morning services:

> Look down from the heavens and see that we have fallen to shame and ridicule among the nations. We have been considered as sheep led to slaughter, to kill, to destroy, to beat, and to shame. But, in spite of all this, Your Name we have not forgotten. Please do not forget us.

The Jewish people, wandering in the Exile, moved from country to country suffering persecution wherever they went. They made their homes in the country that accepted them, stoically suffering abuse and persecution for as long as that country accepted them. When that country tired of its own hospitality and they were expelled, the Jews made their way to another country where they faced the same fate.

The liturgy cited above describes, with pathos, the pathetic heroism of the long-suffering Jew. The power that gave them the strength to persevere, to hope, and to survive, was their faith that the Almighty would not forget them as they did not forget the Almighty.

For generations their faith remained firm, their loyalty to the Torah unswerving. And the generation of 1939, as earlier generations, was steady and undoubting.

But human beings have their limits and the Jewish people had reached theirs. The Jews of succeeding generations could no longer bear to be the shame and ridicule of nations, as a sheep led to slaughter. They wanted to be like the other nations. They would forget the name of the Almighty.

The prophet Ezekiel has said:

> And that which ascends upon your spirit shall not be, that which you say, 'let us be like the nations, like the families of the lands, to serve wood and stone.' [20:32]

In the twentieth century that which Ezekiel had prophesied was coming to pass. There was ascending upon the Jewish people the desire to be like all other nations.

But it was the will of the Almighty that the Jewish people, the bearers of the Torah, would not forsake the Torah. The present generation of righteous would not be the last. The ambition of the coming generation to be like all the nations of the world would not be.

The Almighty knew that the oppression of the Jewish people had to end or the sun of Torah would set. The Jewish people had to be redeemed and returned to the Land of Israel. Only in the Land of Israel would they find freedom from the suffering that was inevitably their lot in the lands of their exile.

When they would be returned to their land and the burden of oppression lifted from their backs, the heaviness would be removed from their hearts. When their hearts and minds would be free, they would seek and find themselves. The pintele yid, the spark of Judaism that is in the heart of every Jew, would be awakened. The sunshine of Torah would rise.

This was therefore the moment in the Divine history of the Jewish people that the Almighty judged to be the time for the beginning of the process of Redemption.

The Talmud describes the process of Redemption. There are four stages in the process. They are: Redemption from oppression, ingathering of the exiles, the restoration of Jerusalem, and the crowning of the King-d-om of David, which is the Kingdom of the Almighty.

The prophet Ezekiel has said:

> As I live says the Lord that only with a strong hand and an
> outstretched arm, and with fury poured out will I be King over
> them. [20:33]

The road to the Kingdom of the Almighty, beginning with redemption
from oppression, would be preceded by "fury." Not just fury, but a fury of
unprecedented magnitude - a "fury poured out."

In the twentieth century the Almighty decreed the unfolding of the prophetic process. It meant the coming of the fury. It meant the Shoah. The
Almighty, the Guardian of Israel, hid His Face and He did not protect His
people from the evil that was lurking in the hearts of His enemies.

The Shoah came. The hatred that was inside the hearts of the enemies
of the Almighty and His people burst out in an explosion of unmatched
savagery. And in the midst of the savagery, before the eyes of the murderer, came to life the most incredible saga of sacred heroism ever displayed by a people.

6,000,000 Jews were burned in the flames. Millions of them were
marched to the woods to dig their own graves in which they died from the
bullets of Nazi machine guns. Millions more were marched to meet their
death in the gas chambers. And while they dug their graves and while they
went to the gas chambers, they sang and danced. Their hearts were filled
with love and their mouths filled with praise of the Almighty Who decreed
their deaths.

They scorned the murderers. What power did they have over their souls!
They sang Ani Maamin, "I believe," and Sh'ma Yisrael, "Hear O Israel"--
in affirmation of their belief in the Wisdom and Mercy of the Almighty, the
Lord of the Universe, to Whom they entrusted their souls.

The following account is related by M. Prager in Tnuat Hachasidut
Bitkufat Hashoah[5]:

> When the murderer Globotchnik came to Lublin at the end
> of 1939, he commanded that all the Jews be gathered together in an
> empty field at the end of the city. When all the Jews assembled,
> trembling with fear, he announced that everyone should start
> singing a happy Chassidic song.
>   Someone in the frightened crowd began to sing the sweet
> Chassidic song "Lomer Zich Iberbeten Avinu Shebashamayim,"
> "Let us Make Up, Our Father in Heaven." But the song did not

catch on. At once Globotchnik commanded his troopers to beat the Jews who were not following his orders. The Nazis swooped down upon the Jews and began to beat them mercilessly. Suddenly a loud clear voice rose up in song. "Mir Vellen Zei Iberbeten Avinu Shebashamayim," "We Will Outlive Them, Our Father in Heaven," singing the same Chassidic melody. In a second, the song caught on. Everyone began singing and then they all joined together dancing a stormy, whirling dance before the eyes of the murderers. The Jews were so intoxicated with feelings of hope and faith that Globotchnik stood there bewildered and confused and began to scream with a shrill voice, "Stop! Stop at once!"

As they waited for their salvation, they went on with their lives as Jews, finding courage, hope, and even joy in their Jewish heritage. They studied Torah and observed Jewish practices. Neither suffering, nor pain, nor fear of death discouraged them.

The following account was related by Zalman Kleinman at the Eichmann trial and published in Ani Maamin by Mordecai Eliav:

> One day as I was lying on my bunk in the children's ward in Auschwitz. I saw a guard carrying a big rubber hose, going to whip someone. I jumped from my bunk to see whom they were going to whip. The guard went over to one of the bunks. The boy that was lying there already knew what was coming and he was waiting. The guard said, "Get down." He came down and bent over. The guard began to whip him.
>
> I and the boys who gathered around watched and counted. The boy did not cry, did not shout, did not even sigh. We were astonished, we did not understand....and the whipping went on. He had already passed twenty-five lashes; as a rule we were given twenty-five lashes. He passed thirty. When he passed forty, he turned the boy over and began to whip him on his head and on his legs. The body did not groan, did not cry, nothing....a boy of fourteen and he did not cry.
>
> The guard angrily finished fifty and left. I can still see this great red blotch that streaked the boy's forehead from one of the blows of that rubber hose.
>
> We asked the boy why he was whipped. He answered, "I brought some prayer books to my friends. It was worth it." He did not add a word. He got up, went to his bunk and sat down.

Yaakov Kurtz in Sefer Ha'aidut[6] tells of the time during the holiday of Succos[7] when he saw an old Jew sitting in a succah and singing zmirot[8] in a loud voice. He entered the succah and asked the old man if he realized the great danger of what he was doing. The old man shook his head this way and that and continued to sing. After a while he turned to him and said,

"What can they do to me? They can take my body but not my soul. They have no authority over the soul. Their power is only in this world. Here they are powerful. But in the Other World they are powerless!"

The following event, related by Rabbi [Ephraim] Oschry in Churban Lita[9], took place in the Kovno Ghetto:

> On the eleventh day of Tammuz 5701 [Sunday, 6 July 1941-- Ed.] a group of great Rabbis were gathered in the ghetto of Kovno and were studying Torah. Suddenly the gates were burst open and a group of Lithuanian fascists sprang into the room. They were all deeply engrossed in their study and ignored the intruders. When the murderers saw that no one was paying attention to them, they began to fire their revolvers, and the Rabbis trembled and arose....
> The order was given: "Line up! Come with us!"
> The Rabbis understood what the order meant. They stood in line. While they were getting ready to march, Rabbi Elchanan Wasserman turned to the prisoners and said, "It seems that in the Heavens they have seen amongst us great righteous men, for they want us with our lives to bring forgiveness upon the people of Israel. We must therefore repent now, immediately, on this spot, for time is short. We must remember that we will surely sanctify His Name. Let us go with heads held high and let no imperfect thought enter it lest it blemish our sacrifice. We are now fulfilling the greatest commandment, to sanctify His Name. The fire which will consume our bones is the fire that will give birth again to the Jewish nation."
> Thus they marched, the march of the holy. With pride and honor they went to bring forgiveness to the people of Israel. Thirteen of the elders of Israel, and at their head the great holy Rabbi Elchanan Wasserman, were killed that day....

The sanctity of the Shoah martyrs pierced the heavens, and the Almighty redirected the course of Jewish history. The process of Redemption began to unfold.

On May 6, 1945, World War II ended. The Shoah was over. A pitiful remnant of Jews emerged from darkness to freedom. But their freedom was not pure light. Where were they to go? They would not go back and make their homes in the countries which were the graveyards of their loved ones. The image of their neighbors and countrymen laughingly participating in their murder swam before their eyes like a nightmare.

They emerged from the Shoah left with nothing but a dream. That dream was Palestine, the Holy Land, the Promised Land of the Jews. They waited in the Displaced Persons Camps until they were ready to leave for Palestine.

They walked through countries and climbed over mountains, always hounded by the British who were determined to prevent the refugees from settling in Palestine. They tracked them through Europe, scouted their boats, stopped them before they could dock. They boarded the boats and took off the passengers, peacefully or forcefully. And many of the boats were turned back to Europe.

In the book Illegal Immigrants Cross the Seas, one of the immigrants who made it from Italy to Palestine describes the feelings of the refugees who participated in the escape:

> We escaped through Czechoslovakia, through the plains of Hungary, through the snow-covered mountains of the Alps, and through the sun-drenched land of Italy. We crossed borders and wire fences. The darkness of the night covered us. We disguised ourselves in various ways. We used every means to get to the sea ports from where we could got to the Promised Land.
> We know that many long days of waiting are ahead of us. Days of wandering in strange ports will be our lot before we reach the miraculous day when we take our first step towards aliyah [immigration--Ed.]. We surely will sail in a small boat, one of those boats which sail the seas with assumed names and strange flags. Many days we will sit crowded below the decks, and the stink of the rats and the salt water will choke our throats. The British birds of prey will follow us threateningly. But the hour will come, and through the dark clouds we will see the harbors of Palestine. And our eyes, red from sleepless nights, will be fixed upon the shores of the Promised Land and our hearts will beat.

Vienna was the stopping point for thousands of Jews wandering through Europe. Dr. Garcia Granados who was a member of the United Nations Special Committee on Palestine describes the visit of the Committee to the Rothschild Hospital in Vienna in 1947:

> Little by little, as we began slowly to explore this incredible building, it dawned upon me that I was in the presence of one of the greatest shames of modern times. We began with what had once been a hospital ward. Beds were placed head to feet almost completely filling the room and where there were no beds, there were cots and mattresses. There was no place for people to stand and so all of them either sat or lay on their beds.

We moved through other rooms in which every possible inch of space was similarly taken by cots and mattesses occupied by men, women, and children. Some lay on the floor.

Hundreds of people swarmed in the corridors. I could scarcely push my way through. In the courtyards hundreds more men and women were camping. There was no room for them inside. Wherever I looked men, women, and children were sitting or trying to sleep curled up on the earth. I descended to the basement of the hospital. It had been divided into large window-less rooms. After our eyes became accustomed to the gloom, we realized there were scores of people lying there. Huge pipes, part of the water system, crisscrossed the ceiling, and from them clothes were spread to dry.

The heavey odor seemed to permeate my being. I felt I was going to be sick....By a tremendous effort, I pushed my way through the people to the door. There I found the Iranian alternate Dr. Ali Ardelan. His face was haggard. He said in a trembling voice, "This is a crime against humanity. I never thought I would witness anything like this." I crossed the doorway and ran to a window opening on the courtyard. I remained there for two or three full minutes breathing deeply and sick at heart for all mankind.

The plight of the Jewish people and the same of the Shoah aroused the sympathy of the world. On November 29, 1947, the General Assembly of the United Nations, aided by an unusual demonstration of agreement between the United States and the Soviet Union, voted for the establishment of a Jewish State.

On May 14, 1948, the government of Palestine proclaimed its independence as the Jewish State of Israel. On May 15, 1948, the British handed over the authority for the government of the State of Israel. The Jewish people were free to return to their Promised Land.

After World War II, along with the gathering hope for the birth of the State of Israel, and its subsequent independence, a new spirit of hope, pride, and self-respect came over the Jews of the world. The sun of Torah began to rise in the United States and in Israel.

No longer were Torah-minded parents losing their children. Their children were joining them to live a Torah-true life. And the parents who were not Torah-minded were, surprisingly, sending their children to Torah Day Schools and learning to become Torah-observant. Many parents were returning to Torah step-by-step with their children.

Before 1939, in all of the United States, there were a handful of Torah elementary schools and Yeshivos teaching Torah to approximately 5,000 Jewish youth. In 1985, there were over 500 Yeshivos and Day Schools teaching Torah to well over 100,000 students.

And in Israel, whereas in 1939 there were about 20,000 students learning in the Torah elementary schools and Yeshivos, in 1985, there were more than 150,000 students in the Torah elementary schools and 50,000 in the Yeshivos.

The prophecy of Ezekiel includes three phases: first, "that which ascends upon your spirit;" second, "with fury poured out;" and third, "I will be King over you" [20:33].

Ezekiel prophesied, first, that there will be a time when, although the Jewish people will be pure and devoted to the Almighty, there will come upon the spirit of the Jewish people, the desire to be like other nations. The youth will feel the urge to leave the Torah. In 1939 the prophecy was exactly correct. The desire of the youth was abundantly clear. They were dreaming to be like other nations.

The prophecy speaks then of the second phase. The desire of the new generation will be arrested by the "fury poured out." There will follow a period in Jewish history when they will be caught in the destructive power of the "fury poured out," a fury of monumental devastation.

The Shoah was a tragedy which surely reached the dimensions of the "fury poured out."

The final phase of the prophecy is that as a result of the Shoah, "I will be King over you." The process leading to His Kingdom spans an unspecified number of years. And, as Ezekiel prophesied, the process began directly after the Shoah, with the rebirth of Israel and the resurgence of Torah.

The Shoah and its effects were the fulfillment, in our day, of the prophesy of Ezekiel and the beginning of the process leading to the King-dom of the Almighty.

II. The Truth of Ezekiel's Prophecy

The explanation of the Shoah advanced above came to me from a conversation with Mr. Abraham Aharon Rimler while we were walking home from the synagogue on the Sabbath in the early 1970's.

Mr. Rimler was born in Poland. As a young man he was trapped into the Shoah and taken to a concentration camp. We spoke often about his life in

Poland. On that Sabbath he said to me, "Don't think that the religious Jews in Poland were not having any problems with their children. More and more of them were leaving the synagogue and their parents' way of life to join Zionist organizations and all sorts of clubs."

I was taken aback by the statement. It was a totally unexpected remark.

Ever since I studied the Talmudic commentary on the prophecy of Ezekiel about "the fury poured out," it struck me that the prophet may very well have been referring to the Shoah. But that possibility was rejected by me, as it would be immediately rejected by every American Jew. For, as every American Jew knew, in the twentieth century in Eastern Europe the Jewish people boasted a citadel of Torah which was among the strongest in modern Jewish history.

The Jews in Eastern Europe were famous all over the world for their Torah scholarship and dedication. Eastern Europe was the center of famous Yeshivos headed by world-renowned Roshei Yeshivos[10], with thousands of devoted students studying the Torah day and night. It was the home of great Rabbinic community leaders and of Torah-observant Jews living in the legendary cities and shtetlach[11]. In the twentieth century, Eastern Europe throbbed with Torah living. How could the prophet Ezekiel be referring to this period as being a time when there was "ascending upon the spirit of the Jewish people the desire to be like the other nations" [20:32]?

But when I heard the statement from Mr. Rimler and I recovered from my disbelief, I thought, "If it were really so and not just a personal, mistaken observation, and if the Eastern European youth were actually leaving their parents' way of life, and if the same were true in the other centers of Jewish living in the world, and if their elders, the generation then existing, were still loyal to the Torah up to and during the Shoah, and if after the Shoah, and, as a result of the Shoah, Israel was born, and if, after the Shoah, there was a reverse in Torah loyalty in any center of Jewish population, then the "fury poured out" would have been the Shoah."

I studied the history of the Jewish people in the twentieth century researching every one of the points I indicted above. I found that in all the history of the Jewish people at that time in all of the world there was not one iota of inconsistency with the prophecy.

I studied dozens of shtetlach in Eastern Europe. Most shtetlach of Eastern Europe had compiled Memorial Books describing the life in their shtetl before the Shoah. In all of them the pattern was the same. The youth were searching for new horizons. I studied the big cities with large Jewish populations. The pattern was the same. Growing numbers of young people were leaving the Torah life of their parents. And it was also true that in every place the problem was concentrated completely on the youth. Their elders were all of one voice, loyal and true to the Torah.

I studied the major centers of Jewish living in the world. Every-where the pattern was the same as in Eastern Europe, but worse. The youth were leaving or had already left the influence of their parents. Many cut themselves off from their parents' life-style so sharply that hardly an impression was left. In the Soviet Union Jewish life seemed to be already gone. In America and in Israel the youth were going their own way and it would be long before the Torah of their elders would be forgotten.

I studied the Shoah and it was true as the prophecy declared. The martyrs died proclaiming the Kingdom of the Almighty.

And I studied the period after the Shoah. What the prophecy pre-dicted was true beyond all doubt. The Kingdom of the Almighty was being established over the people of Israel. The re-birth of Israel after the Shoah, and clearly linked to the Shoah, meant that the Almighty was returned from His Own Exile to the seat of His Kingdom. And there could be no doubt that after the Shoah and the birth of Israel, Torah education and Torah observance took a giant step forward.

I began to write my book. And while I was writing I knew I was making historical predictions. The coming of the Kingdom of the Almighty is a process. It begins with freedom from oppression and continues to the complete Redemption. All the while Torah will be growing until the realization of the prophecy of Isaiah, who declared, "All the world will be filled with the knowledge of the Almighty as water fills the ocean bed" [11:9]; and the fulfillment of the prophecy of Zachariah, who said, "And it shall be that the Almighty will be King over all the world. On that day, He will be One and His Name will be One" [14:9].

According to the explanation offered, it meant that there would be a continuing, uninterrupted growth of Torah in our day. I knew that the truth of the explanation was being tested even while I was researching and writing. Sure enough, the figures kept going up from year to year.

In the mid-1970's when I began my study until the mid-1980's when I completed my writing, the figures rose steadily. In the United States in 1975, there were 427 Torah Day Schools with approximately 80,000 students. In 1985, there were 500 Torah elementary schools with 100,000 students. In Israel, in 1975, there was approximately 100,000 in the Torah elementary schools. In 1985, there were close to 200,000 students.

Since I completed writing the book, and as of today's writing, the figures have gone up again. In 1990, in America, there were 560 Torah elementary schools with 120,000 students and in Israel there were approximately 275,000 students in the Torah elementary schools.

In analyzing Jewish history in the twentieth century, I linked the prophecy of Ezekiel to the prophecy of King Solomon, who said, "The sun rises," and then, "the sun sets"[12], meaning that before the sun of Torah sets in its central source, there will be a new sun of Torah rising somewhere in a new central source. This implies that during the transition from one center to another, the brilliant sun of the past shall be replaced by a sun which, though destined for future brilliance, is still small.

Therefore, while the rising sun of Torah is growing in brilliance, there are, sadly, places of darkness and shadow which it may not ever light up. Many Jewish lives would never be brightened by the sun of Torah. Would the sun of Torah rising in America and Israel come to the Soviet Union?

At the time of the writing of With Fury Poured Out, I did not conceive of the possibility that Torah would ever enter the Soviet Union. I could not imagine that the Jews of the Soviet Union, so engulfed in the darkness of Atheism and Communism, would ever accept Judaism. And I could not believe that the powers of the Soviet Union would ever let the Torah in or the Jews out. I did not include anything about the Soviet Union in the rising sun of Torah.

But the Almighty is the God of Compassion, and He did not forsake the Jews of the Soviet Union. He included them in His Promise. The Almighty directed the course of the Jews of the Soviet Union to bring them back to Him.

In October, 1990, an interview was held with Yaakov Gorodetsky, the famous "refusenik" and activist from Leningrad. Gorodetsky is today the Director of the International Commission of Sh'vut Ami ["Redemption of My People"--Ed.], which is the primary institution for the religious absorption of Soviet Jews in Israel.

Gorodetsky, who was harassed by the KGB since he applied to go to Israel in 1980, was finally "expelled." He left for Israel in 1986. There, in Israel, he and his wife became Torah observant.

At the interview Yaakov discussed the beginnings and the development of religious awareness in the Soviet Union. He was asked what event was the inspiration that sparked the return to Torah among Soviet Jews. Unhesitatingly, without equivocation, he named the Six-Day War [of 1967--Ed.].

Up until the Six-Day War, the Jew of the Soviet Union carried his Judaism like a badge of shame. His papers were different than the identification papers of all other citizens. His "nationality" named no region in the Soviet Union, as did the documents of others. His "national-ity" was Jewish. He was scarred and was regularly the victim of a beating by his "friends." He felt apart from, and beneath, the citizens of the Soviet Union.

But, Gorodetsky said, in 1967 with the lightning victory of Israel in the Six-Day War, the word "Jew" took on a new meaning. The Jews looked at themselves with pride. They saw themselves as members of a proud and strong nation. Gorodetsky declared that after the miraculous victory, the Jews said, "We are also men of courage and strength like the mightiest of nations. The Jew is somebody."

The new interest of the Jew in his Jewishness began to take movement in the late 1970's. A leading figure in the movement for return was Rabbi Alexander Miller who was disciple of the world-renowned Torah leader, the Chofetz Chaim, of blessed memory. He sat and studied in the Bais Medrash [Jewish school--Ed.] in Moscow. Several students gravitated to him. Among them was Eliahu Eses.

Eses began to spread Torah among his friends. He organized classes in his home, braving the watchful eyes of the KGB. He influenced his friends to learn Torah, to teach Torah, and to organize classes in their [own] homes. Soon there were groups of 15-20 students learning Torah in various homes.

At the same time that Torah activity began to spread in the Moscow area, a similar movement was taking place in the Leningrad area. In 1977 Grisha Wasserman, a successful electrical engineer, author and lecturer, became disillusioned by antisemitism in the Soviet Union. He became inspired with a desire to learn about Judaism. He visited the only syna-gogue in Leningrad. There he befriended an old man who surreptitiously helped him learn Torah.

He began to organize classes in his home. In 1981 he started with three students. In 1985 he had about 15 students and each of them had 15 of their own, all of them between the ages of 18-25. Grisha travelled all over the Soviet Union, teaching and lecturing, to arouse the interest of the Soviet Jews to Torah study.

By the end of the 1970's, the seeds of Torah had taken hold in the Soviet Union.

Torah established a foothold in the Soviet Union because of a combination of factors. The first was the inspiration of the Six-Day War. Torah was given added impetus by the "refuseniks" who became inspired with Israel and would not submit to the powers of the Soviet Union who refused to let them go. The publicity they received, and the sympathy that was aroused among their fellow Jews and the world, did much to kindle Jewish feelings in the Soviet Union. And antisemitism spread by the government and quickly communicated to the masses brought home to the Jews of the Soviet Union the fact and the circumstances of their Jewishness.

In the 1970's the doors of the Soviet Union were temporarily opened for Jews to emigrate to Israel. Tens of thousands were permitted to leave. Among them was the "refusenik" Shimon Grilius who had become religious in prison. When he came to Israel he became a leaders in bringing Torah education to the Soviet immigrants. He founded Sh'vut Ami, the primary center in Israel for religious absorption of the Soviet Jews.

In the mid-1980's glastnost, a period of radical change, came to the Soviet Union. With it came to the Soviet Jews a measure of freedom to learn about Judaism and to emigrate to Israel. In 1987 the disintegration of Communism and a new freedom for the people of the Soviet Union brought a great upsurge of antisemitism. The combination of antisemitism and the almost unlimited freedom for the Soviet Jews to emigrate to Israel made for a flood of immigration of Soviet Jews to Israel.

There were now Torah institutions and organizations ready to help the Soviet immigrants in Israel to adjust to a Torah way of life. They were ready to help those still remaining in the Soviet Union to get a taste of Judaism.

Rabbi Abraham Binsky, Director of Shoreshim ["Roots"--Ed.], the organization for religious absorption of Soviet Jews in America, is today on leave from Sh'vut Ami in Israel which he serves as Director of Absorption Services. In an interview held in October, 1990, he described the activity of Sh'vut Ami. Rabbi Binsky said that they began their activity at the airport. They help the newcomer to find jobs and housing. Sh'vut Ami conducts seminars and home study groups all over Israel. In Jerusalem alone their seminars are attended by about 500 people. On the Passover of 1989, about 1,000 people attended a week-long seminar on Jewish history and religion. Sh'vut Ami also encourages the Soviet Jewish immigrant to undergo circumcision when necessary. In the past several years they have influenced some 2,000 men to undergo circumcision.

Shvut Ami has a yeshiva attended by approximately 100 young men. The Yeshiva is producing the rabbis and teachers for the Soviet Jewish community. Thousands of Jews who no longer before hardly knew the existence of the Torah have been exposed to Torah and Jewish religious practice.

The figures for the number of Soviet Jews studying Torah in the Torah elementary schools of Israel are as yet unknown. But without doubt there are today thousands of Soviet Jewish children attending regular Torah schools in Israel.

Torah not only reached the Soviet Jews in Israel. It came to the Soviet Union. Where before there was nothing, today there is something alive and spirited. There are synagogues and yeshivos in several cities in the Soviet Union. There are two Yeshivos in Moscow and Jewish schools in Leningrad, Riga, Kiev, Vilna, and other major cities.

The following article, written by Michael Winerip, appeared in The New York Times of October 31, 1990. The article tells about Steven Springfield, a Jew from Latvia who left Riga for America in 1947. Mr. Springfield returned to Riga as a tourist last fall:

> It was astounding for him, like visiting a nightmare by the light of day. The spookiest was the Jewish school he had attended in the 1930's. In that same building, now crumbling, a new Jewish school had opened on September 1, 1989. Judaism was repressed so long that the founders expected 100. 500 applied.

The Jewish Observer of November, 1990, includes an article entitled "From Kiev with Hope," written by Yehoshua Weber. There he describes the dramatic changes in the spirit and the growth of Torah Judaism in Kiev:

> Focusing on the emerging vitality of one community, Kiev might help bring the religious potential of Soviet Jewry into clearer perspective. Nine months ago....Rabbi Yaacov Bleich, a young American, was appointed the official Rav of Kiev. In the short period of time since then, he and his indefatigable Rebbetzin have spear-headed a quiet revolution among a number of Kiev's 100,000 Jews.
> Under the Bleichs' tutelage, remarkably successful day and sleepaway camps, staffed by energetic young American were organized for both boys and girls. Three hundred wide-eyed children were treated to four weeks of fun and sports, which included potent exposure to tefillin, davening, zemiros [singing--Ed.], and kashrus [dietary laws--Ed.]
> Hundreds of parents hastened to register their children in Kiev's brand new Talmud Torah [for boys--Ed.] and Bais Yaacov [for girls--Ed.]....The parents of a hundred children have somehow gathered the courage to withdraw their children from the state school system and have entrusted the religious and secular educations of their children to the vicissitudes of an incipient, non-registered Talmud Torah.
> ....Two hundred and fifty other children are enrolled in a Sunday Torah program, while another fifty attend a more intensive daily after-school program....Twenty budding talmidei chachamim [students--Ed.] spend their entire day in an advanced all-day yeshiva.

The melamdim [teachers--Ed.], mohelim [ritual circum-
cisors--Ed.], and shochtim [ritual slaughterers--Ed.] who came to
Kiev....were deluged by an unexpected large number of requests
for brissim [ritual circumcisions--Ed.].

I had the zechus [merit--Ed.] to teach groups of adults in
Kiev for a period of three weeks this past summer. A hundred to
one hundred-fifty people religiously attending daily classes, many
of them sitting through three consecutive two-hour lectures!

The Soviet Jews came to Israel as fast as the planes could take them.
And Israel welcomed them with love. In 1990 200,000 Jews came and
300,000-400,000 are expected in 1991. Where before there was darkness for
the Soviet Jews, today there is new light and opportunity. As yet, only a
small fraction of them have been brought to Torah Judaism. But as the
process of Redemption marches along, the numbers rise steadily. The Jews
of the Soviet Union will, with His help, join their brethren in the Kingdom of
the Almighty.

III. For What Purpose?

The question "Why?," which is the theme of this essay, has several
aspects to it. One can direct the question "Why?" at the cause of an event.
"Why?" would then mean: "What caused you to act in such a manner?" Or it
could be direct at the effect: "To what purpose have you acted in such a
manner?"

Ezekiel prophesied why the Shoah would take place both from the aspect
of the cause and of the effect. Ezekiel proclaimed what would be the
problem in the twentieth century which the Almighty would judge was to be
corrected by the Shoah. And Ezekiel prophesied what would take place after
the Shoah and would correct the problem.

But though the question "Why?" was explained by Ezekiel from these two
aspects, there remains another aspect of "Why?" which may trouble the
witness to the Shoah: Why did the Almighty choose to permit the Shoah to be
the instrument to achieve the desired effect?

In the book of Genesis, the Torah related the event of the Binding of
Isaac, the final and ultimate test of Abraham's readiness to serve the
Almighty. The Lord says to Abraham, "Please take your son, your beloved
son Isaac, and bring him as a burnt offering upon the mountain which I will
show you" [22:2]. Abraham arose in the morning, hurrying to fulfill the Will
of the Almighty with love.

The test of the Binding of Isaac is the ultimate test not only because he was being called upon to sacrifice his beloved son. It was the supreme test because that command seemed to contradict everything that Abraham believed and everything that he was teaching to the world. He believed with all his soul in the Truth of the Almighty and this command seemed to contradict His Truth. For, the Almighty had promised Abraham, "From your son Isaac shall come forth your eternal seed." And here, the young innocent Isaac was being sent to his death by the Almighty.

Abraham dedicated his life to teaching the world that the Almighty, the Creator of heaven and earth, is the God of Compassion Who blesses mankind with goodness and kindness. And behold, Abraham is called upon by the Almighty to perform an act of seeming cruelty.

In the liturgy of Yom Kippur[13], the poet tells the story of the Ten Martyrs, the great classic epic of martyrdom that took place during the days of the Roman Empire about two thousand years ago. And thus says the poet:

> These will I remember, and my soul will pour out. Evil men have swallowed us and eagerly consumed us. In the days of the tyrant there was no reprieve for the ten who were put to death by the Roman government....
> "Give us three days," they said, "so that we may ascertain whether this has been decreed from heaven. If we are condemned to die, we will accept the decree of The One Who is All-Merciful."
> Trembling and shuddering, they turned their eyes to Rabbi Ishmael, the High Priest, and they asked him to pronounce the name of God and ascend to the heavens and learn whether the decree was issued from God.
> Rabbi Ishmael purified himself and pronounced the name of God in awe. He ascended to the heavens, and inquired of the angel robed in linens, who said to him, "Accept the judgment upon yourselves, you beloved and pure, for I have heard from behind the curtain that this is your fate."
> Rabbi Ishmael descended and related to his friends the word of God. Then, the evil man commanded to slay them with force. And two of them were taken first for they were the leaders of Israel, Rabbi Ishmael, the High Priest, and Rabbi Shimon ben Gamliel, the President of Israel....

They did not question the Judgment of the Almighty; they did not complain. They wanted only to know whether "this has been decreed from heaven." If so, they would accept it with love. Or was their fate still hanging in the balance in Judgment before the Almighty. If that were so, they would pray and beseech the Almighty for compassion. Rabbi Ishmael ascended to the heavens. He was told that the decree from Heaven was sealed. He went down to the earth and informed his colleagues. They accepted their fate. They trusted in the Perfect Judgment of the Almighty and no questions left their lips.

But the Torah tells us that Moshe[14] did ask "Why?" Let us proceed to examine the question of Moshe, what he asked, and why he asked it.

The Torah tells us of the following events that took place before the Exodus, and the ensuing dialogue between the Almighty and Moshe.

The Almighty heard the cries of the people of Israel and decided to take them out of their bondage. He called on Moshe and told him to go to Pharaoh and tell him that the God of Israel said to let His people go into the desert and celebrate a holiday in HIs Name. Pharaoh refused the request, saying to Moshe that the children of Israel want to sacrifice to their God because they are lazy. He thereupon ordered that their work be increased. He commanded that they no longer given the straw to make the bricks and that they should themselves have to gather all the necessary quantities of straw. But the number of bricks that they had to provide each day would be maintained. When the Israelites could not meet that order, they were beaten by the slave masters who shouted, "Why did you not complete your quota of bricks as you did yesterday and the day before?"

When Moshe saw what had resulted from his mission he said to me:
"Why have You done harm to this people? Why have You sent me? From the time that I came to Pharaoh to speak in Your Name, he has dealt harshly with this people, and You have not saved them."

In the sentence quoted, the Hebrew word for the question "Why" differs. In the first sentence, the word is madua. In the other sentence, it is lamah. Targum Onkelos[15] translates each of them differently. In the earlier sentence, "Why did you not complete your quota of bricks?" Onkelos translates madua as mah dein, meaning "What is this?" In the sentence "Why did You do harm to this people?" Onkelos translated lamah, why, as l'mah dein, which means "to what is this?"

There is a clear distinction between these two question.

Mah dein, meaning "what is this," is aimed at the act. What is the explanation of the act?

It may question the cause, or the justification, or it may be a request for clarification. The word for this question is madua.

L'mah dein means "to what is this." The question is directed at the effect. To what effect was this act done?

The word for the question of Moshe is lamah. Moshe, the leader of Israel, had the duty to pray for his people. He therefore need to know the effect that the Judgment of the Almighty would have upon the people so that he could pray to have it changed. Thus, when the Almighty sent him to Pharaoh to send the people of Israel out of Egypt and instead of sending them out Pharaoh intensified the slavery, Moshe complained to the Almighty and asked, "Why did You do harm to this people? Why did You send me?"

Moshe asked of the Almighty "What is the effect that You intended to happen when You sent me? Was it not to save the people?" Moshe did not question the wisdom and justice of the Judgment. Rather, he beseeched the Almighty to bring another effect to His people and bring to them an immediate salvation.

The history of the Shoah is the history of the Binding of Isaac repeated six million times. Six million martyrs died, not with complaints, not with questions, but with love and faith. They recited Sh'ma Yisrael, "Hear O Israel, The Lord our G-d, the Lord is one." They died proudly proclaiming their love for their Father, the King of the Universe. And they died singing Ani Maamin, "I believe with perfect trust in the Faith and Promise of the Almighty."

Leaders of Israel were like unto Moshe, speaking of the effect that they knew would come from the death of the martyrs. So did the holy Rabbi Elchanan Wasserman who spoke to the Jews of Kovno as they were ready to march to their deaths. He said to the assembled prisoners:

> We are now fulfilling the greatest commandment, to sanctify His Name. The fire which will consume our bones is the fire that will give birth again to the Jewish nation.

We have said that the question lamah is aimed at understanding the effect of an action. The question madua is aimed at understanding the action.

When one asks "Why did the Almighty choose to permit the Shoah to be instrument of the desired effect?" one questions the wisdom of the action. The question asked of the Almighty is madua, and this question the Torah does not ask nor answer. When Moshe was confronted by an Act of the Almighty which he sought to understand, he did not ask madua. He asked only lamah. He did not question the act. He questioned only the effect.

The following comment by the classic Talmudic commentator Maharsha[16] in the section Brachot[17] will help us understand why Moshe limited his questioning of the Almighty to the effect.

The Talmud states that when the Almighty appeared to him in the Burning Bush, Moshe did three things for which he received three corresponding blessings. The Torah says, "And Moshe hid his face for he feared to gaze at the Almighty." He "hid his face" and "he feared" and "he did not gaze at the Almighty."

The Maharsha explains the three meritorious qualities of Moshe evident in that passage. He writes that a human being hesitates to come close to the Almighty for three reasons. One, he has an instinctive rever-ence for One so Great and Awesome and does not step forward to stand close to Him. Secondly, he recognizes the limitations of man and hesitates to analyze the concepts of the Almighty lest he err. And third, he understands the infinite nature of the affairs of the Almighty, and knows that man cannot truly understand them.

At the Burning Bush, "he averted his eyes," meaning "he did not delve into the Ways of the Almighty," for he "feared" his own inadequacy and "he did not gaze at the Almighty" for he realized the infinite nature of the Ways of the Almighty.

The Torah is a "Book of Life," a guide to the human being. It teaches him how he should conduct himself for the peace of his body and soul. It teaches man the qualities of the Almighty so that he should emulate them in his conduct.

But, it does not teach man to judge the affairs of the Almighty. In the Sh'moneh Esray[18], recited on the Day of Judgment, we proclaim the Almighty as "the King of the Judgment," meaning "the Only King of all Judgment." The Almighty has relegated the judgment of the world to Himself.

We are consoled with the knowledge that the 6,000,000 martyrs have taken their places in the presence of the Almighty in Heaven. We praise Him and thank Him for the blessings which came to the Jewish people after the Shoah. We sanctify Him for His Judgment of Truth, for He is the True Judge. We pray that we, and all His people, be blessed with His favor of peace forever..

For Richard Rubenstein, whose book After Auschwitz: Radical Theology and Contemporary Judaism[1], may correctly be understood as the harbinger of the "second phase" of Shoah studies, as Professor Haas correctly notes-- that of thinking about the Shoah--his essay, like that of Fackenheim, is a "summing up" of more than two decades of reflecting on the theological enormity of the Shoah. Many of the themes which have occupied him in his writings over the years are likewise found here: the essential modernity of the Shoah building upon the past; concern with "superfluous populations" as existing "outside the universe of moral obligation;" parallel phenomena to the Shoah existing in other cultures, notably the Austrialian; and what, for him, may be in fact the most pro-foundly religious question of all: "Who is to have a voice in the political community?"[2]

APOCALYPTIC RATIONALITY AND THE SHOAH[3]

[c] Richard L. Rubenstein

I. The Modernity of the Shoah

From the time of the National Socialist seizure of power, liberal think-ers in the West, imbued with the spirit of the Enlightenment, have tended to view both Nazism and its most characteristic expression, the Shoah, as anti-modern and irrational in its hatred, paranoia and quest for volkisch homoge-neity.[4] While there can be no doubt about its hatred, paranoia or aims, the Shoah was a thoroughly modern event in both its method of implementation and in the "problem" it sought to "solve." The Shoah was also an apocalyptic event. Far from being an aberration, regression from, or rejection of modern Western civilization, the Shoah was in reality an expression of some of its most significant demographic, economic, political, moral and religious tendencies.[5] The Greek word apocalypsis means "an uncovering." In ancient times, apocalyptic characterized a movement within Judaism and early Christianity which claimed that God had revealed secrets of the imminent end of the world.[6] The Shoah's ultimate objective was to bring the entire Jewish world to an end; as we know, it succeeded in utterly destroy-ing Eastern European Judaism. Unlike the ancients, today's Jews, whether in Israel or the Diaspora, do not await an imminent cataclysm. We stand in its terrible shadow. Moreover, if history is any teacher, were Jews faced with yet another apocalypse, such as the destruction of the State of Israel, many governments, both East and West, would in all likelihood regard the event as a convenient excuse in problem solving.

The modernity of the Shoah is best understood when the elements of continuity linking that event to other instances of catastrophic misfortune in the modern period are understood. It is, however, important to stress that the uniqueness of the Shoah is by no means diminished when it is viewed in historical context. No matter what continuities can be discerned between the Shoah and other destructive events, there is one way in which it is absolutely unique. In no other twentieth-century instance of mass extermination has the fate of the victims been so profoundly linked to the religio-mythic in-heritance of the perpetrators, whether we look to Christianity or to National Socialist neo-paganism. For German neo-paganism, the Jews were the Wiedergeist, the counter-power that must be exterminated root and branch. For Christianity, the inherited religion of the perpetrators, the Jews, alone among the twentieth century's victims of mass murder, have been depicted as the God-bearing and the God-murdering people par excellence. No other religion is thus portrayed in the classic literature of a rival tradition. Moreover, starting with the fall of Jerusalem in 70 C.E., Christianity has taken the disasters of the Jewish people as a principal historical confirmation of its own truth. As we know, Jewish misfortune has been interpreted in the classical Christian sources to be God's punishment of a sinful and deicidal Israel. The practical consequence of this view has been to facilitate the exclusion of Jews from a common universe of moral obligation with the Christians among whom they were domiciled. In times of acute political and social stress, this view has had the effect of decriminalizing any assault, no matter how obscene, visited upon them, as Hitler and the leading National Socialists fully understood. The implementation of the Shoah was greatly facilitated by the deicidal and demonological interpretation of the Jewish people in the Christian religious imagination.

If we wish to comprehend the Shoah as a phenomenon of modernization, we must keep in mind the question, "Why did it happen in the twentieth century and not before, given the radical demonization of the Jews and their powerlessness within Christendom?" Moreover, our inquiry must commence with the beginnings of the modernization process in England, the world's first country to undergo the wrenching dislocation of the "great transformation."[7] Those beginnings are to be found in the acts of Enclosure of the Tudor and Stuart periods which transformed the agrarian subsistence economy of pre-modern England into the depersonalized market economy of the modern era. In the process, the customary rights to land usage of the economically unproductive English peasant class were abrogated and that class was largely transformed into a congery of dispossessed individuals whose survival was dependent upon their ability to find wage labor. Many turned to vagabondage or outright crime. A tragic social by-product of the beginnings of England's modernization was the creation of a large class of people who were superfluous to the new economic system.

The acts of Enclosure can be understood as the first modern, state-sponsored program of population elimination. The Shoah was, of course, the most radical such program. All such schemes share a common objective, the elimination of a target population from its habitual place of domicile. They differ, however, in their methods of implementation which range from dispossession, to encouragement of immigration, to outright expulsion, and finally to outright extermination. In the case of the Enclo-sures, a large portion of England's peasant population was no longer needed or wanted where they and their ancestors had lived and worked for centuries. The decision was taken to remove them from their place of habitation. Little or no thought was given to what was to become of them.

A class of more or less permanently superfluous people is a potential source of acute social instability and is more likely to be the object of fear than compassion. Having no hope of receiving society's normal rewards, such a class has little incentive, save fear of punishment, to abide by society's customary behavioral constraints. Even if such a group is tied to the rest of the population by common ethnicity and religion, it is likely to be perceived and to perceive itself as having been cast outside of society's universe of moral obligation. A measure of self-sacrificing altruism rather than self-regarding egoism will normally characterize the behavior of members of such a universe towards each other. At a minimum, members will not normally regard other members as potential sources of injury or even personal destruction. To the extent that trust is possible between human beings, the actors within a shared universe of moral obligation are more likely to trust each other than those whom they regard as alien. Such attitudes have less to do with the moral virtuosity of individuals than with the way social relations are structured.

As England modernized, it was confronted with a growing shortage of food and a growing surplus of men. As early as 1597 England passed "An Acte for Punyshment of Rogues, Vagabonds and Sturdy Beggars" [39 Eliz. c. 4] which provided that such "Rogues....be banished out of this Realm....and shall be conveyed to such parts beyond the seas as shall be assigned by the Privy Council." If a banished "rogue" returned to England without permission, he or she would be hanged. In 1717 a new act [4 Geo. I, c. II] provided that the sentences of offenders subject to branding or flogging could be commuted to transportation to America for seven years while capital offenders who were recipients of "the King's Mercy" could be transported for fourteen years. The "rogues" and vagabonds trans-ported overseas were very largely displaced peasants, or their descendants, who had been rendered both redundant and desperate by the acts of Enclosure. Between 1717 and 1776, some 30,000 people from Great Britain and 10,000 from Ireland were transported overseas compelled to work at jobs no free settler would accept.[8]

II. The Case of Australia and Beyond

The American Revolution crated a crisis for England's transportation system. England could no longer use that country as its dumping grounds for its unwanted human beings. In 1788, five years after the signing of the treaty of peace between England and the United States, the first group of 736 men and women convicts were transported from England to Botany Bay, Australia.

According to Professor Tony Barta of La Trobe University, Melbourne, Australia, the basic fact of Australia's history has been the conquest of the country by one people and the dispossession "with ruthless destructiveness" of another people, the Aborigines, those who were there ab origine.[9] While it was by no means the initial intention of the British government to destroy the Aborigines, Barta contends that Australia is a "nation founded on genocide" which was the inevitable, though unintended, consequence of the European colonization. Far from being a consequence of the actions of isolated men acting out their aggressions on a lawless and distant frontier, the destruction of Australia's Aboriginal population was very largely the projected outcome of modernizing transformations in the mother country.

Neither North America nor Australia were unsettled territories when white settlers arrived. In the case of Australia, the aboriginal people had developed a viable human ecology which was altogether incomprehensible to the settlers. Moreover, sheep raising and the settlers' rationalized and desacralized agrarian economy were incompatible with Aborigine land use which was deeply rooted in the Aborigines' sacred cosmos. Since both sides were unconditionally dependent upon the land, each in its own way, loss of the land necessarily entailed the complete destruction of the de-feated way of life. Coexistence was impossible.

The issue was decided, as it almost always is, by superior arms and power. With their survival at stake, the Aborigines had no choice but to resist. As in North America, the predictable settler response was to root out the menace. There were bloody massacres. There were also government-sponsored attempts to diminish settler violence, but even without overt violence the Aborigines were destined to perish. Deprived of a meaningful future, most of the Aborigines who survived white aggression "faded away." Between 1839 and 1849 there were only twenty births recorded among the seven aboriginal tribes around Melbourne. Barta concludes that, whatever the official British intent, the encounter between the white settlers and the Blacks was one of living out a relationship of genocide that was structured into the very nature of the encounter.

The basic colonizing pattern described by Barta, namely, white settlement, native resistance, violent settler victory, and, finally, the disappearance of most if not all of the natives, was played out in North and South America as well.[10] If Australian society was built upon a genocidal relationship with that of the indigenous cultures, so too was American society. There was a time not so long ago when it was taken for granted that "the only good Indian was a dead Indian."

Barta distinguishes between a genocidal society and a genocidal state. National Socialist Germany was a genocidal state. The latter's genocidal project was deliberate and intended. Settler Australia was a genocidal society. It had no genocidal project. Nevertheless, its very existence had genocidal consequences for the original population. The basic pattern of the colonization of Australia was everywhere the same. It consisted of white pastoral invasion, Black resistance, violent victory of the whites, and finally the mysterious disappearance of the Blacks.

Although Barta confines his description to Australia, the process he describes was repeated in other European colonial settlements. In his biography of Oliver Cromwell [1599-1658], the English historian Christopher Hill comments,

> A great many civilized Englishmen of the propertied class in the seventeenth century spoke of Irishmen in tones not far removed from those which the Nazis used about the Slavs, or white South Africans use about the original inhabitants of their country. In each case the contempt rationalized a desire to exploit.[11]

What Hill could have added was the Cromwell was fully prepared to exterminate those Irish Catholics who resisted exploitation and refused to turn their lands over to Protestant colonizers. When the towns of Drog-he-da and Wexford refused to surrender to Cromwell in 1649, they were sacked and those inhabitants unable to flee were massacred. In the case of Wexford, after all the inhabitants had been killed, Cromwell reported that the town was available for colonization by English settlers. An English clergyman commended the place for settlement: "It is a fine spot for some godly congregation where house and land wait for inhabitants and occupiers."[12] Even in the seventeenth century, it was clear to England's leaders that the more Ireland was cleared of its original Catholic inhabitants the more available it would be for Protestant English settlement.

The extremes to which England was prepared to go to empty Ireland of its original inhabitants became clear during the famine years of 1846-48. It is estimated that within the period the population of Ireland was reduced by about 2,500,000 out of an estimated 1845 population of 9,000,000. Approximately 1,250,000 perished in the famine. About the same number were compelled to emigrate in order to survive.[13]

The famine relief given by the English government to the Irish, who were technically speaking British subjects at the time, was deliberately kept at levels guaranteed to produce the demographic result it did. Moreover, the deaths by famine and the removal by emigration were welcomed by leading members of England's society and government as doing for Ireland what the Enclosure had done for England: The land had been cleared of uneconomic subsistence producers and made available for rationalized agricultural enterprise.[14] The candor of an 1853 editorial in The Economist on the benefits of the elimination of redundant Irish and Scots is instructive:

> It is consequent on the breaking down of the system of society founded on small holdings and potato cultivation....The departure of the redundant part of the population of Ireland and Scotland is an indispensable preliminary to every kind of improvement. [Underline added.][15]

Unfortunately, the "departure" entailed mass death by famine and disease for a very significant proportion of Ireland's peasant class. In the eyes of the British decision-making class of the period, Catholic Ireland was an inferior civilization with a primitive, superstitious religion.[16]   An upper class that was indifferent to the fate of its own peasants was hardly likely to be concerned with that of the Irish.

Just as the rationalization of the English economy from the sixteenth to the twentieth century resulted in the rise of both surplus people and experiments aimed at their elimination, so too the nineteenth-century rationalization of the German economy had a comparable result.   Germany's predicament was succinctly summarized in 1891 by Bismarck's successor as Chancellor of the Reich, Leo von Caprivi, who declared: "Germany must export either goods or people."[17]   Hitler, however, was determined that the people who left the Reich would not be Germans. He sought to solve what he regarded as Germany's "population problem" through his Lebensraum program. He was determined that there would be no surplus German population even if Europe's Jewish population and a significant portion of Germany's Slavic neighbors were exterminated to provide the "living space" for German settlers. Hitler proposed to repeat in Europe, albeit with infinitely intensified viciousness, the exploitative colonialism practiced by other Europeans overseas. They were to be displaced, uprooted, enslaved and, if necessary, annihilated, to make way for Germany's surplus population.

Unlike the earlier European colonizers, Hitler had no illusions concerning the genocidal nature of such an undertaking. He had the historical precedents of earlier European efforts at colonization and imperial domination. He regarded the defeat of native cultures by white settlers and colonists as evidence of the truth of his version of Social Darwinism. As is well known, the same Social Darwinism became an important component in the legitimating ideology for the extermination of Europe's Jews during World War II. In Hitler's eyes, the Jews were the most contemptible of all of the inferior races destined by fate and German strength for destruction.

Unlike the destruction of the Australian Aborigines, the extermination of the Jews was fully intended. Nevertheless, the behavior of the English in Ireland and Australia, as well as that of other Europeans in the New World, shows that the destruction of the indigenous population never constituted a reason for calling colonial and imperial ventures to a halt. Nor ought the difference between intended and unintended extermination obscure the fact that both were attempts at population riddance aimed at solving a similar problem, the relatively humane elimination from the mother country of a sector of its own population rendered redundant or threatened with redundancy by the rationalization of the economy. The very success of the earlier experiments in population-elimination invited their repetition. One's own surplus population problem was to be solved by a combination of emigration, colonization and expulsion. Those who inhabited the lands selected as dumping grounds were threatened by an infinitely harsher fate.

Nor ought we to forget the millions of Europeans considered expendable by their own governments during World War I. The modernization of hygiene and medicine permitted an unprecedented number of Europeans to survive to young adulthood; the modernization and industrialization of military technology made possible their slaughter by the millions in battles such as Verdun, the Second Battle of the Somme and Gallipoli. Can anyone believe that governments that permitted the killing on so monumental a scale of their own men would be disturbed by the elimination of people for whom they felt neither moral nor political responsibility? There is thus historical continuity between the unintended genocides of Europe's demo-graphic projection beyond its original territorial limits, Europe's auto-cannibalization during World War I, and the Shoah.

Some may object that, at least in Western Europe before World War II, the Jews were not a surplus population. True enough, but they were a surplus people in the East, as is evident by the massive emigration of Eastern European Jews westward after 1881. Moreover, the Jews of the West occupied slots which surplus members of the majority were prepared to take from them. The question, Who is to have a voice in the political order? is fundamental to the decision to initiate a state-sponsored program of population elimination. That decision is in turn related to the question of the universe of moral obligation. In ancient Greece, members of the polis [city-state--Ed.] belonged to a common universe of obligation. This was especially evident in war. Only those who shared common origins belonged by inherited right to the same community, and saw themselves as partaking of a common fate could be trusted in a life-and-death struggle with their community's enemies. Neither the slave nor the stranger could be so trusted. Hence, they were regarded as outside of the shared universe of obligation.

A very grave problem arises when, for any reason, a community regards itself as having within its midst a group who are perceived, rightly or wrongly, to be untrustworthy. The problem is urgent in wartime. It is even more urgent when a community has experienced a humiliating national defeat. The perception of disloyalty may be mistaken, as was the case with Germany's Jews in World War I and Japanese-Americans during World War II. Nevertheless, the majority's perceptions are politically decisive.

Sometimes the issue of a voice in the political community takes on a class rather than an ethnic dimension. When Kampuchea fell to the Pol Pot regime in 1975, the victors had a very clear idea of the kind of agrarian communist society they proposed to establish. They regarded Kampuchea's entire urban population as objectively hostile to the creation of the new political order. This perception was consistent with the Marxist idea that the bourgeois class is destined to disappear with the coming of true socialism. Not content to let this process take its course non-violently, the regime determined upon the immediate elimination of all who were regarded as either incapable of fitting into the new system or of being objectively

committed to its destruction.[18]   In the aftermath of the Russian Revolution, a
very similar logic compelled the departure from the Soviet Union of millions
of "objective enemies" of the new system.   Similarly, the Cuban revolution
resulted in the enforced emigration of over a million Cubans who would not
fit into Castro's system, primarily to the State of Florida.

The question, "Who is to have a voice in the political community?" was
absolutely decisive for National Socialism.   It was also important for the
Vichy government of Marshal Henri Phillippe Petain.   The antisemitic Statut
des Juifs of 3 October 1940 required no encouragement from the Germans.[19]
The political emancipation of the Jews in Europe in the late eighteenth and
nineteenth centuries gave to the Jews a voice in the political communities in
which they were domiciled.   With the sad wisdom of hindsight, the extermination of the Jews can be seen as in part an unintended consequence of
their emancipation.   Emancipation made membership of the Jews in Europe's
political communities both a fact and a political issue for the first time.
Emancipation was opposed by those who believed such membership should be
restricted to Christians.   It was, as we know, also opposed by those who
sought to restrict membership to those who regarded themselves as bound
together by ties of blood.   An important reason why so little was done to
assist the Jews during World War II, both in Germany and throughout
occupied Europe, was the almost universal European acceptance of the
National Socialist objective of excluding the Jews from membership in the
political communities in which they were domiciled.   This was certainly true
of most mainstream Protestant and Catholic churches, which tended to
regard the denial of political rights to the Jews as a beneficial step toward
the creation of a Europe that was culturally, intellectually and political
Christian.[20]   The fundamental difference between Hitler and the churches
was that Hitler had no illusions concerning the extreme measures necessary
to implement such a program.   The churches never faced openly the question
of implementation.   Having no direct responsibility for carrying out the
process of elimination, they preferred to leave the question of implementation to others.   In any event, it is now clear that early National Socialist calls
for elimination of the Jews from membership in the body politic was in fact
a demand for their extermination.

III. Middleman-Minority

An important economic aspect of antisemitic hostility was the fact that
Europe's Jews were largely a middleman-minority.[21]   Sociologist Walter P.
Zenner has observed that, under certain circumstances, middleman-minority
status can be a precondition for genocide.   Like the Jews, the Armenians
were also a middleman-minority.   In the aftermath of the war in Vietnam,
yet another middleman-minority, the Hoa or ethnic Chinese of Vietnam, were
the object of a large-scale, state-sponsored program of population elimination.[22]   Middleman-minorities are usually permitted domicile in a community
in order to do work that, for some reason, is not being done by the in-

digenous population. Their presence as strangers is tolerated because they constitute an <u>economically</u> or <u>vocationally</u> <u>complimentary</u> population. They are most like to be targeted for elimination when their roles can be filled either by the state or by members of the indigenous population. When this development takes place, the minority members become competitors of the majority. Usually, they compete against one of the most dangerous and potentially unstable groups within the larger population, the majority middle class.

In pre-modern societies it was not socially or economically functional for middleman-minorities to share a common religion with the majority. The objective, impersonal attitudes necessary for successful commerce were less likely to develop between people who considered themselves to be kin worshipping the same god. The flow of commerce often depended upon a depersonalized in-group, out-group double standard. With the rise of Protestantism the personalized ethics of tribal brotherhood gave way to the modern, depersonalized attitude of universal otherhood. It was then possible for a universal money economy to come into being.[23]

As an economy modernizes, the situation of middleman-minorities tends to become increasingly precarious. Thus, the condition of Europe's Jews became progressively more difficult as the economies of Western and Eastern Europe were modernized.[24] As the agriculture of Eastern Europe was progressively rationalized during the second half of the nine-teenth century, large numbers of Polish and Russian peasants were dispossessed of their holdings and forced to seek scarce wage labor in the towns and cities of Eastern Europe and later Western Europe and America. The peasants' predicament was further aggravated by yet another aspect of modernization: improved medicine and hygiene which yielded an unprecedented rate of population increase. Desperate for any kind of work under conditions of mass unemployment and underemployment, newly urbanized members of the former peasant class began to compete with the Jews for wage labor and those middleman-minority slots which had previously been predominantly Jewish. In seeking to displace the Jews, the dispossessed peasants and their urbanized offspring had the support of the Tsarist government, which, after the <u>pogroms</u> [riots--Ed.] of 1881 and the May Laws of 1882, made the Jews the target of one of the most highly successful state-sponsored programs of population elimination in all history. Moreover, the beginnings of political antisemitism in Austria and Germany coincide with the beginnings of the westward emigration of Eastern Europe's Jews. From 1881 to 1917, the fundamental objective of the Tsarist government vis-a-vis the Jews differed little from that of the National Socialist regime in Germany. Both sought the elimination of the Jews as a demographic presence in the areas under their control. Most American Jews are alive today because the two regimes did not share a common method of implementation.

Many of the peasants and artisans from Germany and Eastern Europe responded to the demographic crisis by emigrating to the New World. By so doing they unintentionally intensified resentment at those Jews who remained in Europe. Even as a young man in Vienna, Hitler was keenly interested in the problem of emigration. One of the books in Hitler's library whose marginal notes attest to the young Hitler's strong interest was Aus-wanderungs-Moglichkeiten in Argentinien.[25] In Mein Kampf Hitler wrote of the need for land to the east to absorb Germany's population surplus. He came to regard emigration as a poor solution for the emigrant was lost to the Fatherland as a human resource. As we know, his solution was conquest, colonization to the east, and extermination.

IV. The Importance of Military Defeat

Frequently, programs of genocide such as the Shoah are initiated in the aftermath of military defeat, especially under the devastating conditions of modern warfare.[26] An important element in the decision of the Young Turk regime to initiate the program of extermination against its Armenian Christian minority was Turkey's defeat by Bulgaria in 1912. Similarly, Germany's defeat in World War I created the conditions in which a radically antisemitic, revolutionary, revisionist National Socialist movement could come to dominate German politics. As a consequence of defeat, the fringe became the center. In addition to the role of a defenseless minority as surrogate object of revenge for the victorious enemy, military defeat can intensify the urgency with which the question of membership in the community is posed. Who can doubt that France's defeat in 1870 contributed to the atmosphere that made the Dreyfus affair possible? As noted, a fundamental issue in population elimination programs is the question of who can be trusted in a life-and-death struggle. All minorities suffer some discrimination and experience some degree of resentment and incomplete identification with the majority, a situation which is as obvious to the majority as to the minority. In normal times, such tensions can be held in check. In the aftermath of catastrophic military defeat, they can get out of hand. Aggressive energies can achieve cheap victories over a defenseless minority. The reality of defeat itself can be denied and responsibility for the misfortunes of war ascribed to the minority's hidden "stab in the back." The accusation of secret treachery can legitimate genocide against the minority. If such a group is perceived as bringing about national catastrophe, while appearing to be loyal, it can become a matter of the greatest public urgency to eliminate them from the body politic.

Almost from the moment Germany lost World War I, the Jews were accused of being about her defeat through treachery, an accusation that appeared ludicrous in view of the extremely high proportion of German Jews who had served as front-line soldiers and who had made the ultimate sacrifice for what they regarded as their Fatherland.

Elsewhere, this writer has argued that the tradition of Judas betraying Jesus with a token of love, a kiss, provided an enormously potent religio-mythic identification of the Jew with betrayal in the minds of Christians.[27]   A similar identification was influential in the Dreyfus affair. Commenting on Captain Dreyfus' conduct on the occasion of his public degradation on 4 January 1885, the antisemitic newspaper, La Croix, declared, "His cry of 'Vive la France!' was the kiss of Judas Iscariot."[28] Since the identification of the Jew with Judas takes place in earliest childhood and is constantly reinforced by religious tradition, it is more deeply rooted and less subject to rational criticism than beliefs acquired at a later stage in the life cycle. When Hitler and the German right ascribed Germany's defeat to the Jews, they had working for them this immensely powerful, pre-theological archetype. Here, too, we discern a unique religio-mythic element that sets the Shoah apart from other instances of genocide in our times.

V. The Rationality of the Shoah

Given the presence of religio-mythic elements in the Shoah, it is not surprising that many scholars have argued that the Shoah was irrational in its objective if not in its methods. By contrast, this writer has argued against Lucy Dawidowicz and others that the Shoah was, in a nightmarish way, rational in both its objective and its methods.[29] In contrast to spontaneous outbursts of inter-group hatred and violence, modern, systematic, bureaucratically administered genocide can be understood as a form of instrumentally rational [zeeckrational] action in contrast to value-rational [wertrational] action. Max Weber, to whom we are indebted for this distinction, has observed that instrumental rationality is a matter of ends.[30] Above all, it is important not to confuse humane action and instrumentally rational action. The experience of our era should leave no doubt concerning the enormous potential for inhumanity present in morally autonomous instrumental rationality. The perfection of this mode of political and social action is indeed one of the most problematic aspects of both the legacy of the Enlightenment and the modernization process.

The idea that the Shoah could in any sense be regarded as rational has been rejected by Marxist scholar Ronald Aronson. In his book, The Dialectics of Disaster, Aronson argues that the Shoah systematically outraged the norms of the "normal world."[31] He insists that it was a product of madness, which he defines as a systematic derangement of perception, a seeing what is not there. The National Socialists saw the Jews as the source of Germany's problems and regarded their riddance as a major element in the solution. Aronson argues that when rulers organize a society against false enemies and falsely propagate the view that society is mortally threatened by them, we may speak of madness as much as when a paranoid individual behaves in a similar delusionary manner. Aronson insists that the Nazi attempt wholly to eliminate the Jews as a demographic presence first in

Germany and then in all of Europe was insane because the Jews in no way constituted the threat the National Socialists alleged them to be.

Aronson fails to deal with the underlying reason why the question of "Who shall have a voice in the community?" is raised in the first place. As noted, genocide is a violent means of determining who is to have a voice in a community whose members may have to sacrifice their lives in a life-and-death struggle with external enemies in a crisis. When a group regards itself as secure, it can afford to take a relatively benign view of the presence of a limited number of strangers in its midst. However, in times of acute national stress, such as economic dislocation, modern warfare or military defeat, insiders are likely to view outsiders with intensified suspicion and hostility. Even in relatively tranquil times, the growing presence of those regarded as strangers can be destabilizing. In the case of middleman-minority groups specializing in commerce, insiders may suspect that the outsiders' love of gain will outweigh their loyalty to the homeland. Moreover, when minority intellectuals acquire the ability effectively to communicate in the language of the majority, they can become the object of resentment and hostility. In an extreme situation, leaders of the majority may decide upon the total elimination of the outsiders.

Contrary to Aronson, the patent untruth of National Socialist defa-mations is irrelevant to the critical fact that the overwhelming majority of Germans regarded even the most assimilated Jews as aliens whose elimination would be a positive benefit to the nation. The Germans wanted the volkisch homogeneity Hitler promised them. When it was all over, many regretted the method of implementation employed by their government but not the fact that Europe was largely empty of Jews.

Unfortunately, one cannot even say that it is irrational to want an ethnically or religiously homogenous community consisting of those with whom one shares a sense of common faith, values, kinship and trust. After all, that has been an important element in the establishment of the State of Israel. Admittedly, in the urbanized sections of much of the modern world, pluralism is a given. Nevertheless, there is nothing irrational about the desire for a community of moral trust and mutual obligation. An important reason for the astounding success of contemporary Japan has been its ethnic homogeneity. It is not the irrationality of non-pluralistic communities that is the problem, but the extreme cruelty and inhumanity which must be practiced by the modern state in order to transform a pluralistic, multi-ethnic or multi-religious political entity into a homogenous community. Hitler's program of genocide was not irrational in the sense of Zweckrationalitat [instrumental rationality]. It was ob-scenely cruel.

VI. The Role of the Modern State

Finally, we must consider the issue of the modern state, national sovereignty and genocide, an issue which has become ever more urgent with the attainment of sovereignty by so many of the peoples of the world. With the radical secularization of politics in modern times, there is no longer any credible or effective higher authority that the state. In spite of its persistent, one-sided, even obscene hostility to the State of Israel, the United Nations has been singularly indifferent to mass murder and genocide when practiced by favored member nations against their own citizens. The genocidal Pol Pot regime remains the officially recognized government of Kampuchea in the United Nations.[32]   States have accepted limitations upon their actions with regard to those reckoned as possessing a legitimate voice in the nation's political affairs. The problem arises with those who have been deliberately cast outside of the social contract. It is an unfortunate fact that such men and women can be rendered utterly rightless when confronted with a ruthless state apparatus. As long as the leaders of National Socialist Germany were free to exercise sovereignty, no superordinate system of norms constituted any kind of restraint on their behavior. In reality, absent a communal consensus on belief in God and an unconditional willingness to abide by Divine Law, there are only political rights. Human rights exist only insofar as they are guaranteed by a political community with the power to enforce its guarantee. That is why the question, "Who is to have a voice in the political community?" is today one of the most important human questions. Citizenship in a sovereign political community is no absolute guarantee of safety. Nevertheless, to the extent that men and women have any rights whatsoever, it is as members of a political community with the power to guarantee those rights. It is the dolorous fact that made the State of Israel a political imperative in the aftermath of the Shoah. Genocide is the ultimate expression of absolute rightlessness.

Thus, the Shoah cannot be understood apart from the distinctive conditions and culture we identify as modernity. The Shoah was thoroughly modern both in the "problem" it attempted to "solve" and in its value-neutral, rational, bureaucratic methods of implementation.

Let us conclude with a few observations on the Jewish situation in the face of modernity and the apocalypse. The philosopher-theologian, Emil L. Fackenheim, has taught us that the Jewish people has experienced both "root experiences" such as the Exodus and Sinai and "epochmaking events" which challenged the "root experiences" with new and terrible situations.[33]   The "epochmaking events have included the destruction of Jerusalem first by the Babylonians and then by the Romans, and the most radically disorienting epochmaking event, the Holocaust." Rabbi Yohanan ben Zakkai played a crucial role in responding to the "epochmaking event" of the Roman destruction of Jerusalem. Given the choice of resistance unto death on the part of the Jewish people or submission to Caesar, Yohanan chose submission as the only way Torah and Israel could survive. Even Yohanan's theology of history, which God's hand in the churban [destructive devastation--Ed.], made political sense. If the destruction was ultimately due to Israel's sins, then defeat was not the final word. With God's help and mercy, Israel would someday experience a better world.

Nevertheless, Rabbi Yohanan's submission to Caesar made sense only as long as Caesar could be trusted to refrain from using his power to obliterate the Torah and Israel. One of the Shoah's most important lessons is that under conditions of modernity Caesar can no longer be trusted, especially in a time of radical stress. Even Caligula did not have at his disposal the instruments of propaganda and rationalized mass murder available to a modern Caesar. That is why Masada, the name of the other option available to Israel in the aftermath of the ancient Judaeo-Roman War, is once again being uttered with renewed frequency. Let us, how-ever, be mindful of the fact that the Masada option is an apocalyptic strategy which only makes sense if it includes a credible way of radically escalating the cost of killing Jews.

A Masada option can either be a suicidal strategy for an honorable national death or a variant of the Mutually Assured Destruction [MAD] strategy which until recently kept the Superpowers at bay from the time the Soviet Union acquired the capacity for intercontinental delivery of its nuclear weapons. At Masada the Jewish people fought with stones, spears, and swords. Today, there is every likelihood that an apocalyptic threat to Israel's existence will be met with the use of the most modern and the most apocalyptic weapons as a deterrent threat. In the long run, the willingness and the capability to bring on the apocalypse may constitute an important element in Israel chances for survival.

Indeed, it may be possible for us to learn from one who, at least for a time, counted himself among Israel's enemies and who remained stonily indifferent to the apocalypse of the Shoah throughout his life, the German philosopher Martin Heidegger.[34] Heidegger reminds us that "Being-towards-death [Zein zum Tode] belongs primordially and essentially to Dasein's Being."[35] In the aftermath of the our apocalypse, we cannot dismiss the possibility that Zein zum Tode may belong primordially and essentially to Israel as a people. This, of course, was not the view of Heidegger's contemporary, Franz Rosenzweig, who saw Israel as an "eternal people" which "knows nothing of war."[36] In an era when the utter destruction of Israel remains a passionately desired objective of so many in the Middle East and elsewhere, there may be greater wisdom in seeing Jewish existence in apocalyptic terms than with the calm assurance of the indwelling of eternity which permeates Rosenzweig's Denken. He was mercifully spared the apocalypse; we were not.

Half a century after Kristallnacht ["The Night of the Broken Glass," Germany, November 9-10, 1938--Ed.], the situation of world Jewry can be likened to that of the city of Oran as described by Albert Camus at the very end of his novel, La Peste [The Plague--Ed.], when the crowd rejoices at the lifting of the plague. Dr. Rieux, the novel's protagonist, is unable to join in rejoicing that the death-threat to the city has been lifted. He knows better and so should we. We would do well to give heed to his response:

> And, indeed, as he listened to the cries of joy rising from the town, Rieux remembered that such joy is always imperiled. He knew what those jubilant crowds did not know but could never have learned from books; that the plague bacillus never dies or disappears for good; that it can lie dormant for years in furniture and linen-closets; that it bides its time in bedrooms, cellars, trunks, handkerchiefs, and bookshelves; and that perhaps the day would come when, for the bane and the enlightening of men, it would rouse up its rats again and send them forth to die in a happy city.

For Arthur Waskow, critic of so much of contemporary American Jewish society, whose little essay is "midrashic poetry" [i.e. interpretive Scriptural commentary], the analogy between the Biblical text and the Shoah is an obvious one: We are living in the period "between the fires" of Auschwitz and possible thermonuclear conflagration. Unless we learn to affirm life right now through the process of "making Shabbat" [i.e. Sabbath pause], there will be none to affirm any kind of future whatsoever--nor any seed planted for future generations to record what comes next.

BETWEEN THE FIRES

Arthur Waskow

I. Introduction

I am writing during the week of the Torah portion called Lekh L'kha ["Go forth," Genesis 12:1-17:27--Ed.]. In the midst of the portion [Genesis 15] there is the eerie story of how the wandering Abram--not yet Abraham, nor yet our forbearer--experiences the Covenant between the Fires. He has come in spiritual agony, fearful that for him and Sarai there will be no next generation. He places the divided bodies of several sacrificial animals in two rows. They flame up in a "smoking furnace." He stands between the first, and there falls upon a "thick darkness." He slips into a profound trance. In it he becomes a partner in the Covenant of the Generations: he and Sarai will have seed, and they will live in the land bounded by the Jordan and the Sea.

Abram has created a kind of "Shabbat in space." In one direction there is a fire that represents the candles that begin Shabbat; in the other direction, there is a fire that represents the Havdalah candle that ends Shabbat. But what makes the space between these two into a Shabbat-space is that Abram experiences and accepts in it the Dark of Mystery. Shabbat is the emblem and the practice of Mystery. In it we recognize that although we feel sure we know exactly what to do next and feel driven to do it, in fact we do not know what comes next--since there is in life a mysterious element. And so on Shabbat we do nothing, and celebrate the fact of not-knowing with joy, not fear or anger. From our plunge into this Mystery we learn new paths.

Abram lets the mysterious darkness come into himself. He "rests"--not merely pausing, but letting the Mystery absorb him. And so there wells up in him the Covenant that extends through time to future generations. In recognition that this Shabbat is one in space, he receives a promise of a holy space--the Land that is infused with Shabbat.

How does this speak to the meaning of the Holocaust? We are the generation that stands between the fires--behind us the smoke and flame that rose from Auschwitz, before us the nightmare of the flood of fire and smoke that could turn our planet into Auschwitz. We come, like Abram, in an agony of fear that for us--for all of us--there may be no next generation.

Reprinted from Tikkun, Volume 2, Number 1, pages 84-86. Permission grant

an agony of fear that for us--for all of us--there may be no next generation.

II. The Challenge

What will transform the Fire that lies before us? What will turn it into
a light that enlightens rather than a blaze that consumes? What will make
possible for us the covenant of generations yet to come?

The first teaching of this story is to see the Holocaust as both unique and
non-unique: to see its fire reflected in a giant mirror that could dwarf even
its unprecedented horror. To see ourselves living not after the Fire, but
between the Fires. And to see a profound connection between them, not mere
accident.

The second teaching of the story is to make this time between the Fires
into a time of Shabbat: a time of affirming and celebrating Mystery, a time
to pause from the project of modernity and let a new path emerge from the
mysterious darkness.

Let us explore these two teachings in more depth. What does it mean to
experience and connect these two fires?

Both of them flame up from the sparks of modernity. The dark sparks,
struck on the granite face of History by the dark side of modernity. There
are two ways of talking about this: one uses God-language, the other
History-language. Let us start with the second--the one that modern people
are used to--and then to see whether we learn something more from talking
God.

Over the millennia the human race learns, empowers itself. Learns to
organize larger and larger societies, more and more complex patterns.
Learns to make itself, and then reaches a whole new stage--learns that it is
remaking itself. Breaks from the embedded traditions of the past. Decides
that there are no mysteries to be celebrated, only ignorances to be conquered.

The human race creates modernity. Learns the workings of the planets,
the stars, the Galapagos turtles, drosophila, DNA, the proton, the id, the
working class, the historical dialectic. Reunites the two lost supercon-
tinents. Abolishes smallpox. Sets foot on the moon, makes deserts bloom.
Changes the chemistry of the oceans, puts every human voice throughout the
earth in touch with every other, makes five billion people, brings down the
center of the stars to burn and freeze the earth.

And along the way, as a byproduct, it makes possible the Holocaust.
Before modernity, pogroms--but not a Holocaust. Only the social or-

But why was it the Jews who became the target of this runaway modernity?

In the language of modernity, we can say that history put the Jews of Eastern Europe into the most vulnerable position possible when confronting a human race that was drunk on its new-made "modern" power. The Jews were a stateless people. A non-military people. A proto-type people. What is it Elie Wiesel says? That in the face of nuclear annihilation the whole earth is Jewish--like the Jews who faced the Holocaust. Why [say I]? Because now everyone is a stateless person. Every people, even every government, has been disarmed. Because in the face of Plane-tary Auschwitz Camp I [the U.S. nuclear "arsenal"], the Soviet Union has no weapons of defense--only the threat of Planetary Auschwitz Camp II. And vice versa. "To provide for the common defense" is the deadest letter in the American Constitution.

The holy people, the stateless people, the people who had only the Talmud for a Constitution and rabbis for police--they died the soonest. But they point the way for all of us.

We have been talking the language of modernity. I think this language is necessary, but I do not think it is sufficient. If the Holocaust Past and the Holocaust Yet-to-Come are cancers of modernity, then some other language, some language that encompasses and transcends modernity, is necessary. I propose that this language is God-language. But not the old God-language. God in a new key, a new name, a new sensing. For the old God-language was itself transcended, reduced, relativized, by the leap of modernity.

The Hassidic Rebbe of Chernobyl gave us a hint, two hundred years ago. He taught that we must see the world as God veiled in robes of God so as to appear to be material. Alz iz Gott. All is God. Our job is to unwrap the veil to discover that our history is God, our biology is God, our....is God.

In this way of speaking, the Nazi Holocaust and the Bomb are byproducts of the Divinization of the human race.

Even the Holocaust--it is all right to tremble as you read this, for I am trembling as I write it--even the Holocaust was an outburst of light. Those who say we cannot blame God for the Holocaust are only partly right: it was the overflow of God, the outbursting of light, the untrammeled, unboundaried outpouring of Divinity, that gave us Auschwitz....and may yet consume the earth.

Start back, before the Holocaust. Imagine the God Who stood outside the world, but let a spark of Godness flare up in every human being. And over millennia of slow human history, let the spark catch into a glowing coal--

into a sense of God, the Presence, hovering almost among us, almost within us, not quite beyond us.

And then, in the burst of light that is the modern age, the coals burst into flame. Powers once felt to be Divine are now infused into human beings. Powers like the ability to make a revolution [it was God Who made the Exodus from Egypt]. Like the ability to create new species. Like the ability to destroy all species. Flame by flame, the human race in the modern age incorporates into itself the powers that we once called Divine.

And now in this God-language, why the Jews? In this kind of language, the God Who chose us from outside history at Sinai is still choosing us from inside History. We are God's canary-people: the people God sends down the mineshaft first, to test out whether the air breathes ecstasy and revelation or is full of carbon monoxide. If we keel over....
Now God knows, we all know: the air is heavy with poison.

III. Why the Jews?

Why us, how did we get chosen? From inside history--the history that made us the first stateless people is the history that chose us to be the canary-people. No more mysterious than that--but that is plentifully mysterious.

So was the Holocaust inevitable? Were the Nazis God's own arm, in a paroxysm not of punishment--not at all this time "for our sins"--but of untrammeled power striking down its holy victim? Did God forget to put on t'fillin [i.e. phylacteries--Ed.] one morning and the unbound Arm of the Almighty....?

Wait a minute, damn your midrashic poetry, are you saying so many babies and so many bubbes [Grandmothers--Ed.] died because God was coming deeper into the world? How good can such a God be? Very good; but not totally good. Very good, despite and because of the evidence of the Holocaust, because it was the surge of enormous God-power to do good in the world that made it also possible to do such enormous bad in the world. And very good because the teachings from God, about God, teach and taught the human race how to prevent the Holocaust. And very good because the teachings left us free to choose. But not totally good--or we would have used our freedom better.

I do not believe that Auschwitz was inevitable--but the Divine Insurge made it very hard to avoid. I do not believe that the looming Planetary Auschwitz is inevitable, but rather than the Divine Insurge is making it very hard to avoid. Indeed it is a little less hard to avoid because we have already experienced the Nazis. The fact that our canary-people keeled over is one of the weightier rocks that we can roll into the path of the juggernaut. Maybe the most we can hope to gain from Auschwitz is not perfect security for the State of Israel, not the end of anti-Semitism as a Christian dogma, not Mashiach [Messiah--Ed.], but indeed just "never again"--just the minimum, never again.

I do not mean Kahane's "never again the Jews." That one is easy to refrain from doing. Why bother with the Jews again, who needs to prove that one is possible?--But never again, not the whole earth, now that remains to be proved. The Universal Auschwitz, now that is an eternal monument still waiting to be erected by some Super-Hitler who will not even mind that no one will remain to be horrified by his monument. So the warning of "never again?" The warning to the rest of us to prevent such a Super-Hitler, that may remain as the one decently useable product of the Holocaust.

I am not saying that God sent the Holocaust and murdered the Jews in order to warn the planet. I would say, instead, that God and only God made the Holocaust immensely possible; God also made the Holocaust avoidable; we chose. If we can learn from the Holocaust not to destroy the earth, then we could have learned from the murder of Abel not to do the Holocaust.

Why did Abel die? Because the curse of Eden was work-work-work-work until you die. Exhaust yourself. Shabbat comes into the world to reverse the curse of Eden.

What is the teaching? The teaching is to pause. The teaching is to make Shabbat. That teaching is to put a boundary, a loving limit upon the unbridled. God-energy that is bursting its way into the world. As God's Own Self needed to pause after six days of Creation in order to seal the acts of making with a non-act of not-making....so do we.

The modern era, with its works of production, must pause and make Shabbat if the very brilliance of its productivity is not to burn up the earth. It must celebrate Mystery instead of trying to conquer it. Must learn from Mystery that the dark is light enough--is joy, not frightening.

Why is the celebration of Mystery crucial? It is not that Super-Hitler will necessarily come as Hitler came, with full deadly, murderous intention. The idolatry of death may come this time not with deliberate intention, but by putting into a place a potentially lethal system--and then insisting that we can keep it totally under control. No mistakes, never a mistake. All is known, all is controlled. The total rejection of Mystery.

We, the human race, have painted an extraordinary picture. The picture was completed, but we kept on painting. Hiroshima was a brush-stroke too many. The Holocaust was a dozen, a human brush-strokes too many. The painting is marred. It is on the verge of ruination. We must stop our painting, take it off the easel. We must recognize that <u>we do not know</u> what to do next, we must celebrate that mystery, stop doing, make Shabbat, and fine a new clean canvas. Then we will hear the new teaching from within us; we will uncover what to do.

We are the generation that stands between the fires. <u>If we see this</u>, we can make where we stand into a Shabbat. We can, like Abram, receive the Covenant of the Generations--that there <u>will be</u> future generations, despite our deep dread that it will end with us. And our future generations--those of all humanity--will get to live in the land that lies between the rivers and the oceans of space: all earth.

If we do <u>not</u> see the two fires in relation to each other, then the fire behind us will lose all meaning, and the one that is yet to come will consume us.

Between the fires is the place of thick darkness, of impenetrable mystery. Will we celebrate this Mystery and live, or scorn it and die?

NOTES

INTRODUCTION:

WHY THIS BOOK?

Steven L. Jacobs

1. For a thorough analysis and discussion of the importance of "Shoah vs. Holocaust" terminology, see Zev Garber and Bruce Zuckerman, "Why do They Call the Holocaust 'The Holocaust': An Inquiry into the Psychology of Labels," in Modern Judaism, Volume 9, Number 2, May, 1989, pages 197-211.

2. Alan Rosenberg and Gerald E. Myers [Editors]. Echoes from the Holocaust: Philosophical Reflections on a Dark Time. Philadelphia, Temple University Press, 1988.

3. Samuel Pisar. Of Blood and Hope. Boston, Little, Brown and Company, 1979.

4. The current debate among German historians [e.g. Ernest Nolte, etc.] about the role of Nazism and the Shoah in the overall drama of German and Western world history, as well as the reunification of German in 1990, have raised unease among Jews and others the world over. To be sure, right-wing militant fascism has existed in both parts of Germany since the end of the Second World War, counterbalanced, only in part, by proper recognition of primary German responsibility for the murderous deaths of Jews, Gypsies, homosexuals, and others. To date, however, neither the historical debate nor the implications of German reunification have triggered theological reflection by either Jews or Christians. In time, these topics, too, may serve as sources of serious religious debate among religious thinkers in both communities.

JUDAISM AND CHRISTIANITY AFTER AUSCHWITZ

Steven L. Jacobs

1. First presented at the Second Interdisciplinary Conference on the Holocaust, March 30-31, 1987, at The University of Alabama, Tuscaloosa, Alabama.

2. Irving Greenberg, "Judaism and Christianity After the Holocaust," in Journal of Ecumenical Studies, Volume 12, Number 4, Fall, 1975, page 529. This seminal article was reworked and published under the title "Cloud of Smoke, Pillar of Fire: Judaism, Christianity, and Modernity after the Holocaust" in Eva Fleischner [Editor]. Auschwitz: Beginning of a New Era? Reflections on the Holocaust. New York, Ktav Publishing House, 1977, pages 7-55.

3. Arthur Cohen. The Tremendum: A Theological Interpretation of the Holocaust. New York, Crossroad, 1981, page 39.

4. Robert Sherwin, "The Impotence of Explanation and the European Holocaust," in Tradition: A Journal of Orthodox Jewish Thought, Volume XII, 1972, page 99.

5. Arthur Cohen, Op. cit., page 86.

6. Raul Hilberg. The Destruction of European Jews. Chicago, Quadrangle Books, 1961, pages 3 ff. Philosopher Emil Fackenheim sees the recreation of the State of Israel as a response to this schemata when he writes:

> For it [i.e. the State of Israel] responds to the three- fold prohibition so well formulated by Hilberg. 'You have no right to live'--the Jewish State, although it is impossible to discount a second Masada, will never permit a second Auschwitz. 'You have no right to live among us'--the Jewish State cannot end the persecution and expulsion of Jews, but through its Law of Return it gives a home to such Jews as the persecutors permit to leave. 'You have no right to live among us as Jews'--the very name of the Jewish State in effect replies to Christianity, Paul's 'new' Israel, and to its secularist successors, that the 'old' Israel is not a defunct people of a non-people, but alive.
> Emil L. Fackenheim, "Concerning Authentic and Unauthentic Responses to the Holocaust," in Holocaust and Genocide Studies, Volume 1, Number 1, 1986, page 116.

7. Israeli Shoah scholar Yehuda Bauer sees the Shoah as unique for two additional reasons: [1] The annihilation of the Jewish people was to be a total planned annihilation, and [2] Its orchestration possessed a quasi-religious apocalyptic meaning. Reported by Michael Berenbaum, "Our ancient covenant has been shattered," in Sh'ma: A Journal of Jewish Responsibility, 14/272, April 13, 1984, page 92.

8. Daniel Polish, "Witnessing God after Auschwitz," in Helga Croner and Leon Klenicki [Editors]. Issues in the Jewish-Christian Dialogue: Jewish Perspectives on Covenant, Mission, and Witness. New York, Paulist Press, 1979, page 150. Certainly, there is no more poignant expression of the latter than Richard Rubenstein's interview with Dean Heinrich Gruber of the Evangelical Free Church in West Berlin: "The Dean and the Chosen People," in After Auschwitz: Radical Theology and Contemporary Juda-ism. Indianapolis, Bobbs-Merrill, 1986, pages 47-58, and noted in the present essay.

9. David W. Weiss, "After the Holocaust another covenant?" in Sh'ma: A Journal of Jewish Responsibility, 14/272, April 13, 1984, pages 88-91.

10. Martin Cohen, "The Mission of Israel after Auschwitz," in Helga Croner and Leon Klenicki [Editors]. Issues in the Jewish-Christian Dialogue: Jewish Perspectives on Covenant, Mission, and Witness. New York, Paulist Press, 1979, page 159.

11. Here, Greenberg's reference to "burning children" is particularly relevant.

12. Richard L. Rubenstein, "Some Perspectives on Religious Faith After Auschwitz," in Franklin H. Littell and Hubert G. Locke [Editors]. The German Church Struggle and the Holocaust. Detroit, Wayne State University Press, 1974, page 261. Even so eminent a friend of the Jewish People as the late Paul Tillich was theologically of a similar mindset to Dean Gruber. See Albert Friedlander's "A Final Conversation with Paul Tillich," in Albert H. Friedlander [Editor]. Out of the Whirlwind: A Reader of Holocaust Literature. New York, Union of American Hebrew Congregations, 1968, pages 515-521.

13. See especially The Cunning of History: Mass Death and the American Future. New York, Harper & Row, 1975; and The Age of Triage: Fear and Hope in an Overcrowded World. Boston, Beacon Press, 1983.

14. Comments taken from lecture notes for a course entitled "The Holocaust in Historical Perspective," taught at the University of Alabama at Birmingham since 1985.

15. Michael Novak. Toward a Theology of the Corporation. Washington, American Enterprise Institute for Public Policy Research, 1981.

16. Elie Wiesel. Night. New York, Hill and Wang, 1960, page 71.

17. Seymour Cain, "The Question and the Answers After Auschwitz," in Judaism, Volume 20, Number 3, Summer, 1971, pages 263-278.

18.   Michael Wyschogrod, "Faith and the Holocaust: A Review Essay of Emil Fackenheim's God's Presence in History," in Judaism, Volume 20, Number 3, Summer, 1971, page 288.

19.   Richard L. Rubenstein, "Some Perspectives on Religious Faith After Auschwitz," in Franklin H. Littell and Hubert G. Locke [Editors].   The German Church Struggle and the Holocaust. Detroit, Wayne State University Press, 1974, page 267.

20.   Among the many books which deal with Wiesel's writings are the following: Ellen Norman Stern, Elie Wiesel: Witness for Life. New York, Ktav Publishing House, 1982; Ellen S. Fine, Legacy of Night: The Literary Universe of Elie Wiesel. Albany, State University of New York Press, 1982; Ted L. Estess, Elie Wisel. New York, Frederick Unger Publishing Company, 1980; Harry James Cargas, Responses to Elie Wiesel: Critical Essays by Major Jewish and Christian Scholars. New York, Persea Books, 1978; Harry James Cargas, Harry James Cargas in Conversation with Elie Wiesel. New York, Paulist Press, 1976#; and John K. Roth, A Consuming Fire: Encounters with Elie Wiesel and the Holocaust. Atlanta, John Knox Press, 1979.* A fine literary-critical essay is that of Irving Abrahamson in the first volume of the three-volume set edited by him: Against Silence: The Voice and Vision of Elie Wiesel. New York, Holocaust Library, 1985.

#For a discussion of Cargas and his writings, see my essay "Harry James Cargas: Appreciation and Response," in Journal of Reform Judaism, Volume XXXII, Number 2, Spring, 1985, pages 33-43.

*My review of Roth's work appeared in The New Review of Books and Religion, Volume IV, Number 2, September, 1979, pages 13-14.

21. Eliezer Berkovitz. Faith After Auschwitz. New York, Ktav Publishing House, 1973.

22. A position somewhat similar to that of Berkovitz is that held by philosopher Martin Buber in his Eclipse of God: Studies in the Relation between Religion and Philosophy. New York, Harper & Row, 1952. See, also, the masterful study by Maurice Friedman, Martin Buber's Life and Work. New York, E. P. Dutton: The Early Years 1878-1923 [1981]; The Middle Years 1923-1945 [1983]; and The Later Years 1945-1965 [1983].

23. Emil Fackenheim. Quest for Past and Future. Bloomington, Indiana University Press, 1968, page 19. Repeated in God's Presence in History. New York, New York University Press, 1970, page 86.

24. Gerald S. Sloyan, "Some Theological Implications of the Holocaust," in Interpretation, Volume XXXIX, Number 4, October, 1985, page 408. Emphasis mine--SLJ.

25. Irving Greenberg, "Judaism and Christianity After the Holocaust," in Journal of Ecumenical Studies, Volume 12, Number 4, Fall, 1975, page 544.

26. John T. Pawlikowski, "The Holocaust and Catholic Theology," in Shoah, Volume 2, Number 4, 1979, pages 6 ff.

27. Quoted in Steven L. Jacobs, "Harry James Cargas: Appreciation and Response," in Journal of Reform Judaism, Volume 32, Number 2, Spring, 1985, page 43. Perhaps because of the radical nature of what he is suggesting, Cargas appears to have little, if any, impact on the organized Catholic Church to any appreciable degree. Indeed, one would hazard the guess whether, in fact, many within that community have ever heard of him or his writings.

28. Rosemary Radford Reuther. Faith and Fratricide: The Theological Roots of Anti-Semitism. New York, The Seabury Press, 1974.

29. Michael B. McGarry. Christology After Auschwitz. New York, Paulist Press, 1977.

30. Alan Ecclestone. Night Sky of the Lord. New York, Schocken Books, 1980. See my review in the Anglican Theological Review, Volume LXII, Number 3, Summer, 1989, pages 331-333.

31. Franklin H. Littell. The Crucifixion of the Jews: The Failure of Christians to Understand the Jewish Experience. New York, Harper & Row, 1975.

32. David A. Rausch. A Legacy of Hatred: Why Christians Must Not Forget the Holocaust. Chicago, Moody Press, 1984. Significantly, this volume was published by a conservative, evangelical, fundamentalist Christian publishing house, and, to the best of my knowledge, stands alone and unique because of that.

33. A. Roy Eckardt. Elder and Younger Brothers: The Encounter of Jews and Christians. New York, Charles Scribner's Sons, 1967.

34. A. Roy Eckardt and Alice Lyons Eckardt. Long Night's Journey into Day: Life and Faith After the Holocaust. Detroit, Wayne State University Press, 1982.

35. Alice Lyons Eckardt, "Post-Holocaust Theology: A Journey Out of the Kingdom of Night" in Holocaust and Genocide Studies, Volume 1, Number 2, 1986, pages 229-240.

36. Ibid., pages 229-230.

37. John Roth. A Consuming Fire: Encounters with Elie Wiesel and the Holocaust. Atlanta, John Knox Press, 1979.

38. Steven L. Jacobs, Review of A Consuming Fire in The New Review of Books and Religion, Volume IV, Number 1, September, 1979, pages 13-14. Emphasis mine--SLJ.

39. Alice Lyons Eckardt, Op. cit., pages 230-231. A contemporay evolution of these nightmarish examples is that contained in a footnote to Emil Fackenheim's article, "Concerning Authentic and Unauthenthic Responses to the Holocaust:"

> 36. Consider among counter instances illustrating this point the fundamentalist Canadian Christian minister who sought out Eichmann in Jerusalem, equally sure that a converted Eichmann would find salvation and that his countless unconverted Jewish victims would not. Or the famous American Liberal Protestant theologian who urged his Jewish audience to forgive the German people, but was left speechless when asked by a Jewish layman why Christians could expect Jews to forgive the murder of six million Jews, committed a single generation ago, when Christians had yet to forgive the murder of one Jew, committed two thousand years ago.
>
> Emil L. Fackenheim, "Concerning Authentic and Unauthentic Responses to the Holocaust," in Holocaust and Genocide Studies, Volume 1, Number 1, 1986, page 119.

40. Alice Lyons Eckardt, Op. cit., pages 232-237.

41. Samuel Pisar. Of Blood and Hope. Boston, Little Brown and Company, 1979.

42. Steven L. Jacobs, "[If] There is No 'Commander'?....There are No 'Commandments'!" Originally presented at the Third Annual Conference on Spirituality of the Atlanta, Georgia, Reform Synagogue Council on Sunday, 21 September 1986, under the title, "Reform Jews in Search of God: The Mitzvot--Law or Lore?" Published in Judaism, Volume 37, Number 3, Summer, 1988, pages 323-327. See, also, "A Response to the Critiques," in Judaism, Volume 38, Number 2, Spring, 1989, pages 245-252.

IN A WORLD WITHOUT A REDEEMER, REDEEM!

Michael Berenbaum

1. I am convinced that the Jewish community plays a similar role with respect to Soviet Communism as Jews did in Christianity, i.e. Jews helped bring the Christ and now deny him. By virtue of wanting to leave, Jews deny that community is the kingdom of God on earth and are resented for it.

2. See Yehoshafat Harkabi, The Bar Kockhba Syndrome [Chappaqua, Rossel Books, 1983] for a fascinating discussion of the perils of the 132-135 Messianic uprising and the implications of nationalist historical revis-i-onism surrounding the revolt today.

3. Gershom Scholem. Sabbatai Sevi: The Mystical Messiah. Princeton, Princeton University Press, 1973.

4. Arthur Hertzberg [Editor]. The Zionist Idea. Philadelphia, Jewish Publication Society, 1959, pages 1-103.

5. Joseph B. Soloveitchik. In Aloneness, In Togetherness: A Selection of Hebrew Writings. Jerusalem, Orot, 1976, pages 331-400.Edited by Pin-ch-as H. Peli.

6. Ehud Sprinzak, "Fundamentalism, Terrorism and Democracy: The Case of Gush Emunim Underground," in Occasional Papers. Washington, D.C., The Wilson Center. The paper was originally delivered on September 16, 1986.

7. Zvi Yaron. The Teachings of Rav Kook. Jerusalem, The World Zionist Organization, 1979. [Hebrew]

8. Ibid.

9. Michael Berenbaum. The Vision of the Void. Middletown, Wesleyan University Press, 1979.

10. Yonina Talmon, "The Pursuit of the Millennium: The Relations Between Religion and Social Change," in Norman Birnbaum and Gertrude Lenzer [Editors]. Sociology and Religion. Englewood Cliffs, Prentice Hall, 1969, pages 238-254.

11. See Michael Berenbaum, "Religion and Politics in Contemporary Israel," in Richard L. Rubenstein [Editor]. Spirit Matters: The World-wide Impact of Religion in Contemporary Politics. New York, Paragon House Publish-ers, 1987.

12. Ibid.

13. Yehuda Amital. Ascent from the Depths. Jerusalem, Alon Shevut, 1974. [Hebrew]

14. Scholem, Op. cit., pages 1-102.

15. Gershom Scholem. The Messianic Idea in Judaism and Other Essays on Jewish Spirituality. New York, Schocken Books, 1971, page 35.

16. Sprinzak, Op. cit., pages 11-14.

17. Emil Fackenheim. To Mend the World: Foundations of Future Jewish Thought. New York, Schocken Books, 1982, pages 250-313.

18. Elie Wisel, "Jewish Values in the Post-Holocaust Future," in Judaism, Volume 16, Number 3, Summer, 1967.

19. Richard L. Rubenstein. After Auschwitz: Radical Theology and Contemporary Judaism. Indianapolis, Bobbs-Merrill, 1966.

20. Berenbaum, Op. cit.

21. Maurice Friedman. Abraham Joshua Heschel and Elie Wiesel: You Are My Witnesses. New York, Farrar, Straus, Giroux, 1987, pages 229-259.

22. Elie Wiesel. The Town Beyond the Wall. New York, Holt, Rinehart and Winston, 1964, page 118.

23. Elie Wiesel, "Jewish Values in the Post-Holocaust Future," page 299.

24. See Friedman, Op. cit., pages 247-248, 267-268; and Berenbaum, The Vision of the Void, pages 15-16, 79, 148.

25. Berebaum, Ibid., page 148.

ACADEMIC AND THE HOLOCAUST

Alan L. Berger

1. See, also, Zev Garber, Alan L. Berger, and Richard Libowitz [Editors]. Methodology in the Academic Teaching of the Holocaust. Lanham, University Press of America, 1988. My review of this important text appeared in The National Jewish Post and Opinion, 19 April 1989, page 10.

2. Holocaust is a sanitized word which has entered the public vocabulary. Both inaccurate and inadequate [see below], Holocaust is the name given to Nazi Germany's murder of European Jewry. More appropriate to the horror is its designation as Auschwitz, largest of the Nazi death factories. This essay utilizes the term Holocaust only becuse of its public recognition.

3. Lily Edelman, "A Conversation with Elie Wiesel," in Harry James Cargas [Editor]. Responses to Elie Wiesel. New York, Persea Books, 1978.

4. Richard L. Rubenstein. The Cunning of History. New York, Harper Colophon Books, 1978, page 67.

5. Hannah Arendt. The Origins of Totalitarianism. New York, Harcourt, Brace & World, 1966, III, page 316.

6. Bruno Bettelheim. The Informed Heart. Glencoe, The Free Press, 1960, page 262.

7. Arendt notes that the general mentality of modern German scholars was heavily influenced by intellectuals of German romanticism. This dubious heritage yielded actions which "proved more than once that hardly an ideology can be found to which they [modern German scholars] would not willingly submit if the only reality--which even a romantic can hardly afford to overlook--is at stake, the reality of their position." The Ori-gins of Totalitarianism, II, page 168.

8. Raul Hilberg. The Destruction of European Jews. Chicago, Quadrangle Books, 1967, page 189.

9. Bettelheim. Op. cit., utilizes O. Lengyel's account from her Five Chimneys: The Story of Auschwitz. Chicago, Ziff Davis, 1947, page 147.

10. I. G. Auschwitz was actually located at Buna, the slave center directly adjacent to Auschwitz.

11. Hilberg. Op. cit., page 396.

12. Max Weinrich. Hitler's Professors. New York, YIVO, 1946, page 6.

13. The Nuremberg Trials had specific categories for physicians [most of whom were university professors], attorneys, high ranking military of-ficers, politicians, and for corporate executives. Law professors had spent the war years condemning to death Jews and other opponents of Hitler. Professor Doctor Reinhard Maurach, teacher of Criminal Law at Munich, testified that SS General Otto Ohlendorf [holder of a doctorate in Jurispru-dence, who had studied at three German universities], commandant of Einsatzgruppe D, which murdered 90,000 people, the overwhelming majority

of whom were Jews, had not committed any criminal offense. Ohlendorf, asserted Maurach, had been furthering the aims of the Reich. Maurach continues to be a highly respected law professor. For a vivid and sobering account of Nuremberg and its aftermath, see Benjamin B. Fer-encz. Less Than Slaves. Cambridge, Harvard University Press, 1979.

14. Cited by Hans Jonas in "Tenth Essay Heidegger and Theology," in Jonas' The Phenomenon of Life. New York, Harper and Row, 1966, page 247. Jonas employs the report of Guido Schneeberger, Nachlese zu Hei-degger: Dokumente zu seinem Leben und Denken. Bern, 1962.

15. Hans Jonas has written: "Neither then nor now did Heidegger's thought provide a norm by which to answer such calls [the call of being]--linguistically or otherwise." "The devil," concludes Jonas, "is also part of the voice of being." The Phenomenon of Life, page 247.

16. Littell's study, The Crucifixion of the Jews [New York, Harper & Row, 1975] contains one of the most lucid and perceptive analyses of university shortcomings. See, especially, Chapter I, "The Language of Events," and IV, "The Meaning of the Holocaust." See, also, Littell's chapter "Church Struggle and the Holocaust," especially pages 19-26, "The Treason of the Intellectuals," in Littell and Hubert G. Locke [Editors]. The German Church Struggle and the Holocaust. Detroit, Wayne State University Press, 1974.

17. Elie Wiesel. Legends of Our Time. New York, Holt, Rinehart and Winston, 1968, page 6. Arthur A. Cohen has suggested that the Holocaust be viewed as Tremendum, a caesura in Jewish history. See his lucid, provocative and richly suggestive book, The Tremendum. New York, Crossroad Publishing Company, 1981.

18. Irving Greenberg, "Judaism and Christianity After the Holocaust," in the Journal of Ecumenical Studies, Volume 12, Number 4, Fall, 1975, pages 542-543.

19. Yehuda Bauer. The Holocaust in Historical Perspective. Seattle, University of Washington Press, 1978, page 31.

20. Bauer notes that while certain Gypsy tribes were murdered, others were protected. Moreover, many individual Gypsies served in the German Army. Turning to the Turkish massacre of Armenian citizens in World War I, Bauer observes that, while half the Armenian population in Anatolia was mudered, the Armenians at Istanbul, the heart of the Ottoman Empire, were not killed. Op. cit., page 36.

21. Professor Lucy S. Dawidowicz reports the sordid affair in her article, "Lies About the Holocaust," Commentary, December, 1980. The article

should be required reading for all those interested in the correct usage of academic objectivity. Dawidowicz analyzes the bizarre career of The Journal of Historical Review [JHR] which is attempting to kill the Jews a second time. Nazis physically eradicated Jews; revisionist historians wish to deny their memory. Academics are in the forefront of this ghoulish assault. For example, Arthur R. Butz, Professor of Engineering at Northwestern University and author of The Hoax of the Twentieth Century, in which he reveals the "Holocaust legend," is a leading contributor.

22. Dawidowicz. Op. cit., page 35.

23. Ibid., page 37.

24. Bauer. Op. cit., specifically warns against the danger of moral anaesthesia when writing a "seminar paper about murder," pages 43, 44, and 47.

AFTER AUSCHWITZ AND THE PALESTINIAN UPRISING

Marc H. Ellis

1. For an extended analysis of the themes in Shoah theology, see Marc H. Ellis. Toward a Jewish Theology of Liberation: The Uprising and the Future. Maryknoll, Orbis, 1989, pages 7-24.

2. For an early, radical, and controversial analysis of these themes, see Richard L. Rubenstein. After Auschwitz: Radical Theology and Contemporary Judaism. New York, Bobbs-Merrill, 1966; and The Cunning of History: Mass Death and the American Future. New York, Harper and Row, 1975.

3. Of course, the first priority was to survive as a people so that a future was possible to imagine. This question of survival was described by Emil Fackenheim as the "commanding voice of Auschwitz." See Emil Fackenheim. God's Presence in History: Jewish Affirmation and Philosophical Reflections. New York, New York University Press, 1970.

4. For an interesting exploration of this new framework, see Irving Greenberg, "Cloud of Smoke, Pillar of Fire: Judaism, Christianity and Modernity After the Holocaust," in Eva Fleischner [Editor]. Auschwitz: Beginning of a New Era?. New York, Ktav Publishing House, 1977, pages 7-55; and "On the Third Era of Jewish History: Power and Politics," in Perspectives. New York, National Jewish Resource Center, 1980.

5. Rubenstein, The Cunning of History, page 28; Greenberg, "Cloud of Smoke, Pillar of Fire," page 29.

6. For an extended discussion of Shoah theology's inability to analyze the case of empowerment, see Ellis, Jewish Theology of Liberation, pages 25-37.

7. In effect, a new pragmatism is stressed that allows the "occasional use of immoral strategies to achieve moral ends." With this understanding, the memory of the Shoah enables Israel to be a "responsible and restrained conqueror." See Irving Greenberg, "The Third Great Cycle in Jewish History," in Perspectives. New York, National Jewish Resource Center, 1981, pages 25-26. The recent uprising in the occupied territories and the response of Israeli authorities exemplify the difficult position Diaspora Jews are in relative to Israel.

8. Ibid, page 25. Also, see "On the Third Era in Jewish History," page 6; and "Power and Peace," in Perspectives. New York, National Jewish Resource Center, 1985, pages 3 and 5.

9. Phillip Lopate, "Resistance to the Holocaust," in Tikkun, Volume 4, May/June, 1989, page 56.

10. Ibid. Lopate adds: "A good deal of suspicion and touchiness resides around this issue of maintaining the Holocaust's privileged status in the pantheon of genocides. It is not enough that the Holocaust was dreadful; it must be seen as uniquely dreadful," page 57.

11. Avishai Margalit, "The Kitsch of Israel," New York Review of Books, Number 35, November 24, 1988, page 23.

12. Ibid.

13. Ibid., page 24. All of this is also crucial for the marketing of Israel to the American Jewish community. See Ibid., page 22. For Elie Wiesel's response to the trivialization of the Shoah, see his "Art and the Holocaust: Trivializing Memory," in New York Times, June 11, 1989. To the question of how one transmits the message without trivializing it, Wiesel responds, "Listen to the survivors and respect their wounded sensibility. Open yourselves to their scarred memory, and mingle your tears with theirs. And stop insulting the dead," page 38.

14. Boaz Evron, "The Holocaust: Learning the Wrong Lessons," in Journal of Palestinian Studies, Number 10, Spring, 1981, page 16.

15. Ibid., pages 17 and 18. For an illustration of the need for common struggle within the Shoah, see Helen Fein. Accounting for Genocide:

National Responses and Jewish Victimization During the Holocaust. Chicago, University of Chicago Press, 1979.

16. Evron, "The Holocaust: Learning the Wrong Lessons," pages 17 and 18.

17. Ibid., pages 19 and 20. Evron claims that before the Eichmann trial, Shoah consciousness was waning and the ritualistic system of Shoah commemoration was undeveloped. To immigrants from Arab lands and for Israeli-born youths, "the extermination was a matter of the Jews of Europe, not of Israelis," page 19.

18. Ibid., page 21.

19. Ibid., page 23.

20. Ibid., page 26. For a fascinating response to Evron's article linking the so-called Biblical right of the Jews to Israel and the expulsion of the Palestinians from the land, see Israel Shahak, "The 'Historical Right' and the Other Holocaust," in Journal of Palestinian Studies, Number 10, Spring, 1981, pages 27-34.

21. A. B. Yehoshua. Between Right and Right: Israel, Problem or Solution? Garden City, Doubleday and Company, 1981, pages 101 and 105. Translated by Arnold Schwartz.

22. Ibid., pages 107-147.

23. These themes are annunciated most clearly as a consensus progressive Jewish position by Michael Lerner, Editor of the journal Tikkun. See Lerner, "The Occupation: Immoral and Stupid," Tikkun, Number 3, March-/April, 1988, pages 7-12.

24. Amos Oz, "Granting a Divorce," in American-Israeli Civil Liberties Coalition, Number 10, Summer, 1990, page 15.

25. For the development of this theme, see Muhammed Hallaj, "The Palestinian Dream: The Democratic Secular State," in Rosemary Radford Reuther and Marc H. Ellis [Editors]. Beyond Occupation: American Jewish, Christian and Palestinian Voices for Peace. Boston, Beacon Press, 1990, pages 222-230.

26. On the diversity and complexity of Jewish behavior in the ghettos of Eastern Europe, see Isaiah Trunk. Judenrat: The Jewish Councils in Eastern Europe Under Nazi Occupation. New York, Stein and Day, 1977. For a dialogue on the shifting of the burden onto Palestinians, see "Special

Focus on Iraq," Tikkun, Number 5, November/December, 1990, pages 48-78.

27. Johann Baptist Metz. The Emergent Church: The Future of Christianity in a Postbourgeois World. New York, Crossroad, 1981, page 19. Translated by Peter Mann.

28. For a discussion of these themes, see Robert Gordis. The Dynamics of Judaism: A Study in Jewish Law. Bloomington, Indiana University Press, 1990. See, also, Norman Gottwald. The Tribes of Yahweh: A Sociology of the Religion of Liberated Israel 1250-1050 B.C.E. Maryknoll, Orbis Books, 1979.

29. For earlier discussion of this theme, see Georges Friedmann. The End of the Jewish People? Garden City, Doubleday and Company, 1967. Translated by Eric Mosbacher; and Earl Shorris. Jewish Without Mercy: A Lament. Garden City, Doubleday and Company, 1982.

30. A way of confronting Jewish self-perception with reality is by reading Punishing A Nation: Human Rights Violations during the Palestinian Uprising, December 1987-1988. Ramallah, Al-Haq/Law in the Service of Man, 1988.

31. For an extended discussion of the themes of innocence and redemption, see Marc H. Ellis. Beyond Innocence and Redemption: Confronting the Holocuast and Israeli Power. San Francisco, Harper and Row, 1990. My review appears in Judaica Book News, Volume 22, Number 1, Fall, 1991, pages 46-47.

32. The transformation of segments of Christianity is an important focus of my own work. See, especially, Ellis, Jewish Theology of Liberation, pages 66-90; and Beyond Innocence and Redemption, pages 177-186. For comments on the ecumenical dialogue, see my "End the Dialogue," in Tablet, Number 244, June 30, 1990, page 810.

33. Roberta Strauss Feuerlicht. The Fate of the Jews: A People Torn Between Israeli Power and Jewish Ethics. New York, Time Books, 1983, pages 281-282.

34. Etty Hillesum. An Interrupted Life: The Diaries of Etty Hillesum, 1941-43. New York, Pocket Books, 1985, pages 99-101. Edited by J. G. Caarlandt and translated by Johnathan Cape.

35. Ibid., page 122.

THE HOLOCAUST: A SUMMING UP AFTER TWO DECADES OF REFLECTION

Emil L. Fackenheim

1. On the question of uniqueness itself, see Alan Rosenberg, "Was the Holocaust Unique: A Peculiar Question," in Isidor Wallimann and Michael N. Dobkowski [Editors]. Genocide and the Modern Age: Etiology and Case Studies of Mass Death. New York, Greenwood Press, 1987, pages 145-161; and my review, "Genocidal Civilization," in Judaica Book News, Volume 18, Number 2, Spring/Summer 1988/5748, pages 29-33.

VOLUNTARY COVENANT

Irving Greenberg

1. This text may be read without referring to the notes which are included. A different version of this paper was read at the conference, "God, Covenant and Community," co-sponsored by Conference on Learning and Leadership [CLAL] [then National Jewish Resource Center/NJRC] and the University of Denver Center for Judaic Studies in June, 1981, as part of our joint program, CHEVRA: Society for the Advancement of Jewish Thought, Dialogue and Community. I am grateful to my colleagues and their critique and to the center for Judaic Studies for permission to use this essay in the Perspectives series.

2. Genesis, Chapter 1, especially verses 25, 26, 27, 28. An image of God has infinite value, equality, and uniqueness. Sanhedrin 37a. On the soul quality of animals, see Proverbs 12:10; Nachmanides on Leviticus 22:28; J. Pederson, Israel [London, Oxford University, 1946], page 100. Cf. Maimonides, Guide to the Perplexed [New York, Hebrew Publishing Company, n.d.], Part 1, Chapter 1, page 32, that intellectual perception is the key breakthrough in the human.

3. Rav Abraham Isaac HaCohen Kook wrote: "Only He who is actually Infinite [En Sof] can actualize that which is potentially infinite." "The Doctrine of Evolution," A. I. Kook, Orot HaKodesh [Jerusalem, Mossad HaRav Kook, 1964], Volume 2, Part 5, Section 19, page 537.

4. If people are granted freedom they remain dependent. After being given their freedom, slaves remain psychologically enslaved until they take full responsibility for their own fate and daily life. Thus the Bible portrays the behavior of the Hebrews in the desert, and after the Exodus, as classical slave behavior. The Israelites often turned regressive, were easily thwarted by obstacles, often sought to return to the womb of slavery. See Exodus, Chapters 16, 17, 32; Numbers, Chapters 11, 13, 14, 20, 21.

5. Exodus 19:5-6.

6. See I. Greenberg, "Jewish Tradition and Contemporary Problems," in Relationships Between Jewish Tradition and Contemporary Issues. New York, Yeshiva University, n.d., pages 11-13.

7. Deuteronomy 29:14.

8. Deuteronomy 7.7.

9. Reward and punishment are visited on other people, too, especially in the land of Israel, but the Jews are held on a tighter rein. Genesis 15:16; Leviticus 22:22-26; Amos, Chapters 1, 2, and 3:1-2.

10. Though they do not carry the mark of the covenant in their flesh, Jewish women also experienced the inescapability of being Jewish as a determinant of their fate. Seen through twentieth century eyes, the fact that the central symbol of covenant is carried only by men creates some moral and cultural problematic, i.e., it is gender linked. On another level, however, the special mark on men is the biological analogue of the special status of men in Jewish tradition. For some comments on possible equalization and a new importance to voluntary symbols of covenant, see Note 89.

11. Cf. "To walk in all His ways" [Deuteronomy 11:22], "as He is merciful, so you be merciful" [Sifre Deteronomy, Section 49, page 85a]. See Ronald Green's extended development of this idea in his Religious Reason. New York, Oxford University Press, 1978.

12. See "The Third Great Cycle of Jewish History," pages 1-26.

13. In Ezekiel's lacerating words [20:32 ff], the Destruction is God's "poured our fury," calling Israel to judgment, in other words, holding the people to the covenant--sifting out the rebellious Jews and recalling the others to covenantal relationship with God. Ibid., Chapters 36-38.

14. Hosea 11:8. Cf. Isaiah 50:1, where the prophet, manifestly replying to those Jews who argue that God has rejected Israel, quotes God as saying, "Show me a bill of divorce that I sent your mother [Israel]."

15. See I. Greenberg, "Judaism and History: Historical Events and Religious Change," in Jerry Diller [Editor]. Ancient Roots and Modern Meaning. New York, Bloch Publishing Company, 1978, pages 146-156.

16. It is not just particular texts that can be offered as evidence for this change; the very method and role of the Rabbis was based on this assumption. Cf. footnote 15 above.

17. Mekhilta de Rabbi Ishmael, Section "Bachodesh," Chapter 6, page 298. SOta, 17a; Genesis Rabbah, "Toledot," Chapter 63, Section 6.

18. Mekhilta, loc. cit.

19. Sifra Bamidbar, Section 161, page 221.

20. Sifra Kedoshim, Section 2, Chapter 2, page 86a.

21. Mishnah, Peah 1:1.

22. Menachot 110a, views of Rabbi Samuel Bar Nachmani, Rabbi Yochanan, and especially Resh Lakish and Rabbi Yitzchak.

23. Yalkut Shimoni Isaiah, Section 454. New York, Pardes Publishing, n.d., Volume 2, page 795, Column B, "Amar Rabbi Yehudah amar Rav...."

24. Ibid.

25. Consider the Rabbinic interpretation of hocheah tocheach, "thou shalt surely correct," [Leviticus 19:17]. The Rabbis qualify the mitzvah [commandment]; do not correct the other unless he is prepared to listen; one who is open to the same criticism should not correct another; one who does not know how to speak gently and acceptably should not correct. [Arachin 14b] The divine instruction and the divine correction cannot be purely mechanical or external either.

26. "Since the Temple was destroyed, there is no laughter before the Holy One, Blessed be He" [Yalkut Shimoni, Section 454]. "I am with Him in trouble" [Psalms 91:13]. When a human being is in pain, what does the Shechinah [Indwelling Presence or God--Ed.] say? "My head is heavy [aches], my arms are heavy [ache] [Sanhedrin 46a].

27. Megillah 29a.

28. Yalkut Shimoni, Isaiah, Section 455 [Pardes edition], page 795.

29. Lamentations Rabbah, Portion 1, Section 33.

30. The Talmud refers to Masters of the precedents at Sinai [i.e. one who remembers the record of the past Revelation which began at Sinai].

31. This involved knowing the past commandments, deciding what is foreground and background in the tradition in relation to this case and deciding what is the salient similarity in the present situation. The Talmud calls this the capacity L'damia Milta L'milta--to establish the appropriate analogy or similarity in the two situations.

32. Shabbat 23a.

33. Deuteronomy 21:18 ff.

34. Baba Batra, 121b.

35. Makkot 7a.

36. Gittin 3a; Yevamot 88a; Ketubot 10 ff. See on these and other improvements in the legal condition of wives, "Jewish Attitudes Towards Di-vorce-," in Blu Greenberg. On Women and Judaism. Philadelphia, The Jewish Publication Society of America, 1982, pages 125 ff.

37. See Jacob Neusner. Rabbi Yochanan ben Zakkai: Development of a Legend. Leiden, E. J. Brill, 1970, page 50. The discontinuance of the ordeal is comparable to the end of prophecy and to the passing of the scapecoat ceremony. Through the scapegoat, the sins of the Jewish people were "sacramentally" removed. See Leviticus, Chapter 16, and Maimoni-des, Mishneh Torah, Hilchot Teshuvah, Chapter 1, Paragraph 2.

38. Rosh Ha-Shanah 25b.

39. Baba Metzia 86a; Midrash Shohar Tov Tehillim 4; Deuteronomy Rabbah, Parashat V'Etchanan, Parsha B, Section 14. On this, see Joseph B. Soloveitchik's essay, "Ish Halacha" in Talpiot. New York, 1944, Volume 1, pages 700 ff.

40. Deuteronomy 17:11; Berachot 19b.

41. Cf. Moses' argument to the angels to release the Torah to humanity which needs it: "Is there jealously among you? Is there hatred among you?" Berachot 17a.

42. Joseph B. Soloveitchik, "Ish Halacha," Op. cit., page 702.

43. Cf. Ecclesiastes Rabbah, Parsha 1, v. 10, Section B; Peah 9b, Chapter 2 h. 4; Megillah 19b. Everyone who innovates words of Torah by his own mouth is like one who is being informed from heaven and they are telling him: Thus said the Holy One, Blessed be He. Yalkut Shimoni Shoftim, Section 49 [Pardes edition], Volume 2, pages 707, Column B.

44. Saul Lieberman's view is that the middot, rhetorical analytic devices used by the Rabbis to devise laws from Scripture, are based on Hellenic rhetorical modes. Cf. Lieberman. Jews in Hellenistic Palestine. New York, Jewish Theological Seminary, 1962. This view has been denounced by traditionalists. In the spirit of my interpretation, Lieberman's views would

be compatible with the Rabbinic statement that their teachings are halacha l'Moshe miSinai.

45. Underlining supplied. Matthew 5:18.

46. The Jewish and Christian hermeneutic of the Destruction of the Tem-p-le, the consequences of those views and the implications for Jewish-Christian relationships today, are discussed at length in an essay of mine, presented at a conference entitled Transformations: Judaism and Christianity After the Holocaust, sponsored by CLAL and Indiana University. See, also, my "Judaism and History: Historical Events and Religious Change," in Jerry Diller [Editor]. Ancient Roots and Modern Meanings. New York, Bloch Publishing Compnay, 1978, pages 139-155.

47. Shabbat 88a.

48. Exodus 24:7; Deuteronomy 27:10 ff.

49. Tosafot d.h. Moda'a Rabbah, Shabbat 88a.

50. Shavuot 39a.

51. Jeremiah 31:30; Jeremiah 16:14-15.

52. See my "Lessons to be Learned from the Holocaust." Paper presented at the Hamburg Conference, 1975.

53. A. Roy Eckardt, "The Recantation of the Covenant," in Alvin Rosenfeld and Irving Greenberg [Editors]. Confronting the Holocaust: The Work of Elie Wiesel. Bloomington, Indiana University Press, 1980, page 163.

54. Elie Wiesel, "Jewish Values in the Post-Holocaust Future," in Judaism, Summer, 1967, Volume 16, Number 3, page 28.

55. Jacob Glatstein, "Dead Men Don't Praise God," in Selected Poems of Jacob Glatstein. New York, October House, 1972, pages 68-70. Translated by Ruth Whitman.

56. Gittin 56b. This is a commentary/critique based on Exodus 15:11.

57. Cf. Eckardt, "Recantation," Op. cit., pages 164-165.

58. In a public lecture, Wiesel has used the image that, in light of the evil revealed in the Shoah, the risk in the Jewish mission to the world can be compared to a collective suicide mission. Conversation with the author, May 12, 1982.

59. Note that by Nazi decree, grandchildren of people who were Jewish but had converted to Christianity or assimilated were also identified as Jews and killed. Cf. Emil Fackenheim, "Jewish Faith and the Holocaust," Commentary, August 1967; Emil Fackenheim, God's Presence in History. New York, New York University Press, 1979, pages 70-71. Compare Irving Greenberg, "Confronting the Holocaust and Israel." New York, United Jewish Appeal, n.d., pages 16-17 and 20-22.

60. I. Greenberg, "Cloud of Smoke, Pillar of Fire: Judaism, Christianity, and Modernity After the Holocaust," in Eva Fleischner [Editor]. Auschwitz: Beginning of a New Era? New York, Ktav, 1977, page 43.

61. The term "broken covenant" must be properly understood. A broken covenant may still exercise a powerful magnetism. While its brokenness reflects the wound inflicted on the covenantal people and the damage done to the credibility of hope and redemption, paradoxically enough, the shattering also witnesses to the profound bond between the covenant and the Jewish people. The covenant shares Jewish fate; the Torah is not insulated from Jewish suffering. Thus its brokenness makes the covenant more adequate insofar as it related more totally to the human condition. This helps account for the extraordinary pull it exerts on this generation of Jews. Elsewhere I have cited Rabbi Nachman of Bratslav's famous dictum that "nothing is so whole as a broken heart" and I argued that, after the Shoah, "no faith is so whole as a broken faith." By this logic, no covenant is so complete as a broken covenant.

62. Exodus 24:7. The Jews' response--na'aseh v'nishma--implies commitment before hearing all the risks.

63. The Talmud tells a story which illuminates the faith underlying the response. An opponent once saw Raba so engrossed in learning that he ignored a wound in his hand. The Sadducee exclaimed: "You rash people [You Jews]. You put your mouth ahead of your ears! And you still persist in your recklessness. [You continue to make incredible commitments!] First you should have heard out [the covenant terms in detail]. If it is within your powers, then accept. If not, you should not have accepted." Raba answered: "We walked [with God] with our whole being. [Rashi: We walked....as those who serve God in love. We relied on Him not to burden us with something we could not carry.] Of us it is written, "The wholeness of the righteous shall guide them." [Proverbs 11:3]; Shabbat 88a-b.

64. Joseph B. Soloveitchik, "The Lonely Man of Faith," in Tradition, Volume 7, Number 2, 1965, pages 23, 24, 27, 28-30, 33 ff.

65. Michael Berenbaum has powerfully and convincingly argued that, in his writings, Elie Wiesel has developed a doctrine of "an additional covenant forged at Auschwitz, a covenant that renews Israel's mission despite the

void....[a covenant] between Israel and its memories of pain and death, God and meaning." Berenbaum finds three elements in Wiesel's additional covenant doctrine: sodality, witness, and the sanctification of life. See Michael Berenbaum, "The Additional Covenant," in Rosenfeld and Greenberg [Editors]. Confronting the Holocaust, pages 169, 171 ff. Berebaum has placed these reflections in the context of his important and comprehensive analysis of Wiesel's and others' Shoah theology in The Vision of the Void: Theological Reflections on the Works of Elie Wiesel. Middletown, Wesleyan University Press, 1979. While I differ somewhat from Berenbaum's assessment as to how much Wiesel comes down on the side of theological void after the Shoah, and while my thesis of the voluntary reassumption of the covenant differs from the additional covenantal model, I am indebted to Michael Berenbaum for opening my eyes to the concept of an additional covenant in Wiesel's writings. Eckardt's concept of divine repentance at giving the covenant [See note 53.] particularly, and Beren-baum's formulation of the additional covenant as well, were fruitful intellectual stimulants at the time that I was struggling to articulate this paradigm of the voluntary covenant.

66. See Michael Wyschogrod's review of Eva Fleischner [Editor]. Auschwitz: Beginning of a New Era? [New York, Ktav Publishing Company, 1977] in Tradition, Volume 17, Number 1, Fall, 1977, pages 63-78.

67. "Out of the fierce, came forth sweetness." Judges 14:14.

68. One may offer the analogy of talk about God. Any explanation or description of God may be useful or valid as long as it recognizes its metaphoric essence and its inability to portray the Divine exhaustively or even in its actual essence. Any portrait that "captures" the Divine is an idol, not a representation of God.

69. Cf. Soloveitchik, "The Lonely Man of Faith," Ibid., page 29.

70. When the Rabbis said, "Do not be like servants who serve the Master for the sake of reward, but be like servants who serve the Master not for the sake of reward" [Ethics of the Fathers, 1:3], they were more prophetic than was realized at the time. Continual divine rewards [or punishments] are in tensions with the goal of a relationship based on love.

71. Based on Rabbi Joshua ben Levi's views in Yoma 69b.

72. Cf. I. Greenberg, "Cloud of Smoke," Op. cit., pages 41 ff.

73. That resettlement of the land is proof of the ongoing validity of the covenant is a central theme in Isaiah, Jeremiah and other prophetic books.

74. For the format of the classical ceremony of conversion, see Yevamot 47 a-b.

75. Cf. "Every controversy for the sake of heaven will have a lasting result." [Ethics of the Fathers 5:20]

76. Eruvin 13b.

77. See "The Theoretical Basis of Women's Equality in Judaism," in Blu Greenberg, Op. cit., pages 39-55.

78. Cf. I. Greenberg, "Toward Jewish Religious Unity," in Judaism, Volume 15, Number 2, Spring, 1966, pages 135.

79. Cf. Elie Wiesel. Gates of the Forest. New York, Avon Books, pages 41 ff., page 215, cf. 42-43, and page 223.

80. Elsewhere I have suggested that this is a Messiah who limps even as Jacob did after this struggle with the Angel of the Night left him wounded-- but unbowed. See Shlomo Shamir, "HaShutafim," [The Partners] in Haaretz Weekly Magazine, page 29.

81. I. Greenberg, "Jewish Tradition and Contemporary Problems," in Relationship Between Jewish Tradition and Contemporary Issues. New York, Yeshiva University Press, n.d., page 11; and Samuel Dresner and Seymour Siegel. The Jewish Dietary Laws. New York, Burning Bush Press, 1959, pages 21-30.

82. See above.

83. See Guide to the Shabbat. New York, CLAL, 1981, pages 8-12.

84. Leviticus 19:2.

85. The Talmudic phrase is found in Yevamot 20a.

86. See Nachmanides' analysis in his commentary on Leviticus 19:2 d.h. kedoshim tih'yu.

87. Jeremiah 31:30.

88. The Rabbinic analogue to this concept is the ruling that one who is commanded and performs the act is at a higher level than one who is not commanded but does the act. Cf. Kiddushin 31a. This distinction comes to

serve as an obstacle to the admission of women into liturgical roles. Cf. Blu Greenberg, Op. cit., pages 82-85.

89. Genesis 15:5-18.

90. The Third Era analogue to this concept may be that "greater is the one who is not commanded but voluntarily comes forward than the one who acts only out of command."

91. The author wishes to thank Jonathan Javitch who is much more than the editor of this publication. He assayed, clarified, redirected and shaped this essay. My thanks also to Deborah Greenberg who served as research assistant for this paper.

AUSCHWITZ: RE-ENVISIONING THE ROLE OF GOD

Peter J. Haas

1. A parallel discussion to Haas's thinking may be found in Harold Schulweis's notion of "predicate theology." See his Evil and the Morality of God [Cincinnati, Hebrew Union College Press, 1984], as well as my brief review, "Theodicy Forces Us to Seek Simplicity and Distrust It," in Books & Religion, Volume 14, Number 10, December, 1986, page 13.

2. The most representative Jewish thinker along these lines is, in my view, Eliezer Berkovits. His concept of the hester panim ["the hidden Face of God"--Ed.] draws directly on medieval Jewish conceptualizations. The result of using medieval concepts to explain God to modern people is that God becomes incomprehensible and so dismissable. One example of this phenomenon is Amos Funkenstein, "Theological Interpretations of the Holocaust: A Balance," in Francois Furet [Editor]. Unanswered Questions: Nazi Germany and the Genocide of the Jews. New York, Schocken Books, 1989, pages 275-303.

3. Irving Greenberg makes the point on several occasions that Heinrich Himmler insisted that the members of the SS have a belief in God so that they might be different from the Marxists [for example, in his "Religious Values after the Holocaust: A Jewish Perspective," in Abraham Peck [Editor]. Jews and Christians after the Holocaust. Philadelphia, Fortress Press, 1982, page 76]. This is simply a formal gesture, and not what I have in mind here. The mere invocation of God's name or the use of certain rituals does not amount to religious faith, as the actions of so many "church-people" in Nazi Germany shows.

4. The original edition was copyright in 1961 by Quadrangle Books, New York.

5. Indianapolis, Bobbs-Merrill, 1966.   The book is subtitled "Radical Theology and Contemporary Judaism."

6. Hanover, University Press of New England, 1987. See, especially, pages 2 ff.

7. Rubenstein's writings in After Auschwitz are linked to the "God is Dead" theology associated with, among others, Thomas Altizer. Rubenstein avoids the phrase "God is Dead" as too closely linked to Christian imagery. His phrasing throughout is more passive: "....time of the death of God" and the like. See his discussion of this on pages 243-246.

8. The Tremendum: A Theological Interpretation of the Holocaust. New York, Crossroads, 1988.

9. Spelled out in his God's Presence in History: Jewish Affirmations and Philosophical Reflections. New York, New York University Press, 1970. Also Part Two of The Jewish Return into History. New York, Schocken Books, 1978.

10. Thus he talks of the "614th commandment," the original revelation of 613 [as portrayed in traditional Rabbinic Judaism] having been increased, not replaced, after Auschwitz. See Return, pages 22-23.

11. From her book A Report on the Banality of Evil: Eichmann in Jerusa-lem. New York, Penguin Books, 1963.

12. This has tended to be a more conservative Christian perspective. The most egregious Jewish example is Joel Taitelbaum in his Vajoel Moshe. New York, 1957 and 1957.

13. Related in Night, pages 60-62 in the Bantam Books edition.

14. A Legacy of Hatred: Why Christians Must Not Forget the Holocaust. Chicago, Moody Press, 1984. The book is specifically aimed at combatting white supremacists which portray themselves as true Christianity.

15. As in his Faith After the Holocaust. New York, Ktav Publishing House, 1973.

16. There is no doubt that Arendt did regard Eichmann as personally banal. This is clear from her reaction to his final words [page 252], as well as from her comment that she could not "extract any diabolical or demonic profundity from Eichmann...." [page 288]. Yet she also seems to see Eich-

mann as only an example of a deeper "interdependence of thoughtlessness and evil" [page 288]. Eichmann acted, she concludes, in a wholly meaningful way within the larger framework of which he was a part. Cf. pages 288 ff.

17. Much of what follows is covered in Hannah Arendt's ground-breaking The Origins of Totalitarianism.

18. A good overall treatment is Vamberto Morais. A Short History of Anti-Semitism. New York, W. W. Norton and Company, 1976. The church attitude is the central concern of Edward W. Flannery's The Anguish of the Jews: A Catholic Priest Writes of Twenty-three Centures of Anti-Semitism. New York, Macmillan, 1964.

19. "Concerning the Amelioration of the Civil Status of the Jews." A translated and abridged version is in Robert Chazan and Marc Lee Raphael [Editors]. Modern Jewish History: A Reader. New York, Schocken Books, 1969, pages 1-13.

20. George L. Mosse. Toward the Final Solution: A History of Racism. New York, Howard Fertig, 1978.

21. The most articulate nineteenth-century racial theorist of this type is probably Count J. A. de Gobineau. The full confluence of his theories with Hegel and Social Darwinism is illustrated in the writings of Houston Stewart Chamberlain. Chamberlain championed the idea of the Aryan "race."

22. Published by Harper and Row, New York, 1978. The cited definition is on page 56.

23. Source, Sanction, and Salvation: Religion and Morality in Judaic and Christian Traditions. Englewood Cliffs, Prentice Hall, 1988, page 1.

24.Irving Greenberg makes a similar observation in his paper delivered to a symposium on the Shoah hosted by the Cathedral of St. John the Divine in New York. "No assessment of modern culture can ignore the fact that science and technology--the accepted flower and glory of modernity--now climaxed in the factories of death....There is the shock of recognition that the humanistic revolt, celebrated as the liberation of humankind in freeing man from centuries of dependence upon God and nature, is now reverted..-..to sustain a capacity for death and demonic evil." In Eva Fleischner [Editor]. Auschwitz: Beginning of a New Era? New York, Ktav Publishing House, 1077, page 15.

25. The classic work on this is Thomas Kuhn. The Structure of Scientific Revolutions. Chicago, University of Chicago Press, 1962. Curiously the work of Kuhn was anticipated in its essential insight by Karl Mannheim, who

wrote on the eve of the Nazi ascent power. See, especially, his article "Wissenssoziologie," in Alfred Vierkandt [Editor]. Handwoerterbuch der Soziologie. Stuttgart, F. Enke, 1931.

26. Mannheim comes close to saying the same thing in "Wissenssoziologie." "We will being with the fact that the same word, or the same concept in most cases, means very different things when used by differently situated persons." He then goes on to use as a concrete example the word [or concept] "freedom." Karl Mannheim. Ideology and Utopia: An Introduction to the Sociology of Knowledge. New York, Harcourt, Brace & World, 1936, pages 273 ff. Translated by Louis Wirth and Edward Shils.

27. Alasdair MacIntyre. After Virtue. Notre Dame, University of Notre Dame Press, 1984, pages 27 ff. Second Edition.

28. MacIntyre, Op cit., pages 74-75.

29. I recognize that the extermination of the Jews was implicit in Nazi thinking from the beginning, but it seems to me that it became fully conceptualized and shaped over time. I thus take a functionalist view of the development of the Nazi war against the Jews. For my arguments see my Morality after Auschwitz: The Radical Challenge of the Nazi Ethic. Philadelphia, Fortress Press, 1988.

30. See Irving Greenberg's comments, cited above.

WHY?

Bernard Maza

[Notes supplied by the Editor]

1. Hoboken, Ktav Publishing House, 1986. See, also, my review of it in Holocaust and Genocide Studies, Volume 4, Number 2, 1989, pages 239-241.

2. Ecclesiastes 1:5: "The sun rises and the sun sets, and hurries back to where it rises."

3. Ritual baths.

4. Schools of higher Jewish learning.

5. The Hasidic Movement During the Time of the Shoah.

6. Book of Testimony.

7. Fall festival of "Booths," remembering the harvest in ancient Israel, as well as the temporary dwellings erected by the Israelites when they went out from Egypt.

8. Holiday songs and hymns.

9. The Destruction of Lita.

10. Deans of these Talmudical academies.

11. Eastern European Jewish ghettos, primarily in Russia and Poland.

12. In Orthodox Jewish Religious Tradition, King Solmon is understood to be the author of the Biblical Book of Ecclesiastes.

13. Annual Day of Atonement, ten days after the start of the Jewish New Year [Rosh Ha-Shanah].

14. Hebrew name of Moses.

15. Aramaic translation of the Pentateuch [Five Books of Moses] by Onkelos, First Century of the Common Era.

16. Rabbi Samuel Eliezer Edels [1555-1631], Polish commentator on the Talmud.

17. Blessings.

18. Heart of the Jewish Worship Service, consisting of eighteen para-graphs devoted to the various types and forms of prayers--e.g. petitions, thanksgiving, praise of God, etc.

APOCALYPTIC RATIONALITY AND THE HOLOCAUST

Richard L. Rubenstein

1. Indianapolis, Bobbs-Merrill, 1966.

2. That conclusion is likewise in evidence in his "Afterword: Genocide and Civilization," in Isidor Wallimann and Michael N. Dobkowski [Editors]. Genocide and the Modern Age: Etiology and Case Studies of Mass Death. New York, Greenwood Press, 1987, pages 283-298, especially page 297. See, also, my review "Genocidal Civilization," in Judaica Book News, Volume 18, Number 2, Spring/Summer, 1988/5748, pages 29-33.

3. An earlier version of this paper was presented in Paris, November, 1988, at the Conference "Penser Auschwitz," by the Alliance Israelite Universelle and commemorating the Fiftieth Anniversary of Kristallnacht.

4. See, for example, Lucy S. Dawidowicz. The War Against the Jews 1933-1945. New York, Holt, Rinehart and Winston, 1975.

5. This is the author's fundamental thesis concerning the Shoah as expressed in Richard L. Rubenstein: The Cunning of History. New York, Harper and Row, 1975. See, especially, page 6.

6. Norman Perrin. The New Testament: An Introduction. New York, Harcourt, Brace and Jovanovich, 1974, page 65.

7. This thesis is spelled out by the author in Richard L. Rubenstein: The Age of Triage: Fear and Hope in An Overcrowded World. Boston, Beacon Press, 1983, pages 34-59. See Karl Polanyi: The Great Transformation: The Political and Economic Origins of Our Times. Boston, Beacon Press, 1957.

8. Robert Hughes. The Fatal Shore: The Epic of Australia's Founding. New York, Alfred A. Knopf, 1987, pages 40-41.

9. Tony Barta, "Relations of Genocide: Land and Lives in the Colonization of Australia," in Isidor Wallimann and Michael N. Dobkowski [Editors]: Genocide and the Modern Age: Etiology and Case Studies of Mass Death. New York, Greenwood Press, 1987, pages 237-252.

10. For a study of the fate of the Indians of North America, see Bernard W. Sheehan: Seeds of Extinction: Jeffersonian Philanthropy and the American Indian. Chapel Hill, University of North Carolina Press, 1973.

11. Christopher Hill. God's Englishman: Oliver Cromwell and the English Revolution. New York, Harper Torchbooks, 1972, page 113.

12. R. P. Stearns. Hugh Peter: The Strenuous Puritan, 1598-1660. Champagne and Urbana, Illinois University Press, 1954, page 356. Cited by Hill, Op. cit., page 117.

13. Cecil Woodham-Smith. The Great Hunger: Ireland, 1845-1849. New York, E. P. Dutton, 1980, pages 411-412.

14. Rubenstein, The Age of Triage, pages 120-127.

15. "Effects of Emigration on Production and Consumption," in The Economist, February 12, 1853, pages 168-169. See this author's comments in Rubenstein, The Age of Triage, page 122.

16. See "The Irish Priesthood and the Irish Laity," in The Economist, June 19, 1852.

17. A. J. Ryder. Twentieth-Century Germany: From Bismarck to Brandt. New York, Columbia University Press, 1972, page 40.

18. See Rubenstein, The Age of Triage, pages 165-194.

19. Michael R. Marrus and Robert O. Paxton. Vichy France and the Jews. New York, Basic Books, 1981, pages 3-8.

20. See, for example, J. S. Conway: The Persecution of the Churches 1933-1945. New York, Basic Books, 1968, pages 261-266.

21. The question of the proneness of middleman minorities to genocidal assault has been raised by Walter P. Zenner and a number of other social theorists. See Walter P. Zenner, "Middleman Minorities and the Geno-cide," in Wallimann and Dobkowski, Op. cit., pages 253-281; Zenner, Middleman Minority Theories and the Jews: A Historical Assessment. New York, YIVO Working Papers in Yiddish and East European Jewish Studies Series, Number 31, 1978; Edna Bonacich and J. Modell, The Economic Basis of Ethnic Solidarity: The Case of Japanese-Americans. Berkeley and Los Angeles, University of California Press, 1981.

22. For a discussion of the elimination of the ethnic Chinese from Vietnam, see Richard L. Rubenstein, The Age of Triage, pages 165-194.

23. See Benjamin Nelson: The Idea of Usury: From Tribal Brotherhood to Universal Otherhood. Chicago, University of Chicago Press, 1969. Second Edition.

24. Rubenstein, The Age of Triage, pages 128-164.

25. Robert G. L. Waite. The Psychopathic God: Adolf Hitler. New York, New American Library, 1978, page 73.

26. See Irving Louis Horowitz, "Genocide and the Reconstruction of Social Theory: Observations on the Exclusivity of Social Death, " in Wallimann and Dobkowski, Op. cit., pages 61-80.

27. Richard L. Rubenstein, After Auschwitz: Radical Theology and Contemporary Judaism. Indianapolis, Bobbs-Merrill, 1966, pages 30 ff.

28. Cited by Nicholas Halasz: Captain Dreyfus: The Story of a Mass Hysteria. New York, Simon and Schuster, 1957, pages 57.

29. This assessment accords with the judgment of political scientist, Roger Smith, that genocide is a "rational instrument to achieve an end." See Roger Smith, "Human Destructiveness and Politics: The Twentieth Century as an Age of Genocide," in Wallimann and Dobkowski, Op. cit., pages 21-40.

30. Max Weber. Economy and Society: An Outline of Interpretive Sociology. New York, Bedminster Press, 1968, Volume I, pages 24-26. Edited by Guenther Roth and Claus Wittich.

31. Ronald Aronson. The Dialectics of Disaster. London, Verso, 1983.

32. Richard L. Rubenstein, The Cunning of History, page 90.

33. Emil L. Fackenheim. God's Presence in History: Jewish Affirmations and Philosophical Reflections. New York, Harper and Row, 1972, page 11.

34. See Victor Farias: Heidegger et le Nazisme. Paris, Verdier, 1987; and Richard L. Rubenstein, "Philosopher and the Jews: The Case of Martin Heidegger," in Modern Judaism, Volume 9, Number 2, May, 1989, pages 179-196.

35. Martin Heidegger. Being and Time. New York, Harper and Row, 1962, page 296. Translated by John Macquarrie and Edward Robinson. German edition: Sein und Zeit. Tubingen, Niemeyer, 1953, page 252. Seventh Edition.

36. Franz Rosenzweig. The Star of Redemption. New York, Holt, Rine-hart and Winston, 1970, page 329. Translated by William W. Hallo.

GLOSSARY

Aggadah: [Hebrew] Post-Biblical Jewish literature which includes stories, chronicles, sayings, moral instructions, admonitions and chastisements, as well as consolations.

Akedah: [Hebrew] Reference to the Binding of Isaac as depicted in Bereshit [Genesis], Chapter 22. Oft-times mistakenly referred to in Christian literature as the "Sacrifice" of Isaac, precursor to the death of Jesus.

Aliyah: [Hebrew] Immigration to Israel. Literally a "going up" to the Land of Israel. [Its opposite if **yeridah**, literally a "going down" from the Land of Israel.]

Anamnesis: [Greek] Literally "remembering." Its Hebrew equivalent is **zikkaron**. For Eugene Fisher, Volume II, both Judaism and Christianity are religions of remembering.

Ani Ma'amin: [Hebrew] Literally "I believe...." The opening words to Maimonides' [1135-1204] "Thirteen Articles of Faith," traditional included in the Jewish siddur, prayer book.

Antinomianism: An early Christian interpretation which held that salvation is directly contingent upon faith only rather than obedience to any moral law.

Antisemitism: Hated of the Jewish People and the Jewish Religious Faith, Heritage, and Tradition. Throughout history, the forms antisemitism has taken have included expulsion, ghettoization, forced religious conversion, denial of civil rights, and extermination/annihilation. [Preferred spelling here is without the hyphen; to use it is to imply its opposite: That there is such a thing as "S/semitism," which is non-existent.]

Apocalypse: The idea of the revelation of the End of Days as well as the Day[s] of Judgment. Important to all three monotheistic religious traditions, Judaism, Christianity, and Islam.

Apostasy: The abandonment of the beliefs of one's faith community.

Aryan: The term wrongly employed by the Nazis to designate any "pure-blooded" Caucasian, male or female, possessing no Jewish ancestors, primarily, but, also, one possessing neither Polish or Slavic "blood."

Ashkenazim: German Jews and their descendants. Though the term can be found in the Scriptures [Genesis 10:3; Jeremiah 51:27], it has been used since the ninth century in the above way.

Atheism: The philosophical position that either there is no God or that the proofs which have thus far been presented to prove the existence of God are themselves faulty.

Auschwitz: [German; Polish: Oswiecim; Yiddish: Ushpitzin]. Town thirty miles west of Cracow, Poland. Premier Nazi concentration camp which saw the extermination of between four and five million prisoners, more than one and one-half million of them Jews. It has, also, become the symbolic reference to the entire concentration/extermination camp system of the Nazis.

Bat Kol: [Hebrew] Literally, "daughter of a voice." The term is found in rabbinic literature, especially the Talmud to denote the Divine Voice, available to be heard by anyone.

Bayt Ha-Knesset: [Hebrew] One of the primary functions/roles of the synagogue--to be a "House of Assembly and Gathering."

Bayt Ha-Midrash: [Hebrew] One of the primary functions/roles of the synagogue--to be a "House of Study and Learning."

Bayt Ha-Tefillah: [Hebrew] One of the primary functions/roles of the synagogue--to be a "House of Prayer and Worship."

Bayt Ha-Mikdash: [Hebrew] Literally, "House of the Holy." Reference to the ancient Temple in Jerusalem. Destroyed once by the Babylonians in 586 B.C.E., and, again, by the Romans in 70 C.E.

Beviat Ha-Mashiach: [Hebrew] Literally, the "coming of the Messiah." This term is taken from Maimonides "Thirteen Articles of Faith," and is the general referent to that future moment when, according to Jewish Religious Tradition, he will make his appearance known to the House of Israel. [See above, **Ani Ma'amin.**]

Bureaucracy: According to Webster's New World Diction of the American Language, College Edition, [c] 1959, "the administration of government through departments and subdivisions managed by sets of officials following an inflexible routine....the concentration of authority in administrative bureaus." Particularly relevant in understanding the Nazi administration of the Shoah.

Christology: Christianity's unique faith-claim of the distinctiveness of Jesus as the Christ according to the New Testament texts, and, thus, the very heart and essence of the Christian religious tradition.

Churban: [Hebrew] Literally, "destruction." One of the possibly appropriate words used to describe the wanton murder and callous slaughter of the Jews by the Nazis and their minions during the years 1939-1945.

Chutzpah: [Hebrew] Literally, "brazenness" or "audacity." Sometimes regarded as a uniquely Jewish trait, though in point of fact, not specifically applicable to only one group or individual.

Conservative Judaism: Also known as "Positive-Historical Judaism," this Jewish Religious Movement represents the so-called "middle of the road" approach to religious questions and practices.

Covenant Theology: That theological understanding, originally, of the unique relationship between God and the Children of Israel/Jewish People, first entered into at Mount Sinai, whereby the Jews agreed to observe God's laws as set forth in the Torah in return for Divine protection and favor. Today, there are those theologians who speak of the Jewish Covenant at Sinai and the Christian Covenant through Jesus at Golgotha.

Creed: An authoritative statement of religious belief describing the essence of the group's and/or individual's faith.

Das Nichtige: [German] Literally, "The Nothingness;" a theological reference by Swiss thinker Karl Barth, with far broader religious and philosophical implications. [See the essay by Alan Davies in Volume II.]

Deicide: Literally, "God killer." The ages-old charge against the Jewish People, over which so much innocent blood has been shed, that the Jewish People and its leaders were primarily responsible for the death of Jesus at the hands of the Romans who were only their willing tools. Its roots lie in the New Testament accounts of the events themselves and the invidious statement, "His blood be upon us and upon our children." Despite serious scholarship to the contrary, and the contemporary Roman Catholic position that the death of the Christ was attributable to no one group alone, either historically or since, this charge continues to rear its ugly head even in our own day.

Diaspora: One of the terms, without value-judgment, used to describe the world-wide Jewish communities living outside the Land of Israel.

Die Endlosung: [German] Literally, the "Final Solution," that is, the Nazis' "Final Solution to the Jewish Problem"--extermination or annihilation of approximately six million Jewish men, women, and children, with a world plan to obliterate the Jewish People from the face of the earth.

Displacement Theology: The idea, still prevalent in some Christian denominations, that, with the appearance of Jesus as the Christ, and the rise of Christianity, both Judaism and the Jewish People have been "displaced" from their position as God's favored elect.

Dogma: The authoritative affirmation of the beliefs and principles of one's faith community.

Einsatzgruppe [pl. **en**]: [German] The "Mobile Killing Units" of the SS under the direct authority of Heinrich Himmler, Chief of the SS, responsible for the murder of those Jews found in areas conquered by the Wehrmacht. Oft-times, the Jews themselves were forced to dig their own graves, strip themselves naked, lie down in the trenches and pits and wait to be machine-gunned to death. No regard whatsoever was shown for men, women, children, the aged or the very young.

Einsatzkommando: [German] One of the SS men who considered it their "honorable duty" to put an end to the Jews by such "special operations" as described above.

El Mistater: [Hebrew] Literally, the "Hidden Face of God." Following the idea of German-Jewish philosopher Martin Buber [1878-1965] concerning the "eclipse of God" during the Shoah, for one awful moment in history, God "chose" to "turn His face away" from humankind with the Shoah as result. This concept, interestingly enough, is also found in Jewish rabbinic literature during earlier historical epochs.

En Sof: [Hebrew] Literally, "infinity" or "nothingness." In Jewish mystical literature and tradition, it is the "expanse of God" or "holy nothingness" beyond humanity's full ability to comprehend and understand--the "realm of God."

Eretz Yisrael: [Hebrew] Literally, the "Land of Israel" as distinct from the state and/or government and/or people of Israel. Sacred to all three religious traditions, Judaism, Christianity, and Islam.

Ethics: The system or code by which the morality of a nation-state or any group is put into practice.

Ethnocide: The effort to destroy a people as a cultural entity. [See the essay by Rosemary Radford Reuther in Volume II.]

Evil: That which causes harm to an individual or group usually innocent. In religious circles, the most difficult questions revolve around the role/place/function of evil in a God-controlled world.

Existentialism: That philosophical understanding usually associated with such thinkers as Jean-Paul Sartre and Albert Camus that our world is one of random accident and chance, that whatever happens happens, and we make our way in the world as best we can. Though some have attempted to develop a "religious existentialism," incorporating both the concept of randomness with an interactive God, others feel they are both mutually-exclusive and mutually incompatible.

Fascism: A political system, usually run by a dictator, supported by one party which brooks no dissent, and characterized by intense nationalistic fervor and oppression of both dissidents and minorities.

Galut: [Hebrew] Literally, "exile." That Jewish understanding usually associated with both religious and secular Zionism which regards those Jews who choose to live outside the Land of Israel as living in exile."

Gemilut Hasadim: [Hebrew] Literally, "deeds of loving-kindness." One of the goals of the Jewish Religious Tradition is to heighten human consciousness to better look for ways to perform such deeds.

Genocide: Term coined by the late Raphael Lemkin [1901-1959] Polish-American jurist and "father" of the United Nations Treaty on Genocide to describe the conscious attempt to destroy a people's identity culturally, spiritually, and physically.

Geulah: [Hebrew] Literally, "redemption." That moment in the Jewish journey when universal peace will be achieved and the Jews will have returned to their homeland to dwell in harmony with their neighbors.

Ghetto: Originally from the Italian word 'giotto', that restricted area of settlement, usually in the worst section of the city. Jews were forced into such environments starting in Italy in the Middle Ages, though the term has expanded to include other groups as well.

Gog & Magog: According to the New Testament Book of Revelations [20:8], those nations, under the leadership of Satan, who will contend against God in the coming cataclysm.

Grace: The fullest expression of Divine love and blessing for all of humanity, largely unmerited, and not always understandable by human beings.

Halakhah: [Hebrew] Literally, "The Way." The system of Jewish Law as culled by the Rabbis from the Torah itself and elaborated upon in the Talmud and subsequent and additional Jewish resource literatures. For the Orthodox Jew, Jewish Law governs all facets and aspects of daily and religious living, coming as it does directly from God and interpreted authoritatively by rabbinic spokesmen. Conservative Judaism likewise affirms its sanctity, but attempts to give it a more human cast through its Law and Standards Committee of the Rabbinical Assembly. Reform Judaism has long rejected its sovereignty, acknowledging, instead, that "the past shall exercise a vote, not a veto."

Hallel Psalms: Specifically, Psalms 113-118. Recited in the Jewish worship services for Passover, Shavuot, Sukkot, and Hanukkah.

Heilsgeschichte: [German] According to both Jewish and Christian religious traditions, the working out of human history understood as moving towards an ultimate salvation/redemption.

Hesed: [Hebrew] Literally, "lovingkindness." [See **Gemilut Hasadim.**]

Heshbon Ha-Nefesh: [Hebrew] Literally, "the accounting of the soul." When one's life's journey is at its end, according to Jewish religious tradition, one's good and bad deeds are judged by God and the scale tips one way or the other in terms of admittance into the afterlife.

Hester Panim: [Hebrew] Literally, "[God's] Hidden Face." [See **El Mistater.**]

Higher Criticism: The so-called "scientific study of the Bible," using the best insights of the various academic disciplines. Growing originally out of 19th Century German Protestant scholarship, it was understood by Jews as "higher antisemitism" and an attack on their own religious legitimacy. Roman Catholics, too, saw it in a similar light.

Historikerstreit: [German] Literally, the "historians fight." The movement, among a small circle of contemporary German historians [e.g. Ernest Nolte and Michael Sturmer, among others], to view the Shoah in a far broader context and thus diminish both its uniqueness and minimize an overall sense of German guilt.

Holocaust: Up until recently, the universally-acknowledged English word used to describe the wanton murder of nearly six million Jews by the Nazis and their collaborators. Said to have first been used by the noted writer and Nobel Prize winner Elie Wiesel. Its origin is an Anglicization of the Greek translation of the Hebrew word **'olah,** the totally-consumable offering by fire to God as depicted in the Torah. In recent years, the term itself has become increasingly problematic for obvious reasons. Current thinking is to use the Hebrew term **Shoah** instead.

Hubris: [Greek] Literally, "pride." The excessive, ego-inflating pride that enables one both to perceive himself/herself and to act as if he/she were as God. Understood to be sinful in all three Western religious traditions.

Ideology: Strongly held beliefs, opinions, ideas, values, etc. whether of an individual, group, nation-state, or religious community.

Immanent: The religious belief that the God who is addressed in prayer is close at hand and responsive to human concerns.

Incarnation: The religious belief, primarily of Christianity, following the New Testament, that out of God's love for humanity, He sent His divine son, Jesus, to earth giving him both human form and human nature.

Intifada: [Arabic] Literally, "uprising." The militant response of Palestinians living in the West Bank of Israel to Israeli military and political rule. Begun in December, 1987, it has witnessed the deaths of hundreds of innocent men, women, and children, both Palestinian and Israeli. Perceived by some as a national liberation movement and by others as a terrorist campaign, it continues to be one of the major stalemates to a lasting peace in the Middle East.

Judenrein: [German] Literally, "Jew-free." The ultimate objective of Hitler's extermination policies towards Jews was to free the world of all physical, cultural, and religious evidence of the presence of the Jewish People and Faith.

K'lal Yisrael: [Hebrew] Literally, "all Israel." That term used to designate the world-wide Jewish People in its collective presentation.

Kabbalah: [Hebrew] Literally, "received tradition." The mystical tradition and literature of religious Judaism, arising, perhaps, as early as the 1st Century of the Common Era, and continually influencing all streams of religious expression.

Kabbalat Shabbat: [Hebrew] Literally, "reception of the Sabbath." The onset of the Sabbath according to Jewish religious tradition occurs on Friday Evening at sundown with appropriate blessings, customs, and festive meal.

Kaddish: [Hebrew] Literally, "holy prayer." Aramaicized prayer usually understood to be the "Mourner's Prayer" recited by survivors after the funeral of a loved one either during the Worship Service or at home.

Kadoshim: [Hebrew] Literally, "holy ones," plural form. Reference to the near six million Jews murdered and slaughtered by the Nazis and their cohorts. The use of this religiously-relevant term raises anew the theological problems with which these two volumes are ultimately concerned.

Kibbutz: [Hebrew] Literally, "collective, gathering." The collective farming settlement begun in Palestine in the 1920's prior to the re-creation of the State of Israel in 1948.

Kiddush Ha-Shem: [Hebrew] Literally, "sanctification of the [Divine] Name." The term applied to those Jews who died a martyr's death. Understood now as applicable to all who died as a result of the Shoah.

Kiddush Ha-Hayyim: [Hebrew] Literally, "sanctification of life." The very opposite of the above **Kiddush Ha-Shem.** Understood in the contemporary Jewish world both as an historic Jewish value and a post-Shoah Jewish imperative.

Kristallnacht: [German] Literally, "Night of the Broken Glass/-Crystal." On November 9-10, 1938, the Nazis attacked Jewish businesses [844], homes [171], and synagogues [267] as well as the Jews themselves [72 killed or severely injured] while the state police did nothing to intervene and the government closed its eyes. This "pogrom" was presumably a spontaneous response to the assassination of the Third Secretary of the German Embassy in Paris, Ernst Vom Rath, by a Polish Jew Hershel Grynszpan. A fine of $1,000,000,000 RM [Reich Marks] was imposed upon the Jews of Germany to pay for the damages and clean up operations.

Lebensraum: [German] Literally, "living room." The German understanding, actually given voice prior to World War I, and furthered by Adolf Hitler, that the German people had a/the "natural right" to claim/reclaim those territories both needed for expansion as well as those areas where the majority of the population was German-speaking and, thus, Aryans.

Lebensunwerte Leben: [German] Literally, "life unworthy of life." That German/Nazi understanding that there existed those sub-populations-- the aged, infirm, feeble-minded, handicapped, as well as Jews, Gypsies, homosexuals, and others--who usefulness to the State [economically, politically, militarily, etc.] was nil and thus could be destroyed.

Lecha Dode: [Hebrew] Literally, "Come, my beloved." Title of a popular hymn sung in the synagogue on Friday Evening welcoming the Sabbath.

Limpieza de Sangre: [Spanish] Literally, "purity of blood." A concept which arose in the 15th Century in both Spain and Portugal that only those who were "pure Christians" could perform even the most humble of societal tasks, but especially the more important ones. Its relevance to Nazi ideology is obvious.

Lubavitch Hasidim: Hasidic sect who trace their origins to the town of Lubavitch in Russia. Also known as **Habad Hasidim**, their understanding of traditional Orthodox Judaism is a merging of the intellectual of normative Judaism with the emotional ecstasy of Hasidic Judaism.

Lurianic Kabbalah: An interpretation of the Jewish mystical tradition based on the writings and teachings of Isaac ben Solomon Luria [1534-1572], also known as "Ha-Ari," the sacred lion. His interpretations of the mystical were infused with a hungering for the advent of the Messiah.

Marranos: [Spanish] Literally, "pigs." Term used to designate those new converts to Christianity who were formerly Jews during the Middle Ages. From the Christian perspective, they were not to be trusted as true and sincere converts. From the Jewish perspective, they were equally understood to be "secret Jews" who converted for their physical survival as well as their children, but secretly practiced the rituals of Judaism.

Masada: The summer palace of King Herod in the Judean desert which saw the ultimate suicide of 960 Zealot defenders, men, women, and children. against the Romans at the end of a protracted four-year struggle [66-70].

Medinat Yisrael: [Hebrew] Literally, the "State of Israel." The official term for the contemporary nation-state founded in 1948. Distinguished from **Eretz Yisrael**, the Land of Israel. [See above.]

Megillah: [Hebrew] Literally, "scroll." Generally, any scroll of ancient Jewish text. **Ha-Megillah** or **Megillat Esther** is that associated with the festival of **Purim** and tells the story of the Book of Esther found in the Torah.

Messianism: That religious strain in both Judaism and Christianity which gives voice to the community's yearning for the appearance of the Messiah in Judaism or the return of the Messiah in Christianity. Jewish and Christian thinking on this subject, however, are substantively different.

Metaphysics: A branch of the discipline of philosophy concerned with both first causes and ultimate reality.

Midrash: [Hebrew] Literally, "that which is drawn out." Jewish interpretive literature of a non-legal nature. Commentary on the Torah as well as additional sermonic and story literature "filling in the gaps," so to speak, in the literary record. Some of it is quite fanciful--allowing the Rabbis, the creators of the literature, to give free rein to their imaginations. Others of it are quite insightful morally, ethically, spiritually, psychologically, as well as intellectually.

Mikveh: [Hebrew] [Pl.: **Mikvaot**] Jewish ritual baths used for a variety of religious occasions [e.g. after menstruation, prior to a wedding, conversion, etc.] Early **mikvaot** have been found at **Masada**.

Minhag: [Hebrew] [Pl. **Minhagim**] Jewish religious customs of a given Jewish community at a given historical moment. It is said in Jewish religious life that "the **minhag** of one generation becomes the law of the next."

Mitzvah: [Hebrew] [Pl. **Mitzvot**] Literally, "commanded act" by God to the Jewish People. According to the Rabbis, there are 613 **mitzvot** found through the Torah of both a moral-ethical and ritual-ceremonial nature, of equal sanctity. The **mitzvot** of the Torah given by God ultimately become in the eyes of the Rabbis the legal system--**Halakhah**--of the Jewish Religious Tradition. The word has also taken on a popular form in describing any "good deed."

Monism: The philosophical-theological idea or concept that there exists only one ultimate thing--in religious thought, obviously God.

Morality: Actions which are in accord with the principles of right conduct of a given group, community, religion, or nation-state

Moshav: [Hebrew] Literally, a "settlement." Existing in Israel and distinct from the **kibbutz**, the members of the agricultural **moshav** own their own homes but pool their resources for the purchase of needed farming items and the sale of whatever they produce.

Mussellmann [er] [German] Literally, "muscleman/men." German Nazi term of irony to describe the zombie-like slaves in the concentration and extermination camps, more often than not prior to their murder.

Mysterium Tremendum: [Latin] Literally, "tremendous mystery." Term made "popular" by the late Arthur Cohen [and others] to, somehow, label the Shoah and extend its implications into both the philosophical and theological realms. [A parallel term also used is **caesura**, indicating a break in the natural order and rhythm of things.]

Mystery: That thing, event, idea, etc., for which past and present explanations are not satisfactory. In theological terms, a **mystery** may very well be beyond human comprehension.

Mysticism: That branch of religious expression which sees it as possible to commune with and experience God without recourse to the intellectual and verbal.

Mythology: The collected "stories" of a given religious tradition and/or community often shrouded in the past and expressed in "larger than life" personages.

National Socialism: The "politically correct" term to describe the political philosophy of the Nazis.

Nationalism: Intense patriotic devotion to one's nation-state and its ideals, beliefs, and practices perceived as beyond reproach.

Nazi: Contraction of the German **Nationalsozialistiche Deutsche Arbeiterpartei** [National Socialist German Workers Party]; also abbreviated as **NSDAP.** Founded in 1919 and ultimately given free rein under the organizing genius of Adolf Hitler later to become **Fuhrer** of Germany. It was formally abolished and declared outlawed by the Nuremberg Trials in 1945.

Neturei Karta: [Aramaic] Literally, "guardians of the city." Orthodox Jews already in Jerusalem in Palestine prior to the founding of the State of Israel in 1948. They are intensely opposed to the political rebirth of Israel believing its contravenes the work of the coming Messiah to bring it about.

Nihilism: In philosophical and theological thought, the belief that there is no objective basis for either knowledge or truth. In politics, the belief that all currently-existing political institutions must be destroyed to make way for new ones.

Nostre Aetate: [Latin] Literally, "In Our Time." The 1965 Vatican Declaration on the Roman Catholic Church and the Jewish People which has led to a strengthening and furthering of the inter-religious dialogue between these two faith communities.

Oleh: [Hebrew] [Pl. **Olim**] Literally, "one who ascends." The term used to describe someone who makes **aliyah**, immigration, to Israel and becomes a citizen of that country.

Ontology: The philosophical and metaphysical concern with the nature of being and reality.

Original Sin: The theological concept, found in both Judaism and Christianity, that, as a result of the sin of Adam and Eve in the Garden of Eden, subsequent humanity is born with a "taint" and must work diligently to return to a state of **grace** in God's favor.

Orthodox Judaism: The most traditional and fundamentalist expression of religious Judaism. Orthodox Jews believe the Torah is literally the Word of God and only those who are its authentic and authoritative spokesmen, the Rabbis, can interpret those words for succeeding generations. Orthodox Jews equally claim their religious practices are the only authentic Jewish ritual and ceremonial practices.

Paganism: Religious expression, polytheistic in origin, nature-god oriented, predating Judaism, and today describing a philosophy which is neither Jewish, Christian or Muslim.

Passion of Christ: The suffering of Jesus on the Christ prior to his death. Said to be freely chosen and substitutionary for all humanity.

Pentateuch: [Greek] Literally, "Five Books." Reference to the First Five Books of the Torah: **Bereshit** [Genesis], **Shemot** [Exodus], **Vayikra** [Leviticus], **Bamidbar** [Numbers], and **Devarim** [Deuteronomy].

Pharisees: Anglicization of the Hebrew **Perushim**, "separatists." Religious and political party of the Second Temple Period whose interpretations of the Jewish religious tradition emphasized a "liberal" approach and emphasis on teaching, prayer, ethical behavior, and legal norms. The forerunners of the Rabbis.

Philosophy: The intellectual and academic discipline concerned with such "ultimate questions" as good and evil, knowledge, aesthetics, etc.

Pintele Yid: [Yiddish] Literally, "point Jew." A term of compliment for the Jew who attempts to scrupulously observe all the myriad practices of the Jewish religious tradition.

Pirke Avot: [Hebrew] Literally, "Sayings of the Fathers." Ethical tractate of moral maxims of the Rabbis from the 3rd Century B.C.E. [Before the Common Era] to the 3rd Century C.E. included in the **Talmud** and studied by Jewish religious families on Sabbath afternoons.

Pogrom: [Russian] Literally, "destruction." Historically, in Russia, used to describe an attack, organized, abetted, and oft-times inspired by the authorities which pitted the serfs against the small Jewish enclaves in their midst. More often than not, the Jews witnessed the wanton slaughter and deaths of their own without any retribution whatsoever.

Predicate Theology: A rethinking and re-focusing of theological questions from the author or subject of an act to the act or object itself. For example, the question is not whether God is good, but what is the nature of goodness. [See, for example, Harold Schulweis, Evil and the Morality of

God, Cincinnati, Hebrew Union College Press, 1984, as well as the essay by Peter J. Haas in Volume I.]

Race: An anthropological term used to categorize the different biological divisions of humankind, based on specific characteristics, for example, skin pigmentation. Adapted by the Nazis to the plane of history.

Racism: Discrimination--and worse--against a given biological sub-population based on the above specific characteristics.

Reconstructionist Judaism: The newest Jewish religious movement based upon the philosophy of Rabbi Mordecai Kaplan's [1881-1984] major work Judaism as A Civilization, which called for a "reconstruction" of American Jewish life in all areas, with religious Judaism serving as the hub of a wheel which spokes radiated to all facets and aspects of Jewish living. Kaplan was a professor at the [Conservative] Jewish Theological Seminary of America and was influenced by the writings of American pragmatic philosopher John Dewey [1859-1952].

Reform Judaism: Perhaps the most "liberal" wing of the Jewish religious tradition. Having its start in Sessen, Germany, in 1810 as a movement for liturgical change, it has flowered in the United States and today numbers almost two million adherents. It is also the most welcoming of non-Jews and has pioneered in the area of interfaith dialogue.

Refusenik: [Russian/English] Literally, "one who has been refused." Term used to described those Jews who were **refused** permission to emigrate to either Israel or the United States by the previous Soviet Union.

Resurrection: The belief, central to Christianity, thought originally brought to it from the **Pharisees**, that Jesus was **resurrected** three days after his death on the cross.

Revelation: The belief of Judaism, Christianity, and Islam that, out of God's love for humanity, he chooses to **reveal** himself to us: Though Moses, Sinai, and the prophets for Jews, through Jesus for Christians, and through Mahomet for Muslims. The Hebrew Scriptures, Christian Bible, and Qur'an are the setting down of those revealing moments.

Revisionism: The pseudo-scholarly, antisemitic attempt to "prove" that the Shoah never took place as it has been reported, that it is a "fiction" of the Zionist Jews, who continue to manipulate others, non-Jews, as well as the historical record to win support and allegiance for the beleaguered State of Israel.

Ritual Murder: Already at play in the Middle Ages, the utterly false notion that Jews periodically kidnap and murder Christian children to drain their blood for the making of the **matzot** [unleavened cakes] need for Passover. This libel has been a mainstay of the antisemites up to and including our own day.

SA: [German] **Stormabteilung** or "Storm Troopers." The original Nazi "goon squads," which later become eclipsed into the **Gestapo**[Geheime Statspolizei] or "Secret State Police." The **Gestapo** were the original persecutors of Jews and played a central role in their annihilation and extermination during the Shoah.

Sadducees: The conservative, priestly party of the Second Temple/Roman Period who wished to support and maintain that status quo of Judaism as a cultic religious community. Opposed to the **Pharisees.**

Salvation: The religious belief that the ultimate goal of faith is to be redeemed from death and/or everlasting hell and attain freedom, **grace,** and eternal afterlife in God's presence.

Sanhedrin: Hebrew word derived from Greek origin which identifies the Supreme Court of ancient Israel during the Roman period. Composed of 71 Rabbis, it has headed by a Presiding Judge and rendered both civil and religious decisions and solutions to complexities of the developing Jewish legal tradition. No longer extent in Jewish life after the 4th Century C.E.

Satan: The ultimate personification of evil in Christian religious tradition. Said to have originally been an angel in the heavenly court who found disfavor in God's eyes.

Scylla & Charybdis: Taken from Greek mythology and understood to have been two sea monsters who lured sailors and ships to their death and destruction.   The idiom "between **Scylla & Charybdis"** is equivalent to "between a rock and a hard place" [i.e. between two difficult choices, both of which have both positive and negative consequences].

Second Generation: The term now used to describe the children of Shoah survivors, children of severely-diminished families who are now adults themselves. Many of them continue to struggle with the Shoah, some psychologically, others religiously.

Sefirot: [Hebrew] Literally, "numbers." An essential term in Jewish Kabbalistic and mystical literature to denote the various emanations from God which ultimately become his attributes.

Sephardim: [Hebrew] Literally, "Spaniards." Since the onset of the Middle Ages, the term used by Jews to designate those Jews who trace their ancestry to Spain, Morocco, Italy, Egypt, Palestine, and Syria, as well as the Balkans, Greece, and Turkey.

Shearith Yisrael: [Hebrew] Literally, the "Saving Remnant of Israel." That community of Jews who survives the tragic destruction of large numbers of its own people, and because of its commitments, religious and other, rebuilds itself. After the Shoah, all contemporary Jewish communities throughout the world are "saving remnants."

Shechinah: [Hebrew] Literally, the "Presence." Term used to denote the "Indwelling Presence of God." That is, God's immanence, nearness, to humanity; approachable and reachable.

Shema Yisrael: [Hebrew] Literally, "Hear, Israel!" Taken from **Devarim** [Deuteronomy} 6:4, "Hear, Israel! Adonai is our God, Adonai alone," this sentence has become the Affirmation of God's Unity and is included in all Jewish worship services. It is as close as the Jewish religious tradition comes to a creedal formulation.

Shevirat Ha-Kelim: [Hebrew] Literally, the "breaking of the vessels." Term taken from Jewish Kabbalistic mystical literature to describe the human condition in its estrangement from God. These vessels which held the divine sparks or emanations have been shattered because of human error and can only be put back together through human commitment to God.

Shoah: [Hebrew] Literally, "Destruction, Devastation." The Hebrew, Biblical term now preferred more and more to describe the wanton murder and callous slaughter of almost six million Jewish men, women, and children during the years 1939 and 1945 by the Nazis and their assistants. A singularly unique event in the history of the Jewish People as well as all humankind.

Shofar: [Hebrew] Literally, "ram's horn." Reminder of the **Bereshit** [Genesis] story whereby Abraham sacrificed a ram rather than his son Isaac. Used in ancient Israel as both a military instrument and a call to gather the community. Associated today with the High Holy Days of **Rosh Ha-Shanah** [New Year] and **Yom Kippur** [Day of Atonement].

Shtetl: [Yiddish] Literally, "small town." Term used to denote the village where Jewish lived in Eastern Europe, primarily Russia and Poland.

Shulchan Aruch: [Hebrew] Literally, "Set/Prepared Table." The abstracted and organized Code of Jewish Laws taken from the **Talmud** and elsewhere, originally prepared and added to by Joseph Caro [1488-1575]. Together with the commentary of Moses Isserles [1525-1572], it has become authoritative in Orthodox Jewish religious life.

Shutafut: [Hebrew] Literally, "partnership." The classical rabbinic idea in Jewish religious life that God and humanity are co-partners in the very process of creation. God needs us every bit as much as we need God to bring about a world of which he would be proud.

Sitz im Leben: [German] Literally, "seat in life." Term used to denote one's "situation in life," that is, description of reality as it is, not as we would like it to be.

Social Darwinism: Philosophy popular in the 1920's in both America and Europe where Charles Darwin's twin emphasis on survival of the fittest and evolution of the species were adapted onto the plane of history. The Nazis perverted even this questionable understanding and saw all of history as a battleground between the Aryan, of whom they were its finest representatives, and the Jews, the most evil and lowest ordered among the species.

Socialism: Political philosophy whereby ownership, production, and distribution of goods are held by the collective rather than the individual.

Sonderkommando: [German] Literally, "special commando." Those Jews assigned the grisly task of removing the bodies from the various gas chambers and taking them either to the crematoria or for burial. Their own life expectancy was less than three months, after which they themselves were murdered to prevent witnesses.

SS: [German] Contraction of **Schutzstaffeln,** "Protection Squad." Originally organized as a body guard unit for the **Fuhrer,** it became one of the primary instruments under Heinrich Himmler's direction of the implementation of the Shoah.

Surplus Population: Term used in the writings of Helen Fein, Richard Rubenstein, and others to designate those groups "falling outside the universe of moral obligation," and, thus, liable for Shoah in the case of the Jews and genocide in the case of others.

Synoptic Gospels: Reference to the first three Gospel accounts of Jesus life and death--Matthew, Mark, and Luke--governed primarily by a similar point of view.

Talmud: [Hebrew] Literally, "Teaching." The encyclopedic collection of rabbinic literature following several centuries after the close of the **Mishnah** [the first compilation of Jewish laws completed around 200 C.E.] covering all aspects of Jewish life, based on both discussions in the various rabbinic academies as well as rendered legal decisions. There are both a Babylonian and Palestinian versions, the former ultimately becoming more authoritative in subsequent Jewish religious life.

Talmud Torah: [Hebrew] Literally, "study of the Torah." Term used to designate both the intensive Jewish religious study, especially the **Talmud**

itself, as well as a unique educational system of schools set up for such a purpose.

Teaching of Contempt: Term first suggested by the late French Jewish historian Jules Isaac [1877-1963] to describe the anti-Jewish and antisemitic teachings of Christianity over the course of the centuries. Isaac believed, and rightly so, that such "teaching of contempt" was an indirect contributor to the Shoah which he himself experienced firsthand. His monumental work Jesus et Israel and Genese de l'antisemitisme were said to have influenced directly Pope John XXIII and led directly to the Vatican Declaration **Nostre Aetate**.

Teleology: The philosophical study of the final cause of things and events.

Teshuvah: [Hebrew] Literally, "return." The religious belief of Judaism that the sincere penitent who recognizes the error of his/her ways and **returns** to the path of Jewish life will be accepted by God with open heart and open arms. One finds such an expression in the classic statement, "The gates of repentance are always open."

Theodicy: The religious and philosophical position which attempts to reconcile the goodness of God with the existence of evil in the world.

Theology: The study of the nature of God, God's relationship with the world, and matters pertaining to both.

Theophany: A religious event characterized by the appearance of God to humanity. Jews speak of the **theophany** at Sinai, not necessarily indicating the physical appearance of God.

Tifutzah: [Hebrew] Literally, "dispersion." Parallel term for the **Diaspora** of Jews living throughout the world outside the Land of Israel. Term itself is value-neutral.

Tikkun Olam B'Malchut Shaddai: [Hebrew] Literally, "repairing the world beneath the sovereignty of God." The ethical ideal of Jewish life which impels social action and demands that Jews involve themselves in improving society wherever they find themselves.

Torah She B'al Peh: [Hebrew] Literally, "Torah which is upon the mouth." The Oral Tradition of Rabbinic interpretation later set down in such primary texts as the **Mishnah** and **Talmud**. The so-called "Oral Tradition" continues to be authoritative today for Orthodox Jews, less so for Conservative, Reform, and Reconstructionist Jews.

Torah She B'michtav: [Hebrew] Literally, "Torah which is written down." The written text of the Hebrew Scriptures which begins with **Bereshit** and ends with **Divre Hayamim Bet** [II Chronicles].

Tosafot: [Hebrew] Literally, "addenda." The additional rabbinic commentaries on the **Talmud** compiled by the French Rabbis from the 12th to the 14th Centuries.

Totalitarianism: The political philosophy which has as its goal the complete domination of all aspects of the life of its citizens, usually under the leadership of a dictator, benevolent or otherwise.

Transcendence: The religious belief that God is above and beyond the realm of human approachability.

Tzaddik: [Hebrew] [Pl. **Tzaddikim**] Literally, "righteous or holy man." According to Jewish literary and mystical tradition, in each and every generation, the world is sustained by "thirty-six righteous men" [Hebrew: **Lamed-Vav Tzaddikim**] who, by virtue of their goodness and holiness, bring joy to God. They are, however, unknown to themselves as well as to the rest of humankind.

Unique: Singularly distinct. The issue with regard to the Shoah is whether or not this historical event is **unique** in both Jewish and world history, calling forth new and different responses, or "simply" another in a long list of antisemitic and genocidal world events not mandating significantly different responses.

Untermensch: [German] Literally, "underman." Term of opprobrium used to designate Jews, Poles, Gypsies, Slavs, and others, as "sub-human"--to be disposed of by the Nazis at will and to be enslaved as necessity dictated.

Volk: [German] Literally, "people." The almost mystical reverence shown by the Nazis for the "purely German person and people," the **Aryan.** The German term **blut und boden** ["blood and soil"] equally stresses this idea and its impact upon a generation of Germans willing to do Hitler's bidding.

Weltanschauung: [German] Literally, "worldview." A perspective on the human condition from one's own individual or collective viewpoint, taking into consideration political, economic, religious, and other factors.

Xenophobia: The psychological fear of the different. Said to be at the root of antisemitism in particular and all prejudice in general. Part of the psychological make-up of most human beings, though its conscious manifestation and translation into acts of hatred is a learned response.

Yad Vashem: [Hebrew] Literally, "a hand and a name." Refer-ence taken from the Biblical book of **Yishayahu** [Isaiah], **Yad Vashem** is the Israeli Shoah Memorial Authority created in 1953 to memorialize this tragedy of the Jewish People as well as to do significant archival gathering and research into these events.

Yahadut: [Hebrew] Literally, "Judaism." The Hebrew term for the religious expression of those committed to the belief in the One God of Israel.

Yeshiva: [Hebrew] [Pl. **Yeshivot**] A traditional Jewish parochial school whose primary curriculum consists of the study of the **Talmud** together with other rabbinic literatures.

Yiddish: A cognate, folk language of Hebrew, consisting of linguistic elements of Hebrew, French, Italian, German, and Slavic. Spoken primari-ly by those Jews coming from Eastern Europe [Poland and Russia] and their descendants. A significant literature also arose using **Yiddish** beginning in the late 18th and early 19th Centuries.

Yishuv: [Hebrew] Literally, "settlement." Term used to designate the Jewish community of Palestine prior to 1948 and Israel subsequent to it.

Yordeh: [Hebrew] [Pl. **Yordim**] Literally, "one who goes down, emigre." Term used to indicate that citizen of Israel who leaves Israel, settles somewhere else, and may or may not become a citizen of her/his adopted country.

Zikkaron: [Hebrew] Literally, "remembering." Its Greek equivalent is **anamnesis.** For Eugene Fisher, Volume II, both Judaism and Christianity are religions of remembering.

Zykon B: [German] The trade name of the actual crystalline gas pellets used in the gas chambers in the concentration and extermination camps. Upon contact with the air, **Zykon B,** a pesticide, becomes gaseous suffocating those in its immediate confined space. Death was said to take place within fifteen to forty-five minutes depending upon the size of the gas chamber.

* * * * *

THE BOOKS OF THE TORAH

The Five Books of Moses

Bereshit   Genesis

Shemot	Exodus
Vayikra	Leviticus
Bamidbar	Deuteronomy

Nevi'im: The Prophets

Yehoshua	Joshua
Shofetim	Judges
Shmuel Alef	I Samuel
Shmuel Bet	II Samuel
Melachim Alef	I Kings
Melachim Bet	II Kings
Yishayahu	Isaiah
Yirmiyahu	Jeremiah
Yehezkel	Ezekiel

"The Twelve"

Hoshai'ah	Hosea
Yoel	Joel
Amos	Amos
Ovadiah	Obadiah
Yonah	Jonah
Micha	Micah
Nachum	Nahum
Havakkuk	Habakkuk
Tzfaniah	Zephaniah
Haggai	Haggai
Zechariah	Zechariah
Malachi	Malachi

Ketuvim: The Writings

Tehillim	Psalms
Mishlei	Proverbs
Iyov	Job
Shir Ha-Shirim	Song of Songs/Canticles
Rut	Ruth
Aicha	Lamentations
Kohelet	Ecclesiastes
Esther	Esther
Daniel	Daniel
Ezra	Ezra
Nehemiah	Nehemiah
Divrei Ha-Yamim Alef	I Chronicles
Divrei Ha-Yamim Bet	II Chronicles

*****

THE JEWISH HOLIDAYS

Biblical - Major

Shabbat	Sabbath
Pesach	Passover
Sefirat Ha-Omer	Counting of the Omer
Shavuot	Weeks
Rosh Ha-Shanah	New Year
Yom Kippur	Day of Atonement
Sukkot	Booths
Shemini Atzeret	8th Day of Solemn Assembly
Rosh Hodesh	New Moon

Biblical-Minor

Hanukkah	Festival of Dedication
Purim	Festival of Esther/Lots

Rabbinic

Lag B'Omer	33rd Day of the Omer
Tisha B'Av	9th Day of Av/Collective Day of Mourning
Simchat Torah	Celebration of the Torah
Tu B'Shevat	15th Day of Shevat/Jewish
Arbor Day	

Contemporary

Yom Ha-Shoah	Shoah Remembrance Day
Yom Ha-Atzmaut	Israeli Independence Day

*****

THE MONTHS OF THE JEWISH CALENDAR

Tishri	September-October
Heshvan	October-November
Kislev	November-December
Tevet	December-January
Shevat	January-February
Adar [& Adar Bet/II]	February-March
Nisan	March-April
Iyar	April-May

Sivan	May-June
Tammuz	June-July
Av	July-August
Elul	August-September

BIBLIOGRAPHY

Abrahamson, Irving [Editor]. Against Silence: The Voice and Vision of Elie Wiesel. New York: Holocaust Library, 1985.

Arendt, Hannah. A Report on the Banality of Evil: Eichmann in Jerusalem. New York: Penguin Books, 1963.

Arendt, Hannah. The Origins of Totalitarianism. New York: Harcourt, Brace and World, 1966.

Aronson, Ronald. The Dialectics of Disaster. London: Verso, 1983.

Berenbaum, Michael. The Vision of the Void. Middletown: Wesleyan University Press, 1979.

Berger, Alan L. . Crisis and Covenant: The Holocaust in American Jewish Fiction. New York: State University of New York Press, 1985.

Berkovitz, Eliezer. Faith After Auschwitz. New York: Ktav Publishing House, 1973.

Bettleheim, Bruno. The Informed Heart. Glencoe: The Free Press, 1960.

Birnbaum, Norman and Gertrude Lenzer [Editors]. Sociology and Religion. Englewood Cliffs: Prentice Hall, 1969.

Buber, Martin. Eclipse of God: Studies in the Relation between Religion and Philosophy. New York: Harper and Row, 1952.

Cargas, Harry James [Editor]. Responses to Elie Wiesel: Critical Essays by Major Jewish and Christian Scholars. New York: Persea Books, 1978.

Cargas, Harry James. Harry James Cargas in Conversation with Elie Wiesel. New York: Paulist Press, 1976.

Chazan, Robert and Marc Lee Raphael [Editors]. Modern Jewish History: A Source Reader. New York: Schocken Books, 1969.

Cohen, Arthur. The Tremendum: A Theological Interpretation of the Holocaust. New York: Crossroad Publishing Company, 1981.

Conway, J. S. The Persecution of the Churches 1933-1945. New York: Basic Books], 1968.

Dawidowicz, Lucy S. The War Against the Jews 1933-1945. New York: Holt, Rinehart and Winston, 1975.

Diller, Jerry [Editor]. Ancient Roots and Modern Meanings. New York: Bloch Publishing Company, 1978.

Ecclestone, Alan. Night Sky of the Lord. New York: Schocken Books, 1980.

Eckardt, A. Roy. Elder and Younger Brothers: The Encounter of Jews and Christians. New York: Charles Scribner's Sons, 1967.

Eckardt, A. Roy and Alice Lyons Eckardt. Long Night's Journey into Day: Life and Faith After the Holocaust. Detroit: Wayne State University Press, 1982.

Ellis, Marc H. Beyond Innocence and Redemption: Confronting the Holocaust and Israeli Power. San Francisco: Harper and Row, 1990.

Ellis, Marc H. Towards a Jewish Theology of Liberation. Maryknoll: Orbis Books, 1987.

Estess, Ted L. Elie Wiesel. New York: Frederick Unger Publishing Company, 1980.

Fackenheim, Emil L. Quest for Past and Future. Bloomington: Indiana University Press, 1968.

Fackenheim, Emil L. To Mend the World: Foundations of Future Jewish Thought. New York: Schocken Books, 1982.

Fackenheim, Emil L. God's Presence in History. New York: New York University Press, 1970.

Fackenheim, Emil L. What is Judaism? An Interpretation for the Present Age.
    New York: Summit Books, 1987.

Fackenheim, Emil L. Encounters Between Judaism and Modern Philosophy: A
    Preface to Future Jewish Thought. New York: Schocken Books, 1973.

Fackenheim, Emil L. The Jewish Return into History: Reflections in the Age
    of Auschwitz and a New Jerusalem. New York: Schocken Books, 1978.

Fackenheim, Emil L. From Bergen-Belsen to Jerusalem: Contemporary
    Implications of the Holocaust. Jerusalem: Hebrew University Institute
    of Contemporary Jewry, 1975.

Fackenheim, Emil L. The Religious Dimension in Hegel's Thought. Chicago:
    The University of Chicago Press, 1967.

Fein, Helen. Accounting for Genocide: National Responses and Jewish Vic-
    timization During the Holocaust. Chicago: University of Chicago Press,
    1979.

Feuerlicht, Roberta Strauss. The Fate of the Jews: People Torn Between
    Israeli Power and Jewish Ethics. New York: Times Books, 1983.

Fine, Ellen S. Legacy of Night: The Literary Universe of Elie Wiesel.
    Albany: State University of New York Press, 1982.

Flannery, Edward M. The Anguish of the Jews: A Catholic Priest Writes of
    Twenty-three Centuries of Anti-Semitism. New York: Macmillan
    Publishing Company, 1964.

Fleischner, Eva [Editor]. Auschwitz: Beginning of a New Era? Reflections on
    the Holocaust. New York: Ktav Publishing House, 1977.

Friedman, Georges. The End of the Jewish People? Garden City: Doubleday ,
    1967. Translated by Eric Mossbacher.

Friedman, Maurice. Abraham Joshua Heschel and Elie Wiesel: You Are My
    Witnesses. New York: Farrar, Strauss and Giroux, 1987.

Furet, Francois [Editor]. Unanswered Questions: Nazi Germany and the
    Genocide of the Jews. New York: Schocken Books, 1989.

Garber, Zev, Alan L. Berger, and Richard Libowitz [Editors]. Methodology in
    the Academic Teaching of the Holocaust. Lanham: University Press of
    America, 1989.

Haas, Peter. Morality After Auschwitz: The Radical Challenge of the Nazi Ethic. Philadelphia: Fortress Press, 1988.

Halasz, Nicolas. Captain Dreyfus: The Story of a Mass Hysteria. New York: Simon and Schuster, 1957.

Harkabi, Yehoshafat. The Bar Kokhba Syndrome. Chappaqua: Rossel Books, 1983.

Hertzberg, Arthur [Editor]. The Zionist Idea. Philadelphia: The Jewish Publication Society of America, 1959.

Hilberg, Raul. The Destruction of the European Jews. Chicago & New York: Quadrangle Books and Holmes & Meier, 1961 & 1985.

Hillesum, Etty. An Interrupted Life: The Diaries of Etty Hillesum. New York: Pocket Books, 1985. Edited by J. G. Gaarlandt and translated by Johnathan Cape.

Hughes, Robert. The Fatal Shore: The Epic of Australia's Founding. New York: Alfred A. Knopf, 1987.

Kuhn, Thomas. The Structure of Scientific Revolutions. Chicago: University of Chicago Press, 1962.

Littell, Franklin H. and Hubert G. Locke [Editors]. The German Church Struggle and the Holocaust. Detroit: Wayne State University Press, 1974.

Littell, Franklin H. The Crucifixion of the Jews: The Failure of Christians to Understand the Jewish Experience. New York: Harper and Row, 1975.

MacIntyre, Alasdair. After Virtue. Notre Dame: University of Notre Dame Press, 1984. Second Edition.

Marrus, Michael R. and Robert O. Paxton. Vichy France and the Jews. New York: Basic Books, 1981.

Maurrus, Michael. The Holocaust in History. Hanover: University Press of New England, 1987.

McGarry, Michael B. Christology After Auschwitz. New York: Paulist Press, 1977.

Morais, Vamberto. A Short History of Anti-Semitism. New York: W. W. Norton and Company, 1976.

Morgan, Michael [Editor]. The Jewish Thought of Emil Fackenheim: A Reader. Detroit: Wayne State University Press, 1987.

Mosse, George L. Toward the Final Solution: A History of Racism. New York: Howard Fertig, 1976.

Neher, Andre. The Exile of the Word: From the Silence of the Bible to the Silence of Auschwitz. Philadelphia: The Jewish Publication Society of America, 1981. Translated by David Maisel.

Nelson, Benjamin. The Idea of Usury: From Tribal Brotherhood to Universal Otherhood. Chicago: University of Chicago Press, 1969. Second Edition.

Peck, Abraham [Editor]. Jews and Christians After Auschwitz. Philadelphia: Fortress Press, 1982.

Pisar, Samuel. Of Blood and Hope. Boston: Little, Brown and Company, 1979.

Po-Hsia, R. The Myth of Ritual Murder: Jews and Magic in Reformation Germany. New Haven: Yale University Press, 1988.

Rausch, David A. A Legacy of Hatred: Why Christians Must Not Forget the Holocaust. Chicago: Moody Press, 1984.

Reuther, Rosemary Radford and Herman J. Reuther. The Wrath of Jonah. New York: Harper and Row, 1989.

Reuther, Rosemary Radford. Faith and Fratricide: The Theological Roots of Anti-Semitism. New York: The Seabury Press, 1974.

Reuther, Rosemary Radford and Marc H. Ellis [Editors]. Beyond Occupation: American Jewish, Christian, and Palestinian Voices for Peace. Boston: Beacon Press, 1990.

Rosenberg, Alan and Gerald E. Myers [Editors]. Echoes from the Holocaust: Philosophical Reflections on a Dark Time. Philadelphia: Temple University Press, 1988.

Rosenfeld, Alvin and Irving Greenberg [Editors]. Confronting the Holocaust: The Work of Elie Wiesel. Bloomington: Indiana University Press, 1980.

Roth, John K. A Consuming Fire: Encounters with Elie Wiesel and the Holocaust. Atlanta: John Knox Press, 1979.

Rubenstein, Richard L. After Auschwitz: Radical Theology and Contemporary Judaism. Indianapolis: The Bobbs-Merrill Company, 1966.

Rubenstein, Richard L. [Editor]. Spirit Matters: The Worldwide Impact of Religion in Contemporary Politics. New York: Paragon House Publishers, 1987.

Rubenstein, Richard L. . The Cunning of History: Mass Death and the American Future. New York: Harper and Row, 1975.

Rubenstein, Richard L. The Age of Triage: Fear and Hope in an Overcrowded World. Boston: Beacon Press, 1983.

Scholem, Gershom. The Messianic Idea in Judaism and Other Essays on Jewish Spirituality. New York: Schocken Books, 1971.

Scholem, Gershom. Sabbatai Sevi: The Mystical Messiah. Princeton: Princeton University Press, 1973.

Schulweis, Harold. Evil and the Morality of God. Cincinnati: Hebrew Union College Press, 1984.

Sheehan, Bernard W. . Seeds of Extinction: Jeffersonian Philanthropy and the American Indian. Chapel Hill: University of North Carolina Press, 1973.

Shorris, Earl. Jews Without Mercy: A Lament. Garden City: Doubleday, 1982.

Stern, Ellen Norman. Elie Wiesel: Witness for Life. New York: Ktav Publishing House, 1982.

Trunk, Isaiah. Judenrat: The Jewish Councils in Eastern Europe Under Nazi Occupation. New York: Stein and Day, 1977.

Waite, Robert G. L. The Psychopathic God: Adolf Hitler. New York: New American Library, 1978.

Wallimann, Isidor and Michael N. Dobkowski [Editors]. Genocide and the Modern Age: Etiology and Case Studies of Mass Death. New York: Greenwood Press, 1987.

Waskow, Arthur. Seasons of Our Joy. New York: Bantam Books, 1982.

Waskow, Arthur. Godwrestling. New York: Schocken Books, 1978.

Waskow, Arthur [Co-Author]. The Shalom Seders. New York: Adama Books, 1984.

Waskow, Arthur. These Holy Sparks: The Rebirth of the Jewish People. New York: Harper and Row, 1983.

Vaskow, Arthur. Before There Was a Before. New York: Adama Books, 1984.

Weinrich, Max. Hitler's Professors. New York: YIVO, 1966.

Wiesel, Elie. Night. New York: Hill and Wang, 1960.

Wiesel, Elie. The Town Beyond the Wall. New York: Holt, Rinehart and Winston, 1964.

Wiesel, Elie. Gates of the Forest. New York: Avon Books, 1967.

Woodham-Smith, Cecil. The Great Hunger: Ireland, 1845-1849. New York: E. P. Dutton, 1980.

Yehoshua, A. B. Between Right and Right: Israel, Problem or Solution? Garden City: Doubleday, 1981. Translated by Arnold Schwartz.

Zenner, Walter P. Middleman Minority Theories and the Jews: A Historical Assessment. New York: YIVO, 1978.

SOME QUESTIONS FOR POSSIBLE FURTHER REFLECTION AND FUTURE DISCUSSION

1. Having read all of the essays in this volume, what appear to be the primary concerns/dominant issues of these writers?

2. Do you think Jacobs is correct that the Shoah is an "ignored bit of theology" in light of subsequent Jewish history and its own religious implications?

3. Can one affirm the Jewish idea of Brith or Covenant in historically-traditional ways in light of the Shoah, or do other, innovative and creative ideas suggest themselves?

4. Why do you regard as the central task[s] of both Catholic and Protestant Christian theologies in light of the Shoah and after Eckardt's "essentials?"

5. How do you react to the theology of Rabbi Yehuda Amital? Does it provide a reasoned, reasonable, and logical religious explanation to events in contemporary Israel? Can his thinking, therefore, also be applied to the Shoah?

6. Which metaphor do you prefer that best describes our post-Shoah world: Scattering of divine sparks [Luria]? Rupturing of the vessels [Fackenheim]? The void [Berenbaum]? Other?

7. What is your response to Berenbaum's conclusion that it is "too late" for both God and the Messiah, and that human survival will come about only by virtue of human initiative?

8. Is Ellis correct that one of the lessons of the Shoah is solidarity with all victims of genocide, including the Palestinians? If so, what does it tell us about our responsibilities today?

9. What reasons suggest themselves to you that the reason Shoah theology has failed is because of its inability to now address Jewish empowerment? Is the 'dialectic' between the two over the question of Jewish survival sufficient enough to restore it to its proper place in Jewish thought?

10. Has the "marketing" of the Shoah truly become 'kitsch'?

11. Has the Shoah now truly become 'ahistorical'?

12. Is Fackenheim's term "unprecedented" to be preferred to that of "unique" in describing the Shoah?

13. Now, after the Shoah, is "Man" "infinitely perfectible" or "infinitely depravable?"

14. Would you agree with Fackenheim that "the 'Muselmann' may be called the most truly original contribution of the Third Reich to civilization?"

15. Is the Shoah a crucial event only for Diaspora Jewry? What of contemporary Israel in its relationship to its own immediate past and/or American Jewry?

16. For Jews, is a "return to Zion," therefore, the only viable option and appropriate response after the Shoah? Is it the only understanding of a restored sense of Covenant between God and the Jewish People which now makes sense?

17. Can one write and read poetry after Auschwitz? Can art--of whatever form--truly address horror?

18. Do you agree with Haas that the traditional understanding of **theodicy** is "medieval" in its conception, and, therefore, needs to be re-envisioned by modern people for it to have any relevance today?

19. Was the evil committed by the Nazis truly "banal?"

20. Does Haas's distinction between "ethics" and "morality" place the Shoah, as he contends, in an entirely different perspective? If we can, in fact, speak of the "Nazi ethic," what does this tell us about the nature of human societies?

21. How can Rabbi Maza, in Section III, suggest that the Shoah was an instrument of Divine will?

22. Why is Rubenstein so convinced that the Shoah is a unique and "thoroughly modern event?"

23. Why is his question--"Who is to have a voice in the political order?"-- central to his overall argument?

24. Is the "Masada option" truly an option for Jews, either or both those living inside and/or outside the State of Israel--given the realities of the contemporary world and its political situations and machinations?

25. Does Waskow suggest anywhere in his essay a possible meaning for the murderous deaths of six million Jews, as well as the Shoah itself?

26. Are Jews truly the "canary people of God?"

27. Do you agree with Berger that "abstraction and generalization, professionalism and objectivity" are the "shadow idols" of academia after the Shoah? When, then is the purpose of a university/college education?

ABOUT THE CONTRIBUTORS

ALAN L. BERGER: Alan L. Berger chairs the Jewish Studies Program and teaches in the Department of Religion at Syracuse University. In 1988-1989, he was the Visiting Gumenick Professor of Judaica at the College of William and Mary. He has lectured on the Shoah in Oxford, in Israel at Yad Vashem, in Paris, and throughout America. His articles deal mainly with literature, pedagogy, and the theology of post-Auschwitz Jewish thought. Among his books are Crisis and Covenant: The Holocaust in American Jewish Fiction and Methodology in the Academic Teaching of the Holocaust [Associate Editor].

MICHAEL BERENBAUM: Michael Berenbaum is the Project Director of the United States Holocaust Memorial Museum, and the Hymen Goldman Adjunct Associate Professor of Theology at Georgetown University in Washington, D. C. In the past, he has served as Director of the Jewish Community Council of Greater Washington, Editor of The Washington Jewish Week, and Deputy Director of the President's Commission on the Holocaust, where he authored its Report to the President. The author of six books, more than 100 scholarly articles, and hundreds of journalistic pieces, his writings include The Vision of the Void, After Tragedy and Triumph: Essays in Modern Jewish Thought and the American Experience, A Mosaic of Victims: Non-Jews Persecuted and Murdered by the Nazis, and, together with John K. Roth, The Holocaust: Religious and Philosophical Implications.

MARC H. ELLIS: Marc H. Ellis received his B.A. and M.A. degrees from Florida State University, where studied with the eminent Shoah theologian Richard L. Rubenstein, and his Ph.D. degree from Marquette University in Contemporary Religious Thought. He has written five books, including Towards a Jewish Theology of Liberation [Maryknoll, Orbis Books, 1987], and Beyond Innocence and Redemption: Confronting the Holocaust and Israeli Power [San Francisco, Harper and Row, 1990]. He has lectured extensively in North America, Europe, Africa, Asia, Latin America, and the Middle East. Currently he is Professor of Religion, Culture, and Society Studies at Maryknoll School of Theology.

EMIL L. FACKENHEIM: Emil L. Fackenheim was born in Halle, Germany, in 1916, and studied at the Liberal Seminary in Berlin before World War II. He received his ordination in the year following his release from

Sachsenhausen concentration camp. Emigrating first to Scotland and then to Canada, he received his Ph.D. in philosophy and was a member of the Philosophy Department of the University of Toronto where he served until his retirement in 1983 as a University Professor. He is the author of many distinguished books including The Religious Dimensions of Hegel's Thought [1967]; Quest for Past and Future: Essays in Jewish Theology [1968]; God's Presence in History: Jewish Affirmations and Philosophical Reflections [1970]; Encounters between Jewish and Modern Philosophy: A Preface to Future Jewish Thought [1973]; The Jewish Return into History: Reflections in the Age of Auschwitz and a New Jerusalem [1978]; To Mend the World: Foundations of Future Jewish Thought [1982]; What is Juda-ism?   An Interpretation for the Present Age [1987]; and The Jewish Bible After the Holocaust: A Re-Reading [1990]. He now lives in Israel with his family and is a Fellow of the Institute of Contemporary Jewry at Hebrew University in Jerusalem.

IRVING GREENBERG: Rabbi Irving Greenberg is President of the National Jewish Center for Learning and Leadership [CLAL].   He has served as Professor and Chair of the Department of Jewish Studies at the City College of New York and Rabbi of the Riverdale Jewish Center. He has explored the religious and ethical implications of the Shoah and the rebirth of Israel in a series of essays and monologues including "Cloud of Smoke, Pillar of Fire" [1977]; "Judaism, Christianity, and Modernity after the Holocaust" [1976]; "The Third Great Cycle in Jewish History" [1981]; and "Voluntary Covenant" included here. He is the author of The Jewish Way [1988], an interpretation of the relationship of the Jewish religion and Jewish history.

PETER J. HAAS: Peter J. Haas, the son of Shoah survivors, teaches Judaism and ethics in the Religious Studies Department of Vanderbilt University, Nashville, Tennessee. After receiving Rabbinic ordination from the Hebrew Union College-Jewish Institute of Religion, Cincinnati, Ohio, in 1974, he served as a United States Army Chaplain for three years, going on to earn his Ph.D. in Jewish Studies from Brown University in 1980. He has published several books and articles in early rabbinic legal and moral discourse. He most recent book Morality After Auschwitz: The Radical Challenge of the Nazi Ethic examines how the Shoah affects our understanding of ethical discourse in the modern world.

BERNARD MAZA: Bernard Maza received his Rabbinic ordination at Mesivtha Tifereth Jerusalem from the famous Rosh Yeshiva Moshe Feinstein, of blessed memory. He also received his M.A. degree from Brooklyn College. He is today the Dean of Bais Midrash REM and the Rabbi of Congregation Emunah Shleima in Kew Gardens, New York. Rabbi Maza is the author of two books of Talmudic commentary; a two-volume work of Biblical commentary entitled Insights into the Sedra of the Week; and a book on the Shoah entitled With Fury Poured Out: A Torah Perspective on the Holocaust

[Hoboken, Ktav Publishing House, 1986], the sequel to which Holocaust Messengers to Mankind is in publication.

RICHARD L. RUBENSTEIN: Richard L. Rubenstein serves as the Robert O. Lawton Distinguished Professor in Religion at Florida State University, Tallahassee, Florida, and the President of the Washington Institute for Values in Public Policy, a public policy research institution based in Washington, D. C. He is the author and editor of eleven books including After Auschwitz: Radical Theology and Contemporary Judaism [1966]; The Religious Imagination [1968]; The Cunning of History [1975]; and The Age of Triage [1983]. His most recent book, co-authored with John K. Roth, is Approaches to Auschwitz: The Holocaust and Its Legacy [Atlanta, John Knox Press, 1987]. In 1988, the Jewish Theological Seminary of America conferred the degree of Doctor of Hebrew Letters, Honoris Causa, upon him at this Centennial Convocation.

ARTHUR WASKOW: Arthur Waskow is the Director of The Shalom Center and Fellow of the Institute for Jewish Renewal. He founded and co-edits the journal New Menorah, and is the author of The Freedom Seder [1969]; Godwrestling [1978]; and Seasons of Our Joy [1982]. He is also the co-author of The Shalom Seders [1984]; and Before There Was a Before [1984], a book of midrashic tales of the Creation for children and adults. His book These Holy Sparks: The Rebirth of the Jewish People [1983] examines the history and meaning of the Jewish renewal movement during the last twenty years. He helped found the National Havurah Committee, and is a member of the Board of P'nai Or Religious Fellowship and the editorial boards of the Reconstructionist, Genesis 2, and Tikkun magazine.

ABOUT THE EDITOR

STEVEN L. JACOBS: Steven L. Jacobs serves as the Rabbi of Temple B'nai Sholom, Huntsville, Alabama, and teaches Jewish Studies at Oakwood College, Huntsville, and Mississippi State University, Starkville. He received his B.A. [With Distinction] from the Pennsylvania State University, and his B.H.L., M.A.H.L., D.H.L. and rabbinic ordination from the Hebrew Union College-Jewish Institute of Religion, Cincinnati, Ohio. In addition to serving congregations in Steubenville, Ohio, Niagara Falls, New York, Birmingham and Mobile, Alabama, and Dallas, Texas, he has taught at Spring Hill College, Mobile, University of Alabama, Tuscaloosa, Uni-versity of Alabama at Birmingham, Birmingham-Southern College, and Samford University, Birmingham. Author of more than fifty scholarly articles and reviews dealing primarily with the Shoah, his books include Shirot Bialik: A New and Annotated Translation of Chaim Nachman Bialik's Epic Poems [Columbus, Alpha Publishing Company, 1987] and Raphael Lemkin's Thoughts on Nazi Genocide: Not Guilty? [Lewiston, The Edwin Mellen Press, 1992]. He serves on the Alabama State Holocaust Advisory Council and as an Educational Consultant to the Center on the Holocaust, Genocide, and Human Right, Philadelphia. He is also the Editor of the papers of the late Raphael Lemkin, Father of the United Nations Treaty on Genocide.